Kristine Juul

Tubes, Tenure and Turbulence

Anthropology and Development

edited by

Thomas Bierschenk

(Institut für Ethnologie und Afrikastudien,
Johannes Gutenberg-Universität Mainz)

and

Jean-Pierre Olivier de Sardan

(Ecole des Hautes Etudes en Sciences Sociales, Marseille)

for APAD

(Euro-African Association for the Anthropology
of Social Change and Development)

Volume 5

LIT

Kristine Juul

Tubes, Tenure and Turbulence

The effects of drought related migration on tenure issues
and resource management in Northern Senegal

LIT

Bibliographic information published by Die Deutsche Bibliothek
Die Deutsche Bibliothek lists this publication in the Deutsche
Nationalbibliografie; detailed bibliographic data are available in the
Internet at http://dnb.ddb.de.

ISBN 3-8258-5673-9

A catalogue record for this book is available from the British Library

© LIT VERLAG Münster   2005
Grevener Str./Fresnostr. 2   D- 48159 Münster
Tel. +49/(0)251-62 03 20   Fax +49/(0)251-23 19 72
e-Mail: lit@lit-verlag.de   http://www.lit-verlag.de

Distributed in the UK by: Global Book Marketing, 38 King Street, London WC 2E 8JT
Phone: +44 (0) 207 240 6649 – Fax: +44 (0) 20 7497 0309, http://www.globalbookmarketing.co.uk

Distributed in North America by:

Transaction Publishers
New Brunswick (U.S.A.) and London (U.K.)

Transaction Publishers   Tel.: (732) 445 - 2280
Rutgers University   Fax: (732) 445 - 3138
35 Berrue Circle   for orders (U. S. only):
Piscataway, NJ 08854   toll free (888) 999 - 6778

FOREWORD

Good, solid research is not something which comes by itself, by sheer luck or accidentally. It requires a steady effort, great enthusiasm and a persistent and unshakable belief in the value of investing time and energy in a basically risky endeavour. It requires not only self-confidence, also in those periods of hardship and missed opportunities which inevitably occur when fieldwork is stretched over several years, but also talent, skill and the ability to become part of the particular context which is being studied. These aspects can all be applied when characterising the work of Kristine Juul, as presented in this book. In addition, she carries with her a strong feeling of social and political solidarity and a will to understand her context on its own premises, rather than as based on preconceived notions. This attitude has made it possible to dig deeper into the history of post-drought rehabilitation and to ascertain and challenge some of the conventional wisdom within the desertification and ecological debates which are often too simplistic if not outright wrong.

As mentioned in her own preface, Kristine Juul has been engaged for years in the life and more particularly the survival strategies of the pastoralists population of West Africa, first as an intern in Mauritania, then as an Associate Expert at the Danida funded UNSO project "Centre de Suivi Ecologique" in Dakar, Senegal and hereafter while conducting the field work in the Ferlo, on which this book is based. It has been a long-time affair, strenuous, cumbersome and often exhausting. However, I am certain it was also a love affair. Still is, in fact.

With her research, Kristine Juul has made an important contribution to our understanding of pastoralists and of their ability to adapt through changing patterns of mobility to shifting conditions not only with regard to the natural habitat but also in terms of socio-economic conditions, challenges which have been perceived not only as threats, but also as opportunities. In her research, Kristine Juul has uncovered the complexities involved, the rather sophisticated ability to adapt to new conditions and the innovative thinking exposed for example when exploring the technological possibilities involved in recycling the leftovers from the battle field of development projects. And her research is now here for you to enjoy!

Henrik Secher Marcussen,
Dept. of Geography & International Development Studies,
Roskilde University.

ACKNOWLEDGEMENTS

This work started life already in 1988 when I made my first visits to the Ferlo region of Northern Senegal and was introduced to the rich life of the region by my fellow sociologist Oussouby Touré and our assistants Mamadou Ka and Moustapha Dia. Since then I have benefited from their immense knowledge of the region, of pastoral management and of tenure issues.

Mamadou Ka made the whole journey with me and assisted me as interpreter, assistant, co-driver and friend throughout the 7 years over which my fieldwork was scattered. I owe much of my rich fieldwork experience to him. Apart from being an entertaining, knowledgeable and analytical companion, he patiently tried to teach me some basic Fulani social skills, some Fulani tact and decent behaviour. When this proved to be in vain he was always ready to make use of his talent for entertainment, transforming our visits in the different Fulani camps from long and irksome interviews with overburdened herders into agreeable social events. Making the outmost use of the institutionalised 'mocking relation' between his patronym 'KA' and the patronym 'BA' held by most of our respondents, he was responsible for the pleasant and lively atmosphere which was created and the close relations that were knit to our main respondents in the course of the years. This gave us the privilege of being well received by our respondents who generously granted us time for endless questioning and who carefully explained their stories. Without this confidence and openness it would have been impossible to get to grips with the many intricate and delicate elements which together constitute the political and social life of post-drought Ferlo.

Although it was all too apparent that nothing was to be gained by them from spending precious spare time on our endless interrogation into their private affairs, we were met with immense generosity and hospitality in all the families and encampments visited. Indeed, this generous attitude is clearly understated in my general portrayal of Fulani pastoralists as profit-maximizing and economically rational entrepreneurs, incessantly concerned with the calculation of opportunity costs. This kindness and disinterested manner characterises the totality of the herders and farmers included in the study. It is, however, particularly true for the families of Yerim Sow, Bathil Ba, Terry Ba, Assane Ndiaye and Abdoul Samba Dieri Ba whom it was always delightful to visit and whose hospitality we exploited ruthlessly.

I am grateful for the ample assistance and the accommodating attitude which representatives of the Senegalese authorities at all levels have shown towards me and my work. Direction de l'Elevage, Institut Sénégalais de Recherche Agricole in Dakar and Centre de Recherche Zootechnique in Dahra provided valuable information and interesting discussions. Institut des Sciences de l'Environement, Université Cheick Anta Diop, Dakar ensured institutional backing and it's Director, M. Tidjane BA even took the time to read and comment some of my early drafts.

It was an extremely instructive and valuable experience to discuss with Christian Santoir from ORSTOM who also convinced me of the need to substantiate my findings quantitatively. Inspiring discussions were also held with Brigitte Thébaud and Marlene Richter, hence associated with the GTZ project in Widou Thingoly. Finally my friends and former colleagues at the Centre de Suivi Ecologique have given me invaluable support and advice throughout the years.

Back home in Denmark, Henrik Secher Marcussen is responsible for awakening my interest in West African pastoralism and natural resource management by sending me off to Mauritania on an internship in 1986 and by encouraging me to pursue my 'pastoral interest' in Senegal. Throughout the years he has challenged and encouraged me, but has also displayed tremendous patience and loyalty in those moments where required.

My colleagues and fellow students at International Development Studies at Roskilde University Centre have contributed with constructive discussions and literature suggestion. Notably the milieu concerned with institutional aspects of resources management: Tove Degnbol, Christian Lund, Tine Breinholdt, Hans Otto Sano, Peter Oksen, Gun Mickels, Runa Midtvåge and Henrik Nielsen has invested precious time and energy in reading messy drafts. Particularly Christian Lund shared his ideas with me and suggested crucial improvements that have significantly contributed to raise the standard of the dissertation. I am very grateful to Roger Leys who patiently read and commented my 'oeuvre' and made a tremendous effort to reduce my long sentences and make the work more readable. Finally I am obliged to my present colleagues at the geography department at RUC who have refrained from pressing me but instead patiently have awaited for me to finish, not least Ingrid Jensen for improving some of the maps and Inge Jensen for providing general support throughout the process.

I also wish to express my gratitude to the Danish Council for Development Research which has been both generous and forbearing.

None of this work could have been done without the incessant support of my family network whot have provided valuable support. Finally, Henrik, Kasper and Peter have endured me when I was absent-minded, and have even managed to remain understanding and supportive.

Map 1.
Senegal by administrative boundaries.

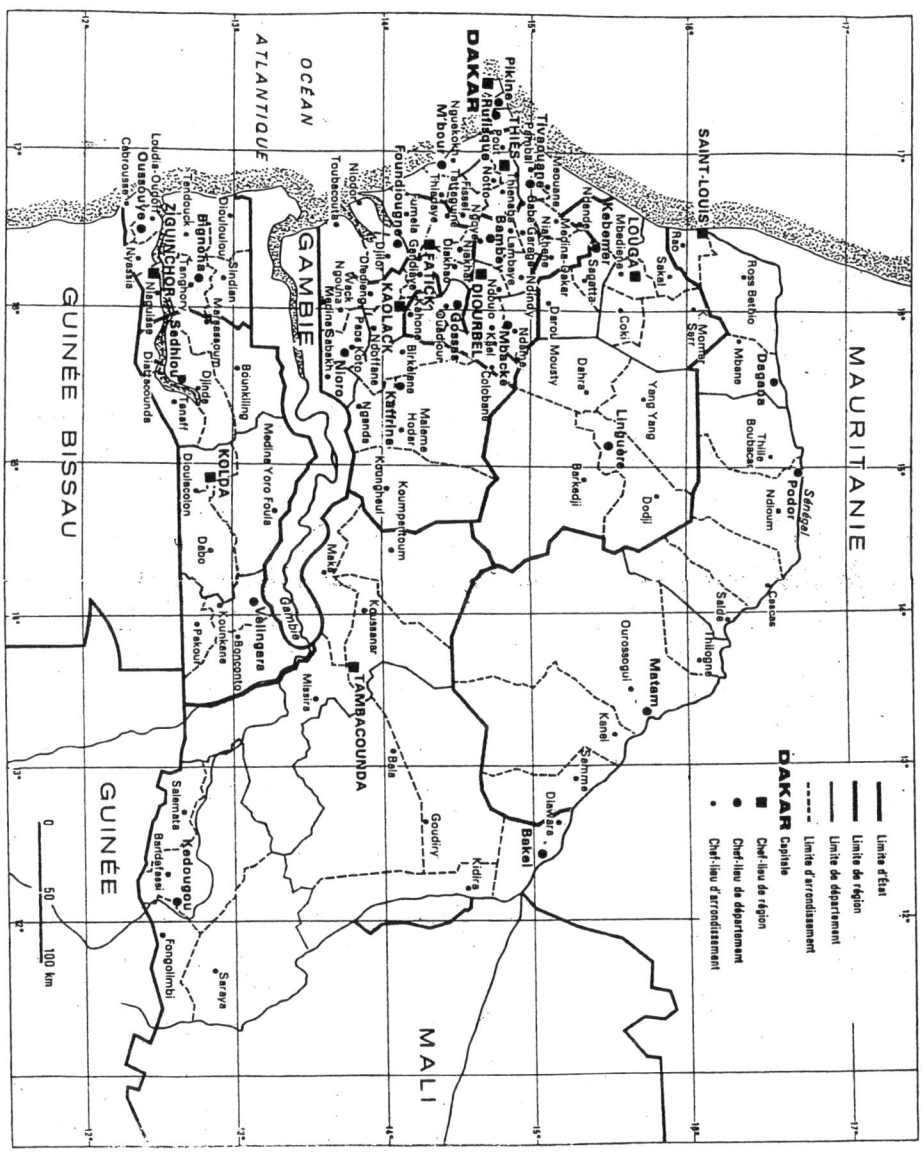

Map 2.
Arrondissement included in the study.

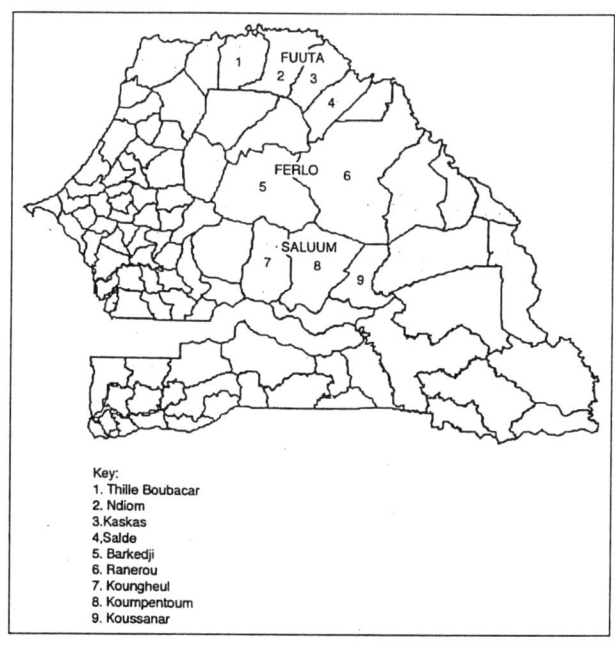

Map 3.
Principal boreholes included,
(by area of coverage)

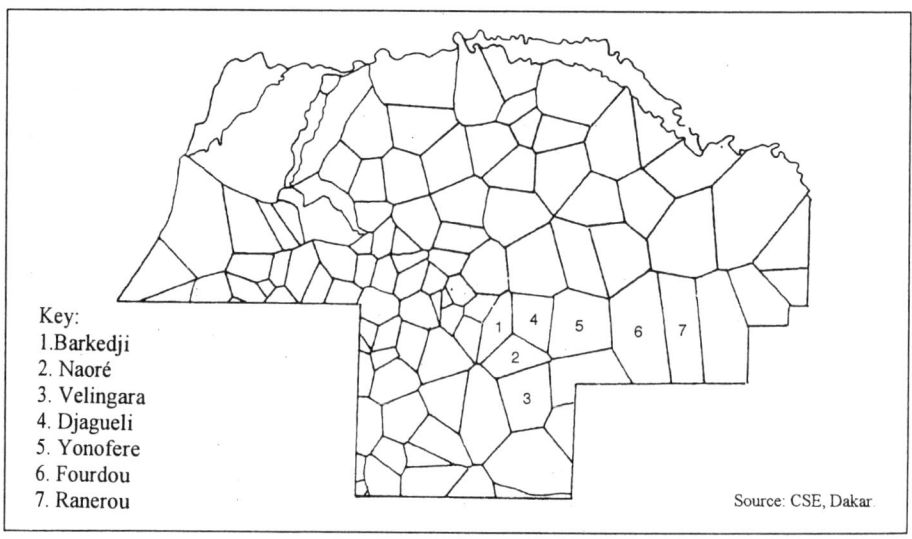

Map 4.
Boreholes and forest or pastoral reserves of the Ferlo

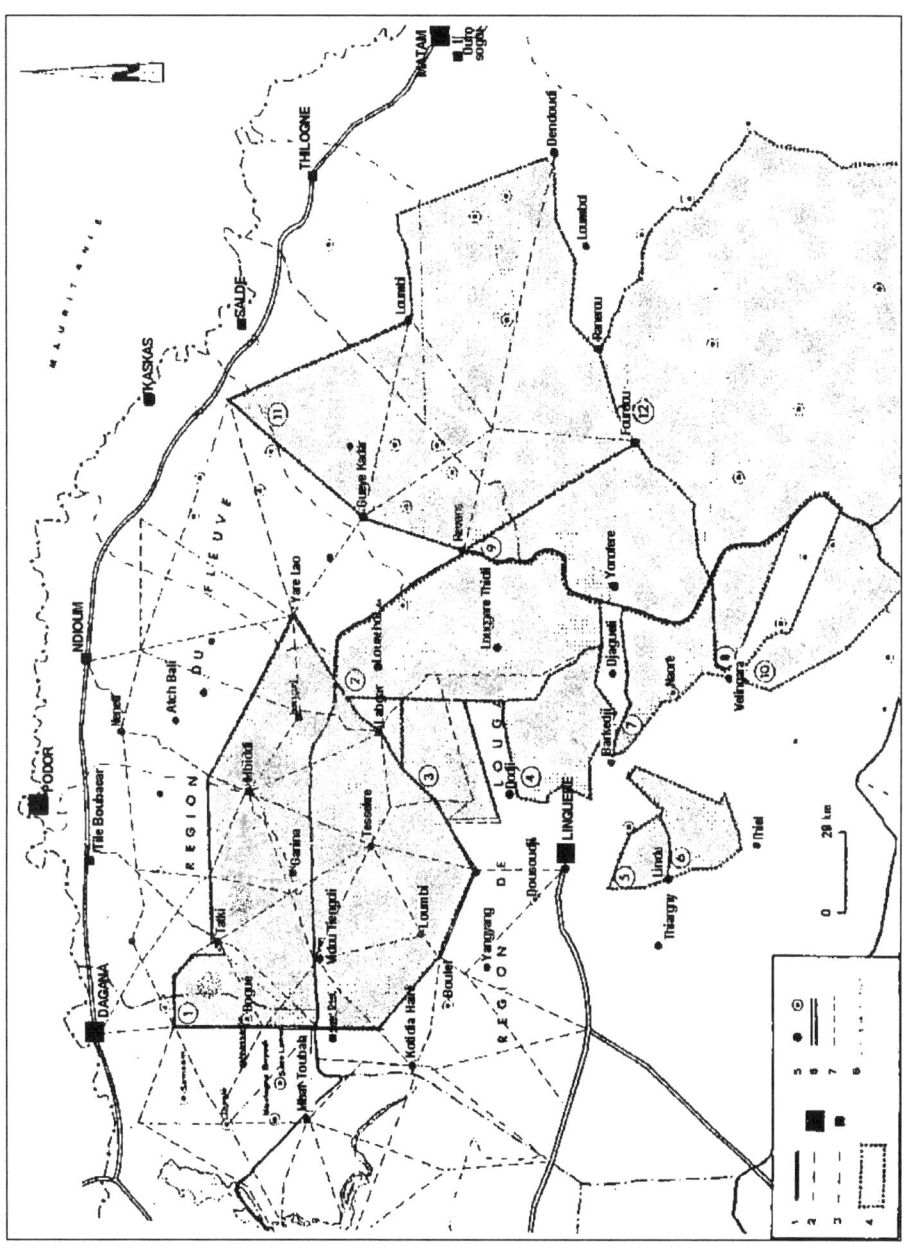

Main gazetted areas:
1. Réserve Sylvo-Pastorale des 6 forages et Sangobé 263.400 ha.
2. Réserve Sylvo-Pastorale de Louggere Thioli 198.000 ha.
3. Réserve Sylvo-Pastorale de Khadar 61.000 ha.
4. Réserve Sylvo-Pastorale de Barkédji-Dodji 65.000 ha.
5. Réserve Sylvo-Pastorale de Khoghé 18.000 ha.
6. Réserve Sylvo-Pastorale de Lindé Sud 30.000 ha.
7 Réserve Sylvo-Pastorale de Velingara 50.800 ha.
8. Réserve Sylvo-Pastorale de Bem-Bem 37.700 ha.
9. Réserve Sylvo-Pastorale de Yonoféré 49.400 ha.
10. Réserve Sylvo-Pastorale de Sab-Sabré 65.900 ha.
11. Réserve de Faune du Ferlo Nord 332.000 ha.
12. Réserve de Faune du Ferlo Sud 663.700 ha

1. INTRODUCTION 5

Drought and mobility: crisis or catalyst for change? 7

The setting 15

Analytical perspective: some initial views 15

The decline of pastoralism or drought as a revelatory crisis? 16

Stagnation or adaptation: 18

Pastoralists, Politics and the State 20

Landscapes and the transformation of the environment 22

Studying change in the making 23

Studying events as part of fieldwork 27

Outline of the study: 29

2. THE DESERTIFICATION DEBATE, THE SAHEL AND THE NON-EQUILIBRIUM PARADIGM 31

Depoliticising environmental change: the desertification debate 33

Uncovering uncertainty; the contours of the non-equilibrium framework 38

Implications for range management 41

Turning a blind eye on local initiatives and the effects of change 43

3. COMMONS, INSTITUTIONS AND BOUNDARIES 47

What is pastoral management about? 48

The indeterminacy of social formations 54

Fitting social dynamics into the study of common property: 55

The embeddedness of social institutions 56

The embeddedness of commons 58

Power, wealth and meaning 59

4. POST DROUGHT MIGRATION AND TECHNOLOCIAL INNOVATIONS 63

Yerim Sow, Barkedji: "The drought enabled herders to get acquainted with new pastures" 63

Bathil Ba, Ranerou: "The Firstcomers don't want us here; they are just waiting for an occasion to get rid of us" 66

Some introductory remarks 67

Perceiving drought in a more open-ended perspective 67

The local context 69

Landscape as a largely anthropogenic creation 69

The borehole revolution 71

Boreholes and environmental degradation 76

Boreholes and agricultural encroachment 77

Post-drought Ferlo as a porous and dynamic formation 82

The effects of drought: expansion of irrigation and out-migration 83

The Egge-egge in the Linguere-Matam area 87

Uneven herd distribution 91

The inner tube and the donkey cart 98

From cattle to sheep 102

Drought recovery through specialisation instead of diversification 104

Changing herding strategies 107

Increased mobility and new grazing techniques 109

Marketing strategies 113

The new herding strategies and the orthodoxy of overgrazing 115

Competition for natural resources and conflicts over access 118

Adaptation to new opportunities 122

The drought as a watershed effect 125

5. STRATEGIES AND MANOEUVRES TO GAIN ACCESS TO AND CONTROL OVER RESSOURCES 129

An example from real life: The borehole of Naoré 131

Fluidity, flexibility, ambiguity and negotiability: 138

Customary regulation of access to pastures 139

Regulation of access to pastures through the control over water? 141

Ultimate dichotomies? Sedentary vs. mobile/indigenous vs. foreigner 145

The local institutional landscape and the myth of the obtrusive state. 150

The Rural Councils 153

The well committees 158

Excessive state centralisation or politisation of institutions? 164

6. POLITICAL AND SOCIAL REALIGNMENT IN A POST-DROUGHT CONTEXT 173

Increased mobility and exclusive management practices 174

Limiting access to water: the technical' solutions 177

Scarcity and other justifications 180

Taking advantage of the drought situation: the economic solution 183

Exclusivity and the heterogeneity of interests 185

The reaction of the FuutankoBe herders 189

Improving the bargaining position 189

Investment in clientelistic networks 193

Straddling between different identities: 199

Transgressing from stranger to local: officialising strategies 200

    a). The role of taxes: 200

    b). the long road to recognition; the appointment of 'foreign' village chiefs: 202

Securing control through private ownership 208

Heterogeneity of interests and politisation of resource management institutions 210

7.   CONCLUSION 225

8.   BIBLIOGRAPHY 225

1. INTRODUCTION

Mobility has always been an integrated part of making a livelihood in rural societies of Sub-Saharan Africa. For millions of Africans being mobile is part of their daily experience. Mobility may take place under many different forms, ranging from travel and trade to labour migration, pastoralism, nomadism and, to an increasing extent, refugism (political, economic or environmental). The ceaseless flux among populations and the variety and dimensions of their movements has made Africa into what Kopytoff[1] terms *a frontier continent,* a continent where populations in comparison with other continents may be relatively recent occupants of their present habitat. Together with a prevalent tendency towards fission and segmentation among African social groups, these population movements have played a significant role in the shaping of African cultural history.

Not least among the pastoral peoples of Africa, mobility and migration have been recurrent responses to turbulent situations such as droughts, environmental change, ethnic rivalry, warfare and disaster. But in spite of its ubiquitous character, migration is often perceived as a special and temporary state, as rupture in society resulting from social systems in disarray. In reality, however, sedentary and mobile worlds often converge. For many people mobility is part of making a livelihood. Through movement new opportunities are explored and connections established through which continuity may be experienced. Mobility becomes a sign not only of rupture but also of continuity, a means to explore opportunities and maintain or establish social relations[2].

Therefore, migration cannot be equated only to a geographical movement between one place and another. Understanding the phenomenon implies an insight in the ways in which people perceive of mobility and into the manners in which they give meaning to the processes it entails in terms of adaptation, integration and social change. Studying how people move within and across social networks, how they negotiate their temporary or permanent stay in new environments and how they manoeuvre to gain access to and eventually control over crucial productive resources in a new environment therefore provides valuable insight into the formation and moulding of contemporary African societies.

---

1 See Kopytoff, I. 1987; *The African Frontier; the reproduction of Traditional African Societies".*

2 For an interesting account on the current status of mobility in Africa see de Bruijn et al. 2001,"*Mobile Africa, changing patterns of movement in Africa and beyond*".

The present book takes as its point of departure the great Sahelian droughts of the 1970s and 1980s where massive population movements southwards were brought about by several years of failing rains. The book is not, however, an account of the immediate consequences of this devastating catastrophe in terms of misery and destitution. Instead, it is the story of how droughts and drought related mobility served as an opportunity for a group of herders in northern Senegal to innovate their systems of production and herding techniques so as to reinvigorate their pastoral lifestyle. It investigates how populations on the move, voluntarily or reluctantly, act to insert themselves into societies, how they take up new economic activities and develop novel forms of social and political relations.

In this account distinction between sedentary and mobile lifestyles and between situations of rupture and those of continuity turn out to be of less pertinence. Even in those cases where mobility does represent serious ruptures in society, as was the case with the Sahelian droughts which caused enormous hardship, the situation of rupture seems blended with that of continuity. Starting as a movement to escape the deteriorating ecological conditions along the Senegal River Valley, the southward movement of the FuutankoBe population continued long after the drought period was over. For more than 30 years the drift has now persisted. To this day relatives to the original migrants continue to flow into the Ferlo to make the best of the economic opportunities found among their kin. At the same time, some of the previously settled agro-pastoralists who took up a mobile livestyle as part of their drought rehabilitation strategy have now again blended these practices into new forms of fixity and belonging.

The text is also an account of the political dimensions of mobility. Moving into new territories necessitates establishment of new arrangements with foreign groups and societies. This can be interpreted as a political process of balancing power and conflict. The book focuses on those changes in access to and control over water and pastures which were triggered by the post drought population movements and explores the institutions and processes through which individuals and groups have gained access to, exploited and exercised control over resources. Through a detailed account of the strategies employed by different herders to ensure for themselves access to key resources, the interaction of local and national political alliances are uncovered as are the manners in which different groups have manoeuvred to make the economic and political system work in their favour. In this manner insight are grained into the micro-politics surrounding the allocation of grazing lands and watering facilities and the changing configurations of power which have ensued.

Finally, taking drought as the starting point obviously entails a closer look into some of the major orthodoxies about droughts, desertification and environmental degradation which dominated the debate in the 1980s and 1990s. The extent of the catastrophe spurred new research interests into the physical and social processes surrounding the arid and semi-arid environments of Africa. New understandings evolved which on several counts challenged previous beliefs on the causes and effects of droughts and desertification. Also the question of human adaptation to changing environmental conditions were challenged and new comprehension evolved on the relations between Sahelian societies and the their environment. Here the systemic importance of adaptation and resilience were stressed rather than balance and constancy of behaviour.

Drought and mobility: crisis or catalyst for change?

In the late 1980s, the issue of drought and migration carried with it connotations of crisis and disaster. Dispossession and forced migration by herders from the affected areas were closely associated with environmental degradation. Development plans, evaluation reports and other types of grey literature were filled of relatives to the original migrants with visions of a population of destitute herders, advancing deserts and a shrinking resource base. Such reports conveyed the message of the need for immediate action to alter the imbalance between natures's supposedly shrinking carrying capacities and the increase of livestock and human population. The general anxiety over the deteriorating state of the natural resources of the Sahel, served to justify a wish for altering the pastoral production systems which were no longer regarded as sustainable. Recommendations therefore emphasised the urgency of stock control and for herders to diversify their sources of income and to find alternative ways of surviving a production system in crisis. Decline of pastoralism was comprehended as an almost irreversible fact and drought-related migration as the ultimate exit option of drought-ridden herders trying to avoid total destitution.

Obviously, these models presented a number of problems. "Drought refugees" were reduced to the role of passive victims, almost a residual category. This left limited space for uncovering the unexpected and innovative ways in which drought victims by themselves adapted or took advantage of new situations. By ignoring the adaptive capacities of the local population a blind eye was cast on the rapid developments which has characterised the recent history in many Sahelian countries. Local skills and management techniques were rendered invisible to researchers and to policy makers whose attention was directed towards the ways in which external intervention could alleviate a stagnant and outmoded system of production and replace it with something more efficient. But in doing so, interesting opportunities for studying the resilience and the adaptive capacities of pastoral societies were lost together with a unique opportunity for studying how and why the actors and institutions involved in the process of transformation acted and operated. Indeed, the limited number of studies concerned with what actually happened to those herders who where forced to migrate could be seen as epitomising the general assumption of crisis and decline of pastoralism. As ends, in terms of decline, were determined in advance, further scrutiny of the adaptation of drought-ridden herders to their new environment became unwarranted and unnecessary.

It is this challenge that the present book aims to take up by suggesting a different picture of post-drought rehabilitation and the effects of the drought-related migration. What is presented here is the story of a conflictive, but nonetheless successful integration of a large group of herders who, in the aftermath of the droughts of 1972/73 and 1983/84, were forced to move southwards in order to save the remnants of their herds. Confronted with the combined effects of poor rains and the proliferation of irrigated agriculture into former grazing lands, these herders abandoned their relatively sedentary agro-pastoral lifestyle along the flood plains of the Senegal River Valley and moved to the southern edge of the Ferlo-region. Many of these herders did not return to their areas of origin once the rains resumed. Instead they remained in the southern Ferlo, transforming their productive assets into a highly specialized and mobile production system based mainly on the raising of sheep.

The outcome of this rather massive influx of foreign herders into the southern Ferlo was quite different to what was anticipated. Post-drought migration in this case acted as a catalyst for technological innovation, leading to a minor revolution of the herding systems, to rising herd productivity and to a dramatic boost in prosperity among both newcomers and first-comers in the area of reception. Within a very short time span, herd sizes increased dramatically, reason for which many herders indigenous to the area started copying the new management techniques. The paradoxical result of this process of migration is therefore that although more livestock is now living in a smaller area than before, it is in better shape and reproduces faster. The single most important factor leading to this success was the invention of a new device for transportation of water. Huge rubber inner tubes from tractors were recycled into water containers. With a donkey cart, the tubes could then be used to transport large quantities of water. The ability to transport water over long distances meant that herders could now camp farther away from the water points and closer to the pastures. This contributed to a significant rise in herd productivity.

Obviously the influx of a large group of foreign herders into this frontier zone between agricultural and pastoral production provoked important changes not only in herding practices but also in land use patterns. In this way post-drought migration contributed to amplify the inherent tenure conflicts in the region. Tensions were, however, not solely the result of increases in population and livestock numbers leading to greater pressure on the resource base as stipulated by conventional environmental wisdom. It was just as much the result of changing relations of power within the institutions controlling access to resources. The new economic and political opportunities triggered by post-drought development also entailed the development of new arenas of struggle.

The present research was undertaken in an area dominated by extensive livestock production systems. It is concerned mainly with resources held in common. Therefore the analysis is focusing on the changes in access to water and pastures that post-drought population movements have triggered and study the changing configurations of power and obligations which have ensued. These developments were neither inevitable nor linear, but have been part of a process of political negotiation and cultural transformation whose ends were largely unpredictable. Because the FuutankoBe herders from the Senegal River Valley acted as catalysts of both conflict and change their post-drought migration and adaptation process provides a convenient lens for examining the often intricate processes of change in access and control which followed the drought of the 1980sand 1990s. On the one hand, the increase in population and animal numbers contributed to intensify competition on natural resources. On the other hand, the innovative production strategies developed by the newcomers provided new opportunities and contributed to a general rise in the prosperity of the micro-region. This contradictory relationship between newcomers and first-comers is reflected in the social manoeuvring over rights to resources and in the struggles to gain political power, and may be traced in the current debates related to political and social identity and in the political struggles over difference and belonging. Hence, the integration process of the FuutankoBe herders into the agro-pastoral societies of southern Ferlo provides a window into the intricate ways in which tenure institutions and struggles over resource access have unfolded in that particular micro-region. Hopefully such an 'unfolding' may contribute to revealing clues as to how political transformations take place both at the local and at the national level.

The setting

The Ferlo, in which this study was conducted, is the northern pastoral zone of Senegal, the dry and sandy territory circumscribed, so to speak, by the 'bend' of the Senegal River. As a territorial entity, the term Ferlo is fairly vague. According to Ba (1986)[3] and Benoit (1988), Ferlo was originally the hinterland: the "non-region" into which one could seek refuge, a wilderness where marginal people and those excluded from power could hide and regain forces. The Ferlo was a space of security and of peace for those with little interest in the exercise of power or those opposing it (Benoit,1988:97). In this way it contrasted the early state formations located along the river valleys - the Jolof kingdom (in the south) and the kingdoms of the Waalo and Fuuta Tooro along the Senegal River.

Map 5.
The Ferlo

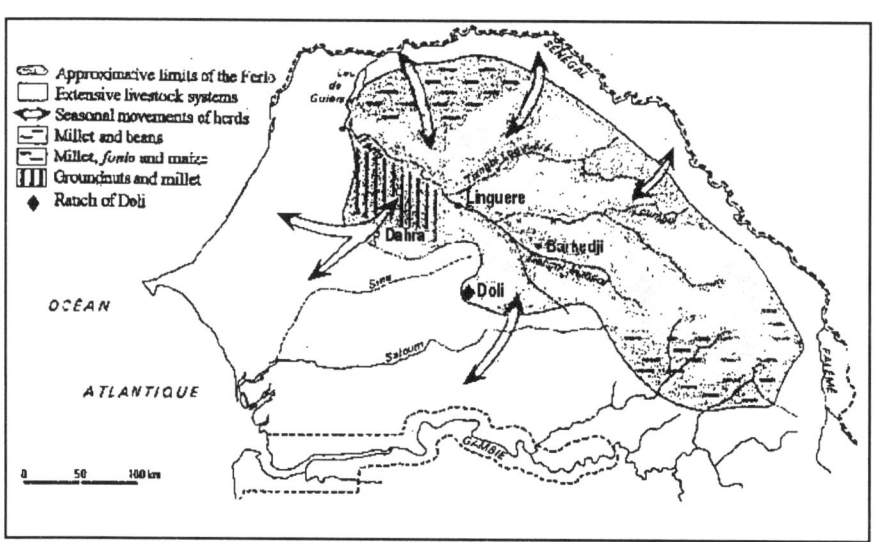

Source: Département d'Histoire et de Géographie de l'Ecole Normale Superieure de Dakar, 1989.

---

[3]According to Ba, Ferlo comes from *ferlaade,* sitting cross-legged, and describes a vast, forested area where one can sit cross-legged, as a sign of freedom (Ba, 1986:369)

While the Ferlo originally referred to one of several hinterlands - the Ferlo of Matam[4] or the Ferlo of the Fuuta Damgan - the term is now widely used to describe the large pastoral zone located west of Lac de Guiers and east of Matam. This zone is distinguished in the north by the flood recession economies of the Senegal River Valley and in the south by the agricultural economies of the Peanut Basin and of Senegal Oriental.

The Ferlo is part of the ecological and cultural transition zone between the savannah woodlands to the south and the more arid environments to the north, a position which has shaped both its land and its people. It is a zone where the flora and fauna of the Sahara is mixed with that of the more humid West African savannah. Although the absolute plant and animal population is not large, the high ratio of species to total population - the biodiversity index - accounts for the great resiliency of the natural environment (Webb, 1995:3). Nonetheless, the richness in species is not matched by a similar high biological productivity which, in these areas, is governed principally by the level of precipitation. Rainfall is low and erratic (between 250-450 mm p.a.), concentrated in a single period of three to four months of the year, and extremely variable in both a temporal and a spatial sense. As a result, the biological production and seasonal composition of the vegetation on which human and animal population subsist, varies significantly: not only from one year to another, but also from one area to another.

Recurrent shifts in climatic conditions have contributed to a constant transformation of Sahelian lifestyles. During long periods of increasing aridity, agricultural communities have been forced southwards while herders on transhumance have been drawn into areas of abandoned once cultivated areas. Similarly, herders have been forced northwards during periods of increasing humidity when risks of trypanosomiasis and malaria were increasing in the southern areas. In such wet periods, farmers have tended to move northwards as conditions for rainfed agriculture in these areas improved. Mobility and flexibility have therefore always been inherent features of the production systems of the area. Not only the livestock-rearing Fulani, but also the agricultural Wolof, although to a lesser degree, have retained high degrees of spatial mobility.

---

[4] Some scholars prefer to use Ferlo to refer only to the Ferlo of Matam, the eastern part of the pastoral area from where the Fulani sub-clan named Ferlanke originate (see for example Bonfiglioli and Diallo, 1988).

When the Ferlo is portrayed as the land of the Fulani, *Les migrateurs aux jambes minces*[5] as they are depicted by Senghor, the former president of Senegal, this image is not very accurate. The Ferlo is also inhabited by Maures, Wolof, Serer and Toucouleurs who in the course of time have mixed with the lifestyles of the Fulani, in such a way that certain Wolof herders have taken on a Fulani identity. On the other hand the sedentary Fulani in Eastern Ferlo have become difficult to distinguish from the Toucouleurs of the Valley. (Grenier, 1960:36). This reflects the fluid and porous character of social relations and identity.

Flexibility and mobility are prominent features also at the intra-household level as individual family members often travel extensively. Young men disposing of a horse or donkey cart may travel to the irrigated fields of the Senegal River Valley in the harvest season to offer their services transporting the harvested grains. Elder men frequently leave during long periods in the dry season to do *maraboutage* i.e. commercialize their 'Fulani knowledge' in the form of amulets (*grigri*'s) and other forms of traditional healing. The women may *go see a relative*, a common paraphrasing for moving over to richer kin in order to alleviate the charges on the household in times of crisis, or look for short term employment in other geographical areas as part of a risk-management strategy. Finally settlements are not very permanent as people frequently move to establish new villages or sections of villages in previously uninhabited bush areas or in places where interesting production opportunities emerge.

As can be seen on map 6, the Ferlo region may be divided into several, but somewhat overlapping production zones[6]; The *Fuuta* region (1), the northern most region alongside the Senegal River Valley, which includes both the *waalo* where flood recession agriculture and irrigated agriculture coexist with pastoral production systems and the *jeeri* the dry hinterlands which are dominated by rainfed millet cultivation and pastoral production. It is from this region that the majority of drought refugees stem. The *Kooya*, or *zone des 6 forages* (2) is known as the 'desertic' zone in which the first boreholes were installed in the 1950s. This area is the traditional heartland of cattle production. Here agricultural production is limited due to insufficient rains. The sandy Upper Ferlo Valley (3), the

---

[5]"The migrants with the skinny legs"

[6] For a more thorough explanation of the different production zones see Touré, O., 1989:" Le zonage du Ferlo, analyse des modes d'exploitation du milieu et de leur evolution.". Rapport partiel , Centre de Suivi Ecologique, Dakar.

lateritic Eastern Ferlo (4) are areas where pastroral production is mixed with agricultural production (predominantly of millet and groundnut). These areas form the borderline between the predominantly agricultural zone of the southern Ferlo (4) and the mainly pastoral production systems in the north.

Map 6:

The production zones of the Ferlo

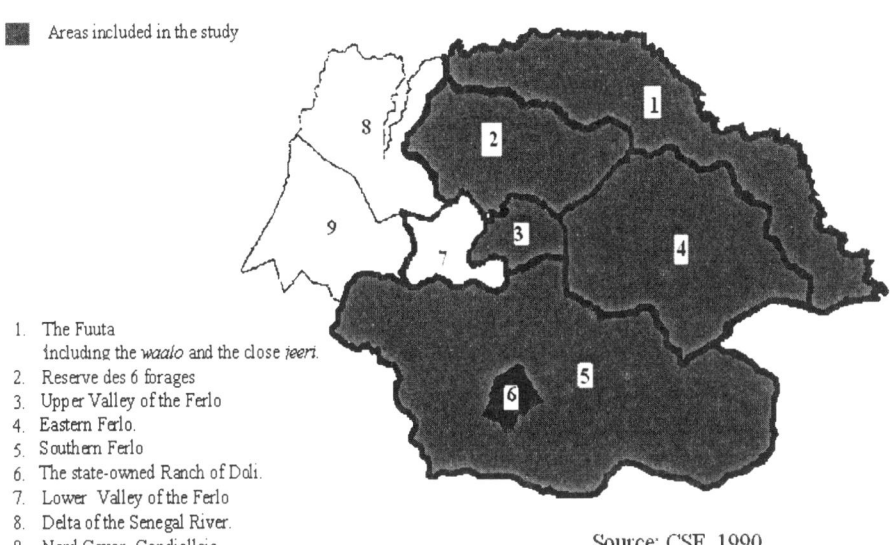

Areas included in the study

1. The Fuuta
   including the *waalo* and the close *jeeri*.
2. Reserve des 6 forages
3. Upper Valley of the Ferlo
4. Eastern Ferlo.
5. Southern Ferlo
6. The state-owned Ranch of Doli.
7. Lower Valley of the Ferlo
8. Delta of the Senegal River.
9. Nord Cayor- Gandiollais.

Source: CSE, 1990

The Upper Ferlo Valley (3) and Eastern Ferlo (4) constitute the core area of the study. They cover the *arrondissements* of Barkedji to the east and the *communauté rurale* of Ranerou[7] to the west. Traditionally, this area has been dominated by semi-sedentarised Fulani who combine cattle herding with limited agricultural production to cover part of the family's consumption of millet. Alongside them, black Maures, former slaves of the Arab-Berber Mauritanians, have specialised in the extraction of gum arabic from the *Acacia senegal* tree. This they have combined with small-scale agro-pastoralism, whereas Wolof farmers provide the bulk of their income from agricultural production.

---

[7] Whereas the study comprises several communautés rurales comprised in the arrondissement of Barkédji, only the vast communauté rurale of Ranerou is comprised from the Arrondissement of Ogo.

Significant differences may, however, be found between the eastern and western parts of the area. The sandy soils of the eastern part attract a large number of Wolof groundnut producers, resulting in significant agricultural encroachment on the grazing lands. In contrast to this, the Wolof farmers have been less tempted by the laterite soils of the east which are more adapted to millet production, the extraction of tree products and livestock production. In this area, raising sheep has traditionally been more important than in the western part of the Ferlo (Touré, 1989). Population pressure is considerably lower in this region than it is in the Barkédji region (4,85 inhabitants per km^2 in Barkédji as opposed to 1,25 inhabitants per km^2 in the vast *communauté rurale* of Ranérou)[8].

During the last 30-40 years several processes of change and adaptation have taken place in the Ferlo region. On the one hand, a significant enlargement of the productive capacities of the region occurred after the mid 1950s. At this time, the drilling programme of the colonial administration established a network of mechanised deep-wells in what had formerly been considered as the "Ferlo desert". Within a few years, a large majority of herders had reorganised their system of annual transhumance to fit with the new opportunities offered (Barral, 1982:43-51; Pouillon, 1988:180). The traditional exchange system between the agricultural and pastoral zones was replaced by a system whereby most herds stayed in the rich pastures of the Ferlo during the dry season. One effect of the drilling programme was a considerable increase in herd size throughout the 1960s and 1970s.

Parallel to this process of enlargement of productive opportunities went a process of diminution. With the expansion of the groundnut economy at the turn of the century, a process started by which large areas of former grazing lands in south eastern Ferlo were converted into peanut fields. This "colonisation process" which is still ongoing, was further spurred by the improved water accessibility in the Ferlo. It included both large-scale pioneer farming communities, the so-called *daara*'s organised by the Islamic brotherhood of the Mourides[9] and individual Wolof

---

[8] The figures are calculated on basis of the 1988 population census: Republique du Sénégal, Ministère de l'Economie, des Finances et du Plan, Direction de la Prévision et de la Statistique, 1988: Répertoire des Villages. Saints Louis, Louga.

[9] The Mouride brotherhood is one of the three Sufi Muslim orders which between them claim spiritual allegiance to the Muslim population of Senegal. Since the turn of the century, the Mouride saints have provided the framework for a mass movement of agrarian settlement which enabled them to expand their activities into vast, hitherto

smallholders. These smallholders had been pushed out of the traditional peanut-producing areas in the south by population increase and deteriorating soils. So when the drought victims arrived from the Senegal river valley, the southern fringe of the Ferlo was under pressure from population movements, not only from the north but also from the south.

The threat of agricultural encroachment on the pastoral economies in the southern fringe of the Ferlo has been analysed in several works (Santoir, 1983; Pellisier, 1966; Weicker, 1993 and Juul, 1993). This is not the case with the influx of pastoralists from the north. Despite its profound effects on both production systems and institutional arrangements in the Ferlo, the influx of drought victims from the north has passed relatively unnoticed so-far, apart from certain hints in the articles on pastoral tenure by Oussouby Touré (1991) and in the works of Santoir on the refugees of the Senegal-Mauritanian conflict in 1989 (Santoir, 1990a; 1990b; 1993). Nonetheless the case is interesting since, on several counts, it challenges mainstream views on common property resource management.

Analytical perspective: some initial views

A major thrust of this work has been to establish a framework that could comprise all the diversities and contradictions observed in the field. Such a framework should help to avoid the perception of pastoral societies as stagnant and marginalised and enable us to go beyond the somewhat unilineal perception of development characteristic of much of the literature on natural resource management and common property. Instead of conceptualising natural resource environments and the landscapes of the Sahel as degrading, they are perceived as transforming as a result of both ecological and social processes. Likewise pastoral institutions will not be understood primarily as means to establish more efficient sets of rules to regulate the conduct of local users. Instead the ambition is to focus on them as part of a process of social manoeuvring involving political negotiation over rights to resources. To set these issues in a context I shall briefly review some of the key understandings germane to the story that follows.

---

uncultivated areas.(This will be explained in further detail in the following chapter). For an exploration of the effects of Mouride expansion on the pastoral economies of the arrondissement of Barkedji, see Juul, 1993).

The decline of pastoralism or drought as a revelatory crisis?

As mentioned above, many authors speak of pastoralism within a crisis scenario (see Baxter, 1991; de Bruijn and van Dijk, 1995; Markakis, 1993; Fratkin, 1997) and consider the 'decline of pastoralism' as an unquestionable and almost irreversible fact. But, as shown by Dietz (1993:85), they seldom define what they mean by decline: Is it the decline in the absolute number of people that can be regarded as pastoralists or is it a question of a decline in the contribution of pastoralism to pastoral communities? And is this happening because of 'depastoralisation' for a proportion of the households or because of a growing importance of non-pastoral elements in the economy of the households? Or is it the absolute and structural decline of the number of animals in the pastoral area, due to either drought or loss of grazing lands?

Compared to decline, the term 'crisis' might be considered a more appropriate concept because it allows for the possibility of recovery (see Markakis, 1993:ix). But as pastoralism may be conceived of as a model of management in an unpredictable environment it may be hard to find periods where the term is not applicable. Statements such as Dyson-Hudson's: "The pastoral strategy so successful in the past is no longer possible", should therefore be the object of further scrutiny (Cited from Markakis 1993:ix)

Looking at the Fulani of the Ferlo, it does not seem that an uncritical adoption of a 'crisis' scenario is likely to generate fruitful insights into the processes of transformation taking place among pastoralists in Northern Senegal. Rather, the 'crisis' or 'decline of pastoralism' perspective tend to work in a unilinear way by which the ends are given beforehand and which is insensitive to the positive and innovative aspects of the post-drought migration process.

An alternative and more open-ended perspective on pastoral crises such as droughts is offered by Jacqueline Solway, who analyses the effects of the 1979 and 1987 droughts of Botswana in terms of a "revelatory crisis". The term revelatory crisis stems from Marshall Sahlins (1972) and describes a situation where socioeconomic patterns are sufficiently interrupted by drought or the like, to lay bare the contradictions in the existing order, disruptions that may have been latent or contained prior to the drought (Solway, 1994:471). In this way, drought may disrupt conventional routines sufficiently to allow actors to innovate normative codes. Hence, drought becomes a time of experimentation where taboos may be violated and moral codes flaunted; a period where something which was unaccepted may become acceptable.

Solway's point is that droughts are perfect scapegoats as all social dislocations and sufferings may be attributed to the drought, while underlying problems such as inequality in access and power relations may be left unacknowledged and therefore not confronted. In a paradoxical manner, the drought therefore reveals and exposes contradictions and deteriorating conditions, while at the same time allowing them to be concealed and mystified (ibid.:473).

In many African societies, the relations existing around reciprocal access to, for example, water sources play a significant role in binding together communities in on-going networks of rights and obligations. But also other items of property lend themselves to reciprocal use. In fact, local concepts of property facilitate reciprocal use because rights to property are simultaneously individuated and dispersed. Most items may be identified with an individual, but at the same time a larger group maintains use rights to the 'family estate'. This is not to say that there is no difference in access, rather that property exists in a continuum. Commoditisation may therefore grant greater, but not complete legitimacy to the rights of the individual or the narrow group of owners. But while one person's claims may rule out the viability of others', it does not preclude the other claims, nor does it negate the legitimacy of these claims. Such a system obviously invites constant redefinition and negotiation. Often it result in a whole series of counter claims being made among kin (ibid.: 482-484).

Depending upon their location in the politico-economic structure farmers and herders have different and at times competing interests and interpretations as to the extent of legitimate claims to property. Whatever their claims, local conceptions of property still render a variety of contradictory claims legitimate. To deny such claims therefore requires a rationalisation that is rarely universally accepted.

In such a situation, a locally recognised crisis such as a drought, offers an opportunity for a redefinition of the range and priority of property relations and claims. Drought to some extent becomes a licence or moral pretext for the denial of communal claims where refusal, before the drought, would have been considered anti-social. In Solway's example, the local emerging commercial Tswana elite have used the drought as a pretext to withdraw economic resources from the pool available for communal purposes. This step by the local elite is part of a process of commoditisation of social relations. Illustrations of this process are for example, when sharing of milk is reduced as part of a shift towards commercial livestock production[10] and when which richer farmers avoid their traditional obligations of lending their draught oxen for ploughing the fields of their destitute kin by converting to tractors that do not so easily lend themselves to reciprocal use[11].

As we shall see later on, the denial of access to water from certain deep wells in Senegal, or the appropriation by herders of private grazing grounds or privately dug wells, are similar examples of transgressions on codes of conduct which, due to the context of drought, have become less improper. Not only may the elite use drought as an opportunity for changing presumably fixed social relations. Drought may also provide an opportunity or a point of entry for the state to insert itself in the life of citizens in new and unexpected ways e.g. as the instrumental effects of drought relief measures[12].

In the pursuit of a less one-dimensional image of the processes of adaptation to the post-drought situation in Northern Senegal, I have sought to avoid the crisis perspective and its derived orthodoxies. By analysing drought in the perspective of a revelatory crisis, a wider perspective is retained. This perspective stresses the multiple and often contradictory courses that development in the region may take. It leaves open the possibility that counter-hypotheses might emerge.

Stagnation or adaptation:

In the 1970s and 1980s pastoralist research was dominated by the cultural ecology framework of adaptation. In trying to explain how pastoralists responded to drought and environmental change anthropologists

---

[10] The longer the calves suckle, the faster they reach maturity which in turn means more frequent calvings.

[11] With regard to transformations occurring at other more ideological levels, Solway points to the experimentation by some of the more wealthy households with 'new' syncretic religions based on western Christian individualism. This illustrates the attempt by the elite to find cosmologies more consistent to their emerging world views than those grounded in the ancestors which affirm principles of mutual responsibility and where ones' wellbeing is inseparable from that of ones' kin.

[12] See Ferguson, 1990, and also chapter 2.

and ecologists emphasised the rationality of pastoral land use systems based on herd flexibility, diversity and mobility[13]. In order to "rehabilitate" herders from the perception that they are irrational destroyers of their immediate environment a counter image was produced. Here pastoralism was seen as the one and only form of resource exploitation which could work out in a sustainable manner under the arduous natural conditions characterizing most pastoral areas. Inherent in this counter image is a tendency to portray pastoral societies as timeless and conservative, often with a "penchant" towards ecological determinism. Because nomads or pastoralist live under such harsh conditions, at great climatic risk, it is held that they are not liable to change the well-adapted and balanced patterns of resource use which they have developed over many generations. Rather the difficult and risky conditions tend to discourage openness to economic and social experimentation[14]. In this way, this perception contributes to reinforce a picture of pastoral societies as stagnant and unchangeable (see also Khazanov, 1984:69-71).

But, as outlined by Pouillon (1990), pastoral societies turn out to be less secluded, less specialised and, not the least, less static than anticipated. As shown by Khazanov (1984:82-84), it is hard to find societies subsisting only on pastoral produce. Rather than being self-sufficient and isolated, pastoral societies relate actively with other parts of society through markets, states etc and are therefore better characterised as a multi-resource system which are capable of adapting very quickly to new opportunities.

In a reflection over his earlier works Salzman notes a propensity for deducing the character of social institutions from the character of the environment[15]. In doing so, he emphasises the environmental impact upon

---

[13] See notably Dahl and Hjort, 1976.

[14] This point is made in Hjort and Dahl's volume on the Beja Nomads of North Eastern Sudan with the illustrative title "Responsible Man". It is, however, important to stress that although Dahl and Hjort underscore the conservative strain in Beja culture in order to explain the structural reasons why innovations are likely to be confined rather than spread in Beja population, they reject the timelessness associated with the traditional stereotype of herders stressing that the Beja have adapted to changes in their surroundings but have done it in a way to safeguard their cultural and social identity as well as their resources from external intrusion.(Hjort af Örnäs and Dahl, 1991:3,8)

[15] The individualistic and uncoordinated nomadic movements of Somali herders were seen as resulting from the scanty, erratic and unpredictable distribution of rainfall and pastures while the regular and well-coordinated movements of the Basseri of South Persia resulted from the predictability and generosity of their natural environment. On the political level

social institutions, while neglecting the underlying cultural components. Instead, adaptations such as pastoral nomadism should be understood as cultural constructions brought to the environment, rather than behaviour patterns generated by it (Salzman, 1995:161). For, although human adaptation to an area takes account of the environmental conditions, it is important to stress that there are many kinds of adaptations. Many independent influences - in terms of knowledge, technology, organisation and values - may in any particular chain of causality lie behind a particular outcome. Therefore it is necessary to adopt a pluralist perspective that stresses multi-causality and focuses upon the interaction of many different factors as the processes generating the patterns of human custom and action that we wish to understand (ibid.: 163).

The concept of adaptation used in this book is not confined to describe the slow and unconscious response to changes in the economic and natural environment. On the contrary, adaptation is conceived as the conscious adoption of a large number of different innovations enhancing the ability to cope with constraints and to take advantage of new opportunities. Needless to say, this does not imply that abilities for taking advantage of new situations are equally distributed among individuals.

Pastoralists, Politics and the State

Most recent studies on nomadic societies argue, explicitly or implicitly, that nomads are becoming increasingly marginalised, not least in their relations with the state. In a summary of some of the most prominent views of the relations between pastoralist and the state, Klute shows how nomads in most cases are perceived as victims of the state they are living in. The relations between nomad and state are characterised by mutual misunderstandings, lack of comprehension and conflicting perceptions in almost every respect (Klute, 1996:3). According to Salih (1990) this is a "hindrance to any meaningful communication between the two parties". It is also argued that nomadic groups are put under enormous political pressure which leads to their economic and/or political marginalisation. Nomads are described as unable to cope with decisions imposed on them by

---

the differences between the contingent polity of the Somalis based on alliances between strong corporate groups of patrilineal kin as opposed to the tribal organization of the Basseri based on political allegiance to a central authority, the Tribal Chief, (i.e. egalitarian vs. hierarchic features) could also be explained with reference to the specificities of the climatic conditions (Salzman, 1995:159).

administrators and development experts. The reaction of nomads is described as either refusal, as retreat or as resistance.

Attempting to give a more balanced view of state-nomad relations, other studies have sought to understand nomads not only as passive victims of the state but also as active agents in the nomad-state relationship[16]. Reviewing the histories of nomadic groups presupposes a far more differentiated relationship, ranging from conflict, over co-operation to incorporation. Just like other groups, they have interfered with, and manipulated, the colonial and postcolonial state, sometimes by reinforcing their ethnic identity and strengthening national identities, at other times by incorporating themselves into the state apparatus and acquiring high-ranking positions or well-paid posts. At the local level too, herders actively manipulate and re-interpret the policy discourses offered by state administrators, bending them to their own advantage. Not least because of the physical distance between the state apparatus and the areas occupied by the herders, Sara Berry's view of state-peasant relationship as being intrusive rather than hegemonic (Berry, 1993:48) seems highly relevant to understand the relationship between herders and the state in the Ferlo region.

Within mainstream natural resource management thinking, it has been fashionable to attribute detrimental resource management practices at the local level to the effects of obtrusive state policies. The panacea to improve local management has therefore been to transfer authority from the centralist state institutions to local user groups considered to be more responsible towards their common productive assets.

But, as shown by Goheen (1992), Peters (1984; 1994) and Berry (1993; 1994), policy initiatives such as the devolution of power over resources to local institutions do not function in a vacuum. Rather, they feed into ongoing local struggles for political power and material gain. For, contrary to what is often believed, these new state-sponsored institutions do not eradicate older political formations. Rather, the new resources generated contribute to re-invigorating older political alliances and divisions or to fuelling new ones (Peters, 1994:45). Hence devolution of power from state to local government contributes to opening new arenas for struggle where

---

[16] See also Bierschenk 1995 for an account of the political and ethnic rituals used by the Fulani of Benin to reinforce their collective political representation and gain access to the central political arena of the State.

local elites can manoeuvre to maintain or re-enforce their political power.

In this process control over key resources such as boreholes becomes a means to acquire political power. The new state-promoted institutions - such as borehole committees and rural councils - become vital institutions in local political and economic life and are used as such by the local political elite. Local struggles over access to resources therefore tend to become politicised as they are mixed with struggles for larger political goals. For these reasons, debates over for example the running and maintenance of boreholes become very political. Consequently, the transformation of livestock and resource management systems in the aftermath of droughts must be regarded as both a social and a political process in which rights and control over boreholes, land and livestock constitute a highly contested terrain. This view is in contrast to the simplistic policy prescriptions presented above which tends to overlook the political and social aspects of resource management. By so doing, such policies do not mesh with the actual realities of social life and are therefore not very meaningful.

Landscapes and the transformation of the environment

In much of the literature with an environmentalist stamp, landscapes are perceived as being almost inevitably in a process of degradation. In the light of the Ferlo case, where overgrazing in spite of rapidly growing animal pressure appears not to be a pressing issue, the need for a more 'spacious' framework for understanding environmental change has surfaced during the process of finishing this work.

Such an alternative view is offered by Leach et al. (1997:14) who stress that landscapes and environmental change may be regarded as "the result of combinations of contingent factors, conditioned by human intervention, sometimes the active outcome of management, and often the result of unintended consequences".

The importance of regarding landscapes as transforming, not only degrading, has been emphasised in recent works by geographers, anthropologists and others (see for example Leach and Mearns, 1996; Leach et al., 1997; Parkin and Croll, 1992; Fairhead and Leach, 1996 and Peet and Watts, 1996). Such works have tried to merge the insights of the new ecology with a better understanding of the land use practices of Africa's farmers and herders. In their view, landscapes should be regarded as the product of both ecological and social history. The application of such an historical approach may, according to them, be a key to reveal the logic and rationality of indigenous knowledge and organisation in Natural Resource Management. When the spatial and temporal variability is stressed, a different view of landscapes as transforming, instead of just degrading, emerges". In such as view non-equilibrium processes and the histories of disturbance events[17] are given a crucial role (Leach and Mearns, 1997:14).

Environmental issues are here framed as 'people in places' and as part of a history. This poses quite different questions about people-environment interactions and the ecological processes driving environmental change. Instead of concentrating on the character and degree of degradation and on how harmony may be reinstalled, we need, as proposed by Leach et al. to ask questions such as: "Which social actors see what components of variable and dynamic ecologies as resources at different times?", "How do different social actors gain access to and control over resources?" or "How does natural resource use by different social actors transform different components of the environment?". (Leach et al. 1997:14). In this way focus is on local communities seen as a group of differentiated social actors, while the undifferentiated 'environment' is replaced or rather disaggregated into a number of particular environmental goods and services. What is being examined is the way in which different social actors gain the necessary capacities to legitimate command over resources. Effectiveness is highlighted in order to emphasise that resource claims often are contested and that, related to the power relations prevailing, some actors are likely to give their claims more weight than others. This is added to the fact that some actors may be unable to mobilise the necessary resources (capital or labour) in order to make efficient use of other assets (for example land). Finally, it is stressed, the issue of legitimacy is central because sources of legitimacy may conflict and different actors may expose different views of the legitimacy of a given activity (Leach et al. 1997:16-18).

Studying change in the making

The conventional wisdom underlying many projects related to post-drought rehabilitation and improved resource management tend to perceive

---

[17] These issues will be elaborated further in chapter 2.

of the drought periods as a year zero; a reference point to which may be attributed a 'before' and an 'after'. 'Before' is synonymous with 'the traditional', where balance of nature prevailed, while 'after' refers to present turmoil or 'crisis'. Obviously, such short-termed historical perspective is not well fitted to understand long term processes of continuity and adaptation out of which present day pastoral societies are formed. The issue of time or historicity is therefore central to the conception of change as disruption or continuity. Emphasising continuity and adaptation and avoiding characterising traditional societies as stagnant implies looking at development in a longer time span.

Evidently this implies a number of problems, which have been summarised by Sally Falk Moore (1994:371, 1987:727). First of all, can change be seen in field work and can fieldwork be done with a historical attitude in localities where there are no or few historical records?[18]. Secondly, how can one unravel the changes occurring at the local level, take hand of the diversities and contradictions observed and, at the same time, distinguish if the changes observed should be interpreted as crisis and disruption or as transition or even continuity? And finally, how does one distinguish the transitory from the durable, cultural change from persistence and how can one generalise from the local and time-specific, from the "small history" to a social and cultural totality.

Drawing on historical records is of course important as it is good to know as much as possible about how the past took form and what type of sequences of transformation came into being before the present acquired its shape (Moore, 1994:371). Without such information many relatively recent relations and practices may appear utterly 'traditional' to the outsider, as it does to the insider. But as the traditional lived in the present no longer is the same object as it was in the lived-in past, little is gained if the social facts

---

[18] Obviously records from the Ferlo can be found in the accounts of the administrative officers in charge of the area during the colonial period. It nevertheless requires a different fieldwork than the type carried out here. In general, Ferlo is not among the best-described areas of Senegalese history. While much work has been done to unravel the histories of the powerful kingdoms of pre-colonial Senegal few attempts have been made to establish a broad historical account of the Ferlo. Singular exceptions are Mark Freudenbergers work on the history of the gum arabic and articles by Benoit (1988), Dupire's work form 1970 on the social organization of the Peul DjengelBe of the Djoloff Greniers work on the installation of the boreholes in the 1950's as well as the historical accounts in the works of Santoir, Barral, Touré and others. In newer works on recent economic and political development of the Senegalese state for example Momar Coumba Diops *"Sénégal , Trajectoire d'un Etat"* and Moctar Dioufs *"Sénégal, les etnies et la Nation"* from 1974, the interior parts of the country are hardly mentioned.

collected during fieldwork are categorized in two different conceptual bins, according to whether they are old or new, traditional or modern. Rather, there is a fair chance that any evidence of change is lost (Moore, 1994:371). If the object of dynamic analysis is how the transformational sequence is generated over time, one cannot, as stressed by Moore, content oneself simply with an historical account in which fieldwork is presented as the terminal point. It is crucial to conceive of the present as a time from which the next moment will emerge.

The proposition offered by Sally Falk Moore is therefore to adopt a time-oriented perspective on both continuity and change, by studying events as part of a process-oriented analysis. In contrast to the idea of a received order that is then changed (the crisis/disruption perspective mentioned above), the analytical emphasis here is on continuous production and construction without differentiating between repetition and innovation. (Moore, 987:729).

Obviously, traditional field work - in-depth interviews etc. - is important for obtaining a general understanding of the setting. But as the focus, is more directed towards peoples' practices, situations and events, it becomes crucial to adopt a field methodology that is open towards, and can capture, the unexpected and unintended. One way of doing this is by looking at events.

Events have, according to Moore, the advantage of taking place at a particular moment in a time stream, giving them a different standing from those forms of data that present themselves as timelessly. This provides the data with a sort of purity as spontaneous local information, in contrast to the interview material elicited and generated directly by the researcher. Events as data comprise both observed and recounted events as well as peoples' reactions to them. The action and reaction is locally constituted and locally produced. Most important, however, is that events often involve a number of persons, who are so to speak situated at the crossroads where many different interests and visions intersect. It is precisely in these intersections that evidence of change may be identified.

"Events situate people in an unedited and pre-analysed context, before the cultural ideas they carry and the strategies they employ are extracted and subjected to the radical reorganisation and the hygienic order of the anthropologist's analytical purpose. They contain the possibility of learning something new" (Moore, 1994:365).

It is while unfolding an event that the locus of certain struggles of control over the future may be identified. Because the people involved are acutely aware of the ways in which they want to shape their future, things that were formerly veiled may become visible as part of a sequence. In this way a processual approach conceptualises the present as an emerging moment, and is concerned with the present as a point in time from which the next moment will emerge.

Obviously not all events have the same explanatory value. Some events have diagnostic qualities and contribute to identify political and economic change by eliciting the interests and strategies of particular social groups. Others may be termed events of articulation since they reveal the situational articulation of different political interests (Moore, 1994:365). As stressed by Lund (1994:13), diagnostic events are obviously not generalisable in themselves, but give hints to certain patterns of processes that should be looked for.

Returning to the issue of resilience versus change, it seems that many cases contain part of both and that larger processes are made up of smaller processes and that these processes, often seemingly separate, interact and spill over into one another. Accordingly the choice of unit of analysis and time perspective will tend to be crucial for whether continuity aspects or transitory values are attributed predominance of explanation (Lund, 1994:15).

In the interpretation of the present case material the notion of 'event' is used in two slightly different ways. In unravelling the immediate effects of drought-related migration on the production systems of the Ferlo in chapter 4, the droughts of the 1970s and early 1980s are described as *watershed events*. In contrast to this, the disentanglement in chapter 5 of the political processes of adjusting the political and social institutions to a new emerging order which followed the 'watershed' has been treated as *events of articulation.*

As will be argued, the severe droughts of 1972/73 and 1983/84 carried with them profound transformations of the herd management systems as well as of the social relations. Hence, the two situations, 'before' and 'after' the drought were according to all standards, highly dissimilar. In chapter 4, the drought and the derived migration will therefore be perceived as the events which form the backdrop for the analysis of the changes on the production systems that ensued. Although process-oriented, in the sense that the open ended perspective hopefully prevails, the concrete disentanglement of the logics of the new range management systems put into work by the newcomers is based on more 'traditional' fieldwork, i.e. a combination of in-depth interviews and more quantitative research methods in terms of questionnaire survey and collection of statistical data. This is in contrast to chapter 5 and chapter 6, where the political struggles and social manoeuvring are unfolded. Here the role of events, understood as local strife or conflicts or just 'events' are far more central.

Studying events as part of fieldwork

A prime source of inspiration has been Sara Berry's proposition that we trace peoples' movements through interviews and observation, as a means of understanding the porosity and flexibility of social and spatial boundaries. In my own attempt to trace herders' movements, I have particularly focused on the opportunities and obstacles faced by herders in their movements and settlements. Following my informants as they travelled from one place to another enabled me to gain insight into the ways in which they organised their diversified patterns of income generation, the labour requirements of the alternating production strategies and how social networks were established and maintained across space and time. In certain cases I have also visited family members remaining in the area of origin in order to grasp the diversity of outcomes from the post-drought situation. Many hours have been spent on bumpy and curved dirt roads in order to join informants who had suddenly moved to new grazing grounds up to 100 km away from their original camp. Here, the exactness by which neighbours could inform us of the whereabouts of our informants also gave a good impression of the effectiveness of *"radio-brousse-sans-fil*[19]*"*. This information is not all incorporated in the present work, but has provided important background material for understanding strategies pursued by the various herders.

In many ways my research method has been as opportunistic as the herding strategies employed by my informants. Often it was more or less by accident that I learned about certain conflicts, which later proved very informative. Although people in the bush were not eager to recount of their conflicting relations in front of strangers my interpreter and I finally acquired such fame as the odd couple crossing through the Ferlo that people ended being more willing to reveal their knowledge and opinions on local

---

[19] "Wire-less bush radio", i.e. rumours.

controversies. Consequently our itinerary was often changed in order to examine more closely certain events and phenomena.

In the course of my fieldwork I became increasingly aware that conflicts related to management of local resources, in many cases, were less associated with the actual competition on access to resources than it was to the competition over political and economic resources generated by the new situation. In order to unravel these intricacies, I realised the need to concentrate on events and conflicts to understand the strategies and motivation as well as the constraints and possibilities faced by the different parties in a conflict. Many of the insights I have gained during my fieldwork on pastoral mobility have been sparked off by such events - whether small or big. In several cases events have contributed to modify stereotypes of power relations that I had acquired through my initial interviews. Such a stereotype is that of the politically well-organised sedentary herders as being powerful vis-à-vis the migrating and therefore marginalised newcomers. This static picture of the relationship between sedentary and migrants obviously did not explain why the migrants, who were becoming progressively richer and more well-established, apparently endured a situation of political subordination. It gave few hints as to the room for manoeuvre possessed by the newcomers. Hence, it was primarily the insights acquired by looking at events that enabled me to look into the unconventional and illicit ways of gaining control over resources.

Nevertheless, the study contains several weaknesses. Being neither a veterinarian nor a botanist my capabilities for making an independent assessment of whether or not rangelands are degrading, or for evaluating more thoroughly the herding skills of my respondents, were severely restrained. Hence I had to accept statements given by my respondents regarding the quality of the pastures, and to accept that when neither newcomers nor first-comers regarded degradation or overgrazing as a pressing issue, the acuteness of the problem was likely to be limited. Where it has been possible I have, nonetheless, incorporated available data on range development[20] and herd structures, but as discussed elsewhere,[21] data on livestock numbers and herd size is notoriously erroneous, and must be used with great caution.

---

[20] Notably the very thorough work carried out by Miehe and the staff of the GTZ project in Widou Tingol (see Miehe 1990, Tluczykont et al.1991).

[21] Juul, K.1990 "Animal Counting in Northern Senegal, (Ferlo). Proceeding from the Danish Sahel Workshop.

Evaluating peoples' level of wealth is equally an issue apt to give a headache to the researcher. As I have normally stayed overnight with those families that have been my primary sources of information, and whose households I have visited regularly over a period of 5 to 7 years, I have been able to observe patterns of expenditures as well to estimate the current size/growth of the flocks. Such a method is of course far from conclusive and could only be made with the 3 or 4 families to whom I had particularly close ties. In order to assess the actual increase in livestock due to the new herding techniques, I have had to rely on the rather unreliable statistics of the Direction de l'Elevage of Dakar and a few other sources.

Finally, the evaluation of just how devastating the effects of the drought actually were in Senegal poses serious methodological problems. First of all it is impossible to get an accurate picture of the individual herd sizes before, under and after the drought, as the temptation for herders to glorify their past is too great for the answer to be attributed more than anecdotal value. Secondly, those who might have been identified as victims are most likely no longer present in the area as it is difficult to survive in the pastoral area without animals. Interrogating the remaining households about those who left is also liable to result in vague and evasive answers as it is considered improper to discuss the unfortunate situation of others[22]. Already trespassing FulBe perceptions of proper conduite on several other counts in my presumptuous questioning into private affairs, I gave up realising that the core of my research was rather to show that a large majority of herders had been able to recover successfully, than to postulate that this was valid for the entire population. Fortunately my general impression that post-drought recovery has been smooth and successful for the majority of herders has been confirmed by other studies, such as Thébaud, 1995; Richter, 1991; Touré, 1991 and Santoir, 1994.

Outline of the study:

The book is organised in two parts: one is mainly concerned with the ideas, ideologies and theories governing natural resource management, the other part with events as they have unfolded in the Ferlo region. In the first part (chapters 2 and 3) what is considered as conventional wisdom on a) land degradation and its causes and b) the institutional arrangements

---

[22] On a few occasion I have met destitute herders living off the backs of their richer kin, but such social ties are to my knowledge not common any longer.

necessary to resolve the problems, is discussed. The limitations and shortcomings of these widely applied theoretical frameworks are discussed, as are the reasons for their longstanding popularity. On basis of this an alternative framework more apt at apprehending the intricate and often contradictory processes of post-drought rehabilitation is developed.

The second part concerns the empirical analysis of the effects of post-drought migration. Here the conceptual analysis and derived frameworks of chapter 2 and 3 are confronted with the realities of the Ferlo.

Chapter 4 discusses the effects that the influx of a large group of drought ridden herders from the North had on the production systems of the South. This is analysed both in terms of constraints and of new opportunities. The changing productive opportunities characterising the region since the turn of the century are described in order to understand the flexible and opportunistic management systems employed both in the area of departure and in the area of reception. On the basis of surveys concerning unequal herd distribution and diverging herd management strategies, the particularities of the new productions strategies are depicted as are the interrelations between newcomers and first-comers.

Chapter 5 analyses the process of political inception of the FuutankoBe herders and its impact on the institutions controlling the crucial resources water and pastures. The emerging changes in rights of access and control to these crucial resources are analysed through the uncovering of the often ruthless struggles centred on the boreholes and not the least representation within the borehole committees.

Chapter 6 deals with the manoeuvres and strategies undertaken by first-comers and newcomers, respectively, to adjust their political power to the new situation. These struggles convey an entrance to understand the constant social manoeuvrings and ongoing debates over political and social identity, often played out in terms of difference and belonging, which constitute the core of local politics in the Ferlo.

2. THE DESERTIFICATION DEBATE, THE SAHEL AND THE NON-EQUILIBRIUM PARADIGM

Mainstream understandings of pastoral production systems and environmental change have been dominated by two equally forceful and interrelated perspectives: one, the desertification paradigm, related to range science, and two, the Common Property perspective related to land use and range management. Although the first perspective is closely associated with the biological processes of range science and the latter more with human action, both have dealt with the interface of biological and social/economic processes. Anthropologically derived concepts such as Herskovits' 'Cattle Complex (1926)' have, together with Hardin's 'Tragedy of the Commons' (1968), have had considerable influence on biologists' perceptions of desertification. At the same time pictures of deserts advancing at x km a year have impelled range managers and government agencies to rapid action in order to change 'the negative impact of man upon nature'.

In this field the metaphor of the Tragedy of the Commons proved particularly forceful. Hardin's now classic allegory of the rational herdowner grazing his animals on a pastures that was held as a common and who in spite of signs of overgrazing would add new animals to the pastures, as the effects of overgrazing was shared by all while the benefit derived from the production of extra animals could be reaped by the individual, fitted well into the prevailing understandings of herders as irresponsible destructors of their own environment. Although the allegory originally was conceived as part of an argument concerning population policies, the idea that "freedom in a commons brings ruin to all" became a common heading under which to portray the presumably irreconcilable conflicts between individual resource users and common resources.

While economic rationality was a dominant feature in the interpretation of Hardin's metaphor, the notion of a so-called "Cattle-Complex" gained popularity due to its ability to explain the presumably irrational social values governing traditional African herd management. As cattle, according to the theorem, is kept as a sign of wealth and prestige herders tend to accumulate large herds, often in excess of what the environment can properly support, and is hence considered inconsistent with ordinary economic rationality[23].

---

[23] This explanation of the cattle complex is far from the intentions of the article by Herskovits from 1926 entitled "The cattle complex in East Africa". Here the notion of complex was used to denote the common traits, a culture-complex among African cattle

The image of the encroaching Sahara introduced already at the turn of the 19th century also contributed to form the powerful image of the African environments as being in a process of increasing desiccation due to population pressure and the derived overuse of existing resources[24]. This shows the close kinship between environmental concerns and Malthusian economics: The more people there are, the more they destroy the long term potentials of their fragile environments and the poorer it makes them and their descendants. Consequently many aid interventions have been based on the premise that African environments are under immediate threat from overuse and that open access and communal tenure exacerbated by population growth has prevented a change towards more productive and more sustainable patterns of use.

Since the earliest versions considerable criticism has been voiced against these images, but attempts to breach the neo-Malthusian assumptions concerning the relationship between society and environmental change underlying these perceptions have not always been very successful. While the majority of researchers and many donor agencies[25] operating in the field of range and resource management agree on the inappropriateness of battered notions such as "The Cattle Complex" and "The Advancing Desert", the myths nonetheless exhibit considerable perseverance among practitioners, bureaucrats or policy makers and continue, at least partially, to guide policies operating at local and national level.

---

keeping population, while posteriority have used the term in its psycological sense, as an emotionally charged idea, a mental abnormality.

[24] Bovill (1921) and Stebbing (1935) were among the first to introduce the idea of the encroaching Sahara. At the turn of the century, environmental concerns had merged into a picture which was to have long-lasting effect on western scientific thinking. The Sahara was said to be encroaching southward onto the Sudan zone along its entire southern front, leading to wells drying up, lake levels falling, pastures being depleted and trees dying. In East Africa alarm was voiced among the colonial administrators already in the 1930's to arrest the cycle of degradation observed in the Machakos district of Kenya (Tiffen et al. (1994). In northern Senegal, colonial administrators aired their concern for the accelerated felling of trees along the Senegal River from the middle of the 18th century (Bernard, 1993:49) and by 1920 several afforestation projects had been launched on both sides of the Valley. Aubreville introduced the notion of desertification in 1949 to describe the creation of desertlike conditions in humid parts of Africa, notably Cote d'Ivoire.

[25] For example the German Gesellschaft für Technische Zusammenarbeit (GTZ),the British Overseas Development Agency (ODA),United Nations Soudano-Sahelian Office (UNSO) and the Danish International Development Agency (DANIDA).

The appeal of these myths or 'development narratives' as they have been termed by Roe (1991), lies primarily in their simplicity. Because rural development in many parts of the developing world is a genuinely uncertain activity characterised by high degrees of unpredictability, one of the principal ways that planners and policy-makers make sense of this uncertainty is to tell stories and set up scenarios that simplify it. Simple theorems like the Tragedy of the Commons have provided the practitioner with a model to understand what is going on and what must be done - and they continuously do so. According to Roe (1991:288), the more uncertain things appear at the micro-level, the greater the tendency to require broad explanations that can be operationalised into standard approaches with widespread application. This is particularly true of the pastoral sector where planned intervention during the last 30 years has produced little but failure.

Depoliticising environmental change: the desertification debate

The presumed relationship between degradation and overstocking, manifested through the focus on issues such as carrying capacity, and sustainability is an old one[26]. Contemporary problems related to imposing more sustainable management practices on local users were experienced in earlier periods, as may be seen in Schneider's description of the frustrations of the colonial authorities in Kenya to limit stock size and preserve the environment among the Pakot:

"The Pakot argue that the government exaggerates the problem of erosion; even though there are large patches of exposed red earth on the plains, they maintain that the area has always been that way. They regard government officials as perennial pessimists who constantly complain that the land is washed into the rivers, and they ignore these warnings because their cattle continue to be fat and sleek." (Schneider, 1959:156)

---

[26] In the Bechuanaland Protectorate, the fear of uncontrolled grazing and degradation of the range that emerged in the 1930's in relation to the first drilling of boreholes mounted steadily in the succeeding decades. Experts warned that stock limits might be necessary to prevent damage to the pasture around boreholes and rules were issued ordering chiefs to lay down a maximum number of animals which may be grazed in reach area (Schapera, 1943 cited from Peters, 1994:79). According to Peters this suggestion seems not to have been followed up, possibly for technical reasons. Nevertheless stock limitation was incorporated into all the later borehole schemes.

But if this is so, then how come that in the mid seventies environmental concerns suddenly turned into the major global environmental issue perceived to threaten not only the drought-ridden Sahelian countries but also the more developed economies of USA, USSR and Australia?

Among the obvious explanations one finds the enormous media-coverage that the droughts received the growing concern for environmental issues in general and the fact that environmental issues had gained political credibility in both the left and the right. Just as important, however, was the way in which the issue of drought and environmental degradation was institutionalised through the UN system, achieving a level of representation and concern within both donor communities and national governments that no other environmental issue has gained so readily. This process of institutionalisation turned desertification into big business, a politically sensitive and major North/South issue.

It was particularly the UN conference on desertification (UNCOD) held in Nairobi in 1977 that provided the great watershed. This conference, attended by representatives of 95 countries, 50 UN offices and a myriad of NGOs, opened a new epoch where desertification entered the popular and scientific vocabulary as a representation of a major environmental problem of great importance for the political agenda (Thomas and Middleton, 1994:1 and 3).

By placing desertification as one of the highest priorities, the United Nations contributed to the creation of what Middleton and Thomas called the institutional myth of desertification. Certainly, desertification involved the interest of state elites and donor organisations, but at the same time the mythology surrounding the concept resulted in the omission of politics from the conceptualisation and perception of the problem. Instead of addressing the role that land use policies and agricultural interests play in the desertification process, it was uncomplicated to view the problem in an environmental light. Rather than blaming internal political or social issues, the Sahelian problems could now be presented in an environmental context where politicians from the developing world legitimately could ask for assistance from the developing world[27]. Desertification turned into what has been called an "ecological taboo", controlling political action on a *prima*

---

[27]The political potential of the desertification argument could also be used internally as is illustrated by President Kountche's use of the need to fight desertification as an excuse to halt the democratic process in Niger (Thomas and Middleton, 1994: 2).

facie basis without examination of the context and underlying issues (Middleton and Thomas, 1994:99).

Much of the research and data collection undertaken in the aftermath of the UNCOD conference focused on ecological explanations and technical solutions, operating almost exclusively with biological rather than social indicators. The focus on biological processes led to a revival of Bovill and Stebbing's old theory of the encroaching Sahara. Much rhetoric was squeezed out of the metaphor of the moving sands, often without much empirical evidence. Further confusion was created by implying that desertification might well happen beyond drylands and in fact affect all climatic zones[28].

Very early in the debate, critics pointed to the lack of scientific foundation for this view of the advancing desert. Le Houérou, characterized the images of desertification as progressing at a more or less constant speed, as "one of the nicest pieces of climate fiction that one could probably find in the specialised literature" (Le Houérou, 1977:29). Later, more sofisticated use of remote-sensing techniques enabled Hellden (1984 and 1988) to show that there was no creation of long lasting desert-like conditions during the 1962-75 period in the Sudan[29] and "that the impact of the Sahelian drought was short lasting followed by fast land recovery". Still referring to the same area, Olsson (1984) could demonstrate how "the boundaries between different vegetation associations appear to be the same as they were 80 years ago".

Nonetheless, desertification remains a very important issue in parts of the donor community. In spite of mixed experience with most anti-desertification activities, the validity of the Plan of Action to Combat Desertification was reconfirmed in 1990 by an external review[30]. At the Earth Summit of Rio in 1992 commitment was given to negotiate and agree

---

[28] In 1987 UNEP writes: "At a rate of 27 million hectares lost a year to the desert or to zero economic productivity, in a little less than 200 years there will not be a single, fully productive hectare of land on earth" (UNEP DC/PAC, 1987 quoted from Thomas and Middleton, 1994:60).

[29] This was the area where Lamprey found evidence of the Sahara advancing at a speed of 5,5 km pr. Year by comparing vegetation maps from 1958 with new maps from 1975 (Lamprey 1988).

[30] Among the shortcomings mentioned by the external review were its lack of focus, the very ambitious goals set and the omission of socio-economic factors (Toulmin, 1993:14).

on a formal convention. In this convention signed in 1994, the term desertification was applied very broadly to "land degradation in arid, semi-arid and dry sub-humid areas" (UNCED, 1992: Convention on Desertification; article 1).

Part of the explanation for the important role given to desertification might be found in what Ferguson terms 'the anti-politics machine'[31]. This refers to the ability of the 'development apparatus' to suspend even the most sensitive political operation from politics (Ferguson, 1990:256) as a sort of unintentional side-effect or instrument-effect of 'development' ideology. Ferguson argues that through these side-effects many development projects, although failing on their own terms, have *"regular effects which include the expansion and entrenchment of bureaucratic state power, side by side with the projection of a representation of economic and social life which denies 'politics' and to the extent that it is successful, suspends its effects"* (Ferguson, 1990:xv).

In the case of the desertification business, the elevation of the problem by UNCOD and its entourage of environmentalists, to be a global environmental problem has contributed to transform the environmentalist/desertification establishment into an anti-politics machine. While making the issue highly political at the global level, an effect of this globalisation has been a depolitisation at the local level. Although environmental plans are formulated as benign and universal human projects, social and political ills eventually causing environmental stress and conflicts over resources are less often addressed. Rather, plans reflect political ambition both at international and national level and act, as in Ferguson's Lesotho case, as a smoke screen for other agendas being played out in the development arena, agendas involving the expansion of state control or the assertion of authority by local elites.

By reducing the issue of desertification to a technical problem and by shifting the perspective from people to the politically more neutral natural resource and soil conservation, problems fundamentally related to poverty and deprivation are no longer addressed as political problems. For national governments the 'crisis' scenario served as a justification for authoritarian interventions in rural land use and for claiming rights of stewardship over resources previously outside their control, as local herders and farmers were assumed to act merely as destroyers of their environment.

---

[31] Inspiration for the term comes from the wondrous 'anti-gravity machine' made famous in science fiction stories that at the flick of a switch suspends the effects of gravity.

For the international donor community the desertification narrative served as a pretext for an unprecedented growth of aid flows and hence of aid bureaucracies enabling them, as stated by Swift (1996:88), to assert rights as stakeholders in the drylands of Africa[32]. In this way they managed to gain legitimacy to participate in the decision making over dry-land resources and to obtain a platform through which they could try and impose their views.

In the Ferlo this process can be observed when ranches[33] or rotational schemes[34] are established. In these cases a *de facto* privatisation is taking place as some groups are given priority access to the range at the expense of others. Nonetheless, the issue is seldom addressed. The same goes for the sinking of boreholes, the establishment of grazing associations or even tree planting, where the issue of who is to hold control over these key resources is most often ignored.

The focus on technical solutions, on context-independent expertise and standardised approaches and the extended use of development narratives in the desertification discourse are partly a product of this globalisation. However the global (or standard) solutions imposed on local problems, such as the ranch model, the rotational schemes and the fenced paddocks, have turned out not to work. This has been particularly true for the livestock sector which, in the vocabulary of the World Bank, has been a 'disappointing experience'[35] (de Haan, 1990:43). Millions of dollars have been spent, with few obvious returns and many donors and international agencies have effectively abandoned the dry zone in their development efforts (Scoones, 1994:3).

This generalised failure within the livestock sector as well as the general high cost and poor performance of many afforestation or other

---

[32] Swift (1996:89) also points to the convenience of the crisis scenarios for part of the scientific community as it provided justification for large scale funding for the development of remote sensing.

[33] This was tried by the GTZ project in Vidou Tingoly in northern Senegal or at the Ranch de Doli.

[34] For example the World Bank funded PDESO project in the Tambacounda area.

[35] As a result of poor performance the World Bank, like many other donors, hastily withdrew from this discouraging sector. After a peak period in 1974-79 where the lending programme to the livestock sector reached 340 million US dollars a year, it declined to 240 million dollars in the period 1980 to 1985. In the second half of the 1980's it has been at around 100 million dollars a year (de Haan 1990:43).

conservation projects has furthered interest for developing a new theoretical framework more suitable to the unpredictability of the Sahelian environment, a framework relying on principles and guidelines rather than blueprints and prescriptions.

Uncovering uncertainty; the contours of the non-equilibrium framework

Fundamental to the range management approach related to the desertification paradigm is the assumption that ecosystems are equilibrial by nature. This conviction draws on Malthus' ideas of populations being regulated by their food supply, through density-dependent feed-back relations. Added to this is Darwin and Wallace's theories of the gradual evolution of plant species through orderly processes of competition and natural selection. Both assumptions presume that conditions outside the system of interest are relatively stable over time, allowing the internal processes of the system to equilibrate and regulate the system structure and dynamics. This equilibrium approach has been one of the most durable ecological theorems since it was launched on the scientific arena at the end of the eighteenth century (Ellis et al. 1993:31).

According to what was later known as succession theory, a single, persistent vegetation, the climax, would dominate a particular site according to the soil and climate of the site. If the climax vegetation was disturbed, the original vegetation could return through a successional sequence to climax (Behnke and Scoones 1993:2). In an adapted form this logic has been the driving force behind most range - and resource management projects in the Sahel. As African pastoral ecosystems in principle are seen as stable, it is possible to identify a threshold of *carrying capacity*, a balance between the grazing pressure and the natural regenerative power of the plants. But when pushed beyond this threshold, the balance will be destroyed and the condition of the range progressively deteriorates. Ultimately this would lead to desertification.

Within this way of thinking, desertification was speeded up during the seventies due to a general increase in livestock densities and improper use by pastoralists that destabilized the potentially stable range systems. Increase in livestock numbers was attributed to: a). Increase in the number of pastoralists triggering a demand for more livestock to support the extra pastoralists and a supply of herding labour to look after the extra stock. b). Improvement of veterinary medicine and services which reduced mortality. c). Traditional and 'irrational' social systems which place a very high social value on the accumulation of livestock numbers rather than on the economic output of the herd or environmental conservation (the so-called Cattle Complex. Preconditions for desertification had been further exacerbated by local inhabitants through land mismanagement, excessive firewood gathering, deforestation and drilling of wells (Glantz 1977:3, Picardi and Seifert 1976:44). Hence, the drought itself was seen primarily as a catalyst which exposed the deleterious effects of long-term degradation by people. Besides unwise cultivation of rangelands, the most important element in the on-setting of the desertification process was attributed to overgrazing by domestic animals. Restoration of the balance of nature in order to avoid desertification has been, so to say, the point of departure of most range management projects in the Sahel for more than 5 decades.

When working with a 'balance of nature' concept in relation to grazing systems, outside perturbations must be treated as 'noise' which confuses and obscures an underlying equilibrium pattern. But by the end of the 1980's researchers working with range management in dry savanna ecosystems found that disturbances, 'noise' and random events turned out to be so dominant, that it proved more useful to think of the 'noise as the system itself' (Scoones and Benhke 1994:8). High degrees of uncertainty seemed to be characteristic of many African ecosystems. Therefore, predicting the levels of production that the systems might yield from one year to the next proved increasingly difficult or even impossible, not to mention prediction of how ecosystem structures would change over time.

Searching for a way out of this impasse, a number of researchers tried to change the focus of research by applying the emerging concepts of complexity, turbulence and non-linearity to ecological systems. These concepts, derived from theories of chaos, complex dynamics and non-equilibrium (as presented by Prigogine, Nicolis, Glieck), stressed the random occurrence of external events and the idiosyncratic and unpredictable effects of externalities on ecosystems dynamics and on populations and species (Ellis et al. 1991:2).

According to chaos theory, turbulence and non-linearity are as evident as periods of stability and order. Both phenomena occur in different phases and time scales of dynamic patterns of cyclical evolution (Spooner, 1993:157). Virtually all processes periodically pass through phases of turbulence, but if turbulence is to been seen in its entirety, the world must be viewed as a continual process of dynamic change over time.

As one of the pioneers of applying chaos theories to ecological systems, Holling (1973) focused his work on the relations between resistance, resilience and stability, while advocating the need to explore the conditions necessary for systems persistence. "If we are dealing with systems profoundly affected by changes external to it, and continually confronted by the unexpected, the constancy of behaviour becomes less important than the persistence of relationships" (Holling 1973:1). Undisturbed natural systems, as well as those under the influence of man, are likely to be continually in a transient state. Therefore, useful insights might be gained by shifting emphasis from the equilibrium states to the conditions for persistence. In contrast to stability, which represents the ability of a system to return to equilibrium after a temporary disturbance, persistence is measured through resilience i.e. through the ability of the system to absorb change and disturbances and still maintain the same relationship between population and stable variables (Holling, 1973:14). Random perturbations such as forest fires, pest attacks etc. may produce instability in the sense of large fluctuations. They may, however, also introduce resilience and capacity to persist. In short, Holling's insistence on persistence emphasises the need for keeping the system open, to view events in a regional rather than local context, to emphasise heterogeneity, and to accept the unpredictability of future events (Holling, 1973:21).

Building on these insights researchers[36] were able to demonstrate that unstable non-equilibrium conditions characteristic of, for example, African savannah ecosystems was a fundamental condition producing a highly resilient system capable of repeating itself over time until a disturbance restarts the sequence. In these areas which are dominated by frequent droughts, population fluctuations prevent plants and herbivores from developing closely coupled interactions as ecosystem development and succession are abbreviated or non-existent. Hence ecosystems seldom reach the climatically determined equilibrium point which is central to plant succession theory and the equilibrium paradigm as mentioned above (Ellis, 1995:38). In non-equilibrial systems, the complex dynamics and the resulting uncertainties arise because of the amplification or positive feedback within systems[37] or due to external forcing. In dryland ecosystems, external climate forcing is the primary case of complex dynamics. This is in contrast to equilibrium systems where populations are more or less in

---

[36] This includes notably Weins (1977) and Walker et al. (1981) and later Caugley et al. (1987), Ellis and Swift (1988) and Westoby (1989).

[37] The so-called butterfly effect (see Glieck, 1987).

balance with resources, other populations or external forces like climate (Ellis, 1995:37).

Implications for range management

If, as hypothesised, it is external factors, such as rainfall, that determine availability of forage, altering the grazing pressure is not likely to have much effect. Instead of trying to manipulate and control the system, both animals and herders are in a position to respond to externally driven change. Pastoralists are therefore likely to move their animals to more favourable areas as forage resources decline. As they have little capacity or imperative to control localised fluctuations in rangeland productivity they have instead adapted to instability through so-called opportunistic management strategies. In short, livestock populations may decline because of lack of fodder, but fodder is scarce because there is too little rain not because of excess numbers of animal (Behnkhe and Scoones, 1994:9). Overgrazing and range degradation is therefore likely to occur only under special circumstances such as when drinking water is a limiting factor or mobility of the herds is constrained (Bartels et al., 1991:26).

Recognition of unpredictable variability as the governing principle in range ecosystems has lead to a growing understanding of pastoral strategies geared towards seizure of opportunities and avoidance of hazards[38]. As rainfall variability increases, so do the opportunity costs. This means that conservative grazing strategies, (i.e. ranches with fenced paddocks, rotations, controlled stocking rates etc. dictated by the long-term carrying capacity of the system) are likely to prove uneconomic under highly unpredictable rainfall conditions. A conservative strategy, defined as one which maintains a population of grazing animals at a relatively constant level without overgrazing through good as well as bad years, would imply that during good years livestock numbers were not allowed to increase to utilise all the additional forage available. In contrast, opportunistic herd management strategies, where livestock numbers vary in accordance to the availability of forage, enables the extra forage available in good years to be converted directly into economic output (milk and meat) or into productive capital in the form of a bigger herd (Sandford, 1982:62). Obviously such a strategy carries the implication of heavy losses periodically and

---

[38] This insight is in no way new. Numerous ethnographic studies have documented in great detail the way pastoral livestock keeping is adapted to environmental variability (Gulliver, 1955; Dupire, 1962; Dyson-Hudson, 1966; Dahl,1979).

unpredictably whenever droughts occur. But such losses can be dealt with in several ways, for example through insurance, diversification and not least spatial mobility.

The competitiveness of indigenous systems of herd management are closely related to the concepts of resilience and adaptation introduced above. One of the principal forms of adaptation is through the matching of available feed supply with animals at a particular site (Scoones, 1995:9) i.e. moving animals to areas where fodder is available. In this way mobile livestock producers can maintain a total livestock population within a wide geographic area which is in excess of what could be sustained by several herds confined to their individual area (Benhke and Scoones, 1993:15).

Another aspect of adaptation and resilience which has been overlooked in previous range management efforts mainly concerned with production increases is the adaptation of animal physiognomy. Recent research has revealed that indigenous zebu cattle, for instance, have energy sparing mechanisms that act as an adaptation to undernutrition and water deprivation. Such mechanisms may off-set increased mortality and increase recovery after drought[39] (Scoones 1995:18). This shows that a) indigenous animals are well adapted to uncertain fodder and watering availability and b) that more animals can be sustained on a given amount of fodder during periods of drought due to reductions in fasting metabolism.

Finally, one could point to the possibilities provided through increasing locally available fodder by importing feed from elsewhere (hay or industrial feed) or by enhancing fodder production through investment in key resource sites. The strategies adopted by herders to mitigate risk display considerable flexibility. According to changing economic, environmental and personal circumstances herders may diversify their production assets by: a) keeping a mix of livestock in terms of species and class, which enables herders to exploit seasonal and annual variability as well as forage quantity and quality on a local and regional basis; b) by diversifying their

---

[39] A trial carried out by Finch and King (1979) showed that increasing the walking distance and decreasing the watering frequency, as might happen in periods of drought, did not result in any significant loss of weight in African zebu. Similar adaptation has been observed among calves of Borana Cattle in Ethiopia. Here reduction in milk supply to the calf did not affect the longer term target weight of the calf, despite reducing the growth rate in the short term. Recovery following drought was equally rapid (Coppock, 1992). According to Western and Finch forage need during droughts may be reduced by as much as 30 per cent through changes in metabolic rate. This is likely to reduce drought induced mortality among zebu cattle considerably (Scoones, 1995:18).

production goals to include not only milk and meat production but also animal traction and accumulation of capital and c) diversifying their economic activities into cropping, wage labour or commerce (Perrier 1994:54). This flexibility involves a far more free flow of investment between different sectors than is usually assumed, often involving a certain degree of occupational straddling. For some it is more profitable to invest surplus from cropping in livestock, for others it is the reverse (Morton 1994:85). If it turns out to be more profitable herders may take up agriculture or farmers take up nomadic herding (or hire a herder). In short, people direct their investments and labour efforts towards the most profitable activity at any given time.

Local producers are opportunists who manage for current conditions rather than for long term means or possible future calamities such as extreme droughts. In highly variable and risk prone environments planning is often a very individualistic undertaking. The tendency of mainstream range management to assume homogeneity of both social group and landscape and consequently planning for averages, has therefore meant that diversity is unaccounted for. Often it is precisely this diversity that allows the pastoral system to sustain itself.

Diversity and flexibility give rise to opportunistic management, management for current conditions rather than for long term means or for rare events such as extreme drought (Sandford 1983). This means that conservation of rangelands is of secondary concern to pastoralists. Because land is in surplus in large parts of the Sahel, especially in areas governed by non-equilibrium conditions, it has relatively low value. Herders have little motivation to manage for stocking rates and prefer to manage for the ratio of livestock to other limiting factors such as labour and water. The benefits to be gained from controlling stocking are simply too small to justify the efforts of enclosure and negotiation (Morton, 1994:177).

Turning a blind eye on local initiatives and the effects of change

The brief historical focus, the tendency of viewing environmental problems in terms of 'before' and 'after' the drought as well as a certain predilection for characterising indigenous production systems as stagnant have furthered a tendency to turn a blind eye to the rapid change which has characterised recent development of most Sahelian societies. Far from being stagnant these societies have to a very large extent been able to adapt effectively to changing circumstances when given the chance. In most cases where technological innovations have proved practical they have also been adopted by the local population, although sometimes in ways that differ from the original intentions.

Often these developments have almost entirely been the result of private initiative. This has been the case with the adaptation of donkey carts and rubber inner tubes, discussed below. These innovations are examples of key technologies which have contributed to break two of the principal constraints of the region: water and transport. Similar cases are reported from Darfur in the 1980s, where major expansion of farming of the previously waterless *goz* regions did not come from sinking of boreholes alone. Here credit for effectively bringing vast areas of land under the hoe also goes to the local adaptation of old Bedford truck axles into flat one-horse carriages fit for carrying water in old fuel drums. Likewise transformation by local blacksmiths of old car springs into cheap tools for clearing and cultivating and simple new inputs like hessian sacks or second hand containers such as plastic cans, tins and bottles have helped overcome constraints related to transportation of goods over longer distances. In most cases these innovations have been provided solely by local traders.

But not all innovations stem from low technology input. Often, considerable local activity remains veiled to the observer simply because the right questions are not asked.[40] Often one is surprised to find large investments, such as expensive four wheel-drive pick-ups or private wells which are financed by individual herders, or when witnessing the large amounts of money which can be raised in local communities when funds are raised for building common assets such as mosques. Indeed, a paradox exists between underdevelopment explained as lack of capital while herders are blamed for accumulating too much capital in their herds. Although unevenly distributed, much seems to suggest that considerable amounts of money may be mobilised locally in cases where interesting investment objects occur. Morton's experiences from Darfur in the 1980's and my own from the Senegalese Ferlo confirm that considerable investments may be directed into trade and public transports, activities which have all contributed to considerable development of local markets. Nonetheless, this remains largely unaccounted for in aid circles, maybe because the need for

---

[40] This point was well illustrated by a Senegalese colleague. In the course of a survey on wealth and consumption habits he was interrupted in his listing of the family properties in terms of torches, mats, kitchenware by the respondent who tried to draw his attention to the brand new Mitshubishi pick-up parked outside the hut (O.Touré 1990).

foreign capital is perceived as more or less axiomatic to developing countries. It is obvious that once development projects are present with their capital intensive portfolio there is no need for local herders or traders to risk their own capital. This dilemma, which can be dealt with only superficially in the present context, is summarised neatly by Jean-Pierre Joseph: "*Le développement, c'est l'entrepreunariat sans le risque*[41]" (see Jean Pierre Olivier de Sardan, 1995:191).

Apart from the tendency to conceal local potentials for rapid growth, the anticipation of catastrophe may also lead the observer to perceive environmental change in a more gloomy perspective than is necessary. Focusing on resilience instead of stability, and on adaptation and absorption instead of on equilibrium and degradation may for example change the perception of some of the phenomena considered by the mainstream view to be indicators of future turmoil. Too often degradation and erosion are defined in terms of reduced productivity, while the question of its significance in terms of impact on people's ability to make a living is left unaddressed. Erosion for example is not disadvantageous *per se*. In some cases certian groups might be perfectly happy for the change. In other cases high soil erosion on slopes may turn out to provide valuable soils and nutrient for production systems that use the valley bottom lands[42]. Equally, the costs of reducing degradation in terms of the opportunity costs of output foregone (of crops and animal produce) may be very high in relation to reduced levels of soil erosion (Toulmin, 1993:5).

Drought related migration is another example of issues which often is often perceived in a negative light. Instead of seing it as people being forced to move to less uncharitable environmental conditions, one may turn the argument upside down. Migration as exploitation of opportunities has long traditions in West Africa and is connected with agricultural expansion, as well as with development of trade and with nomadic pastoralism. As many areas are characterised more by scarcity of labour than by scarcity of land (Berry, 1989), influx of migrants has often

---

[41] "Development is entrepreneurship without risk-taking"

[42] Erosion may be seen not as a hazard but as a resource. By directing the flow of the eroded material, Mixtec farmers can annually feed their fields with fertile soils and can even extend their agricultural land. Before large scale gullying began, the agricultural productivity of the valley was less than it is today as the judicious use of gullying has permitted them to convert poor hill-top fields into rich alluvial farmland (Spooner, 1982:19).

acted as a catalyst for development of new productive activities as is the case in the Ferlo. Far from being restricted many traditional African societies are highly porous, a fact that does not exclude the existence of dispute and conflict over resources. But conflict is not always negative, it may also be the means by which groups can overcome inappropriate or 'unjust' distribution of resources (Morton, 1994:246).

3. COMMONS, INSTITUTIONS AND BOUNDARIES

An issue of primary interest to the present research has been the ways in which access to grazing lands and water have changed as a result of the arrival of a large contingent of 'foreign' pastoralists to the boreholes of the Ferlo region. Understanding how this has affected the indigenous, relatively sedentary agro-pastoralists of the area and what changes it has brought about in terms of transforming social relations requires an analysis of the institutional arrangements related to regulating access to water and grazing lands. It also calls for a more general understanding of how groups of people and societies innovate technologically and institutionally, to accommodate and respond to environmental change. Finally it requires a recognition of the fundamentally political nature of well-committees, rural councils and other social institutions involved in the management of local resources.. Unfortunately these issues are seldom addressed by states and donor agencies who often demonstrate a certain mysophobia for addressing the political nature of institutions.

Institutional arrangements in relation to resources held under common property (as water and rangelands) have been discussed intensely during the last 30 or 40 years. According to mainstream views, environmental degradation arises from unclear institutional arrangements (including property rights) and from the absence of an authority structure to give meaning to such rights (Bromley and Cernea, 1989:55). In pastoral societies, crucial resources such as water or grazing are seldom held as private property. Enhancing more clear use rights on territories attributed to distinct groups of resource users to ensure a more balanced relation between the resources available in a specific setting and the number of users has therefore been a standard aim for many development projects with a pastoral imprint.

These attempts to enforce local management capacities[43] have contributed to changing the outlook of practitioners and policy makers towards recognition of the potentials of common property resource management (Li, 1996:505). Apart from delivering a persuasive counter-argument to the Tragedy of the Commons model, the creation of a "counter-image" of successful intact resource managing communities governed by sound and sustainable resource practices has provided important

---

[43] These constrictions have drawn heavily on the so-called Common Property school, in particular on the works of Ellinor Ostrom (1987, 1990) and Bromley and Cernea (1989) Bromley (1992), Berkes and Farvar (1989) and Runge (1986,1988)

justifications when NGO's and major donor agencies have adopted more community-based approaches.

The emphasis on the potentials of rural communities to ensure sustainable management of local resources has, however often been coupled with a inclination towards perceiving rural communities as distinct and as a relatively stable environments governed by a common interest in preserving the natural resources. Consequently conflicts of interest or diverging resource priorities have tended to be viewed as exceptions, disturbances or "noise", liable to lessen once a workable institutional set up is put in place. But as was the case with the physical environment, it often turns out that it is the "noise", the exceptions and the random events rather than a fictive regularised enactment of rules that hold the clues to the workings of the systems. Hence, it seems that it is precisely in the open struggles over access and control and in the constant social manoeuvring over rights to resources, that an understanding of the institutions and their transformation may be found.

What is pastoral management about?

In areas as the Ferlo, where surface water resources are scarce, improving pastoral production basically involves strengthening the institutions involved in the management and control of water resources.

While **management** refers to the organisation and maintenance of the watering facilities[44], **control** relates to the regulation of access to a water resource and of restricting this access to the number of people considered adequate (Sandford 1983). This central issue is often treated in a rather scant manner, as the technical calculation of the number of animals in relation to the fodder resources available. But in reality the issue of control is an essentially political question, related to the politics of inclusion and exclusion, of autochtony and community. Obviously, the organisation of pastoral watering systems varies from society to society, from season to season between different kinds of water sources and between different years. As recollected by Sandford (1983:9) factors such as the degree of scarcity influences the degree of control and management. Where neither

---

[44] Watering facilities must be organised in such a way that a minimum of time and water is wasted either through slow rates of extraction due to insufficient labour or other types of energy to draw water, through quarrels and fighting about turns to watering, through fouling of watering by animals or through losses from water sources or troughs

water nor grazing is scarce, management tends to be less strict if not non-existent. Where human labour has been invested in the development of a water resource, some marginal control is likely to prevail. In some places, local laws and customs may prohibit local landowners from denying access to water resources. In other cases the powers to do so are vested in individuals through a concept of private property and this can be bought sold or inherited. Finally, ownership may in some areas be vested in the entire society as a whole that grazes on that area. In other cases that ownership is vested only in a section of that society.

All cases above point to the interconnectedness of three factors: water, labour and land. The value of a watering point is, for example, connected to the amount of labour involved in its creation and access to water is crucial for whether pastures are exploitable or not. But as the organisation of pastoral production differ in different settings, so will the rationality and institutional set up surrounding it. Social institutions play a significant role in guiding decisions regarding the use of water resources and these decisions may have wide ranging implications. Creating water points may, for instance, increase the value of adjacent land and hereby increase tensions between different user groups. Likewise handing over of responsibility to what seems to be the group of regular users of a certain borehole will of course have implications for the condition of access of more irregular types of users. But although creation of wells and well-committees is so closely related to issues such as access, power and control, this is often overlooked in development interventions related to natural resource management where focus tends to be on technical-managerial problems on improving efficiency and productivity.

In the Ferlo the most common goal for policy interventions has been to enhance efficiency of herd management by increasing the number of wells and in this way to reduce the amount of energy spent by animals when walking to the watering facilities. Moreover, efforts have been directed towards getting the grazing pressure right, either through different forms of regulations such as fenced rotational paddocks or by establishment of grazing committees in charge of regulating the access of foreign herds on basis of calculations of the available biomass. Also technological innovations such as decentralised troughs located a few kilometres from the water tower have been used to spread the users of a certain borehole over a larger area. Finally efforts have been made to improve water quality as the new water reservoirs are closed and hence inaccessible for the individual user.

Not many of these interventions have proven successful. As will be shown below, herders have seldom followed the designs and restrictions set up by projects and have been reluctant to rely on expert data generated by remote sensing[45] when deciding how much cattle it would be wise to include on the grazing lands. In many cases herders have reverted to their old ways of doing things, once the projects have left. Where new borehole equipment has been installed[46], herders often complain that the capacities of the pumps are too small to cater for the increased number of animals at the height of the dry season. As a result, people often retrieve to the old water towers and their old techniques of water hauling so that the sight of filthy hoses plunged directly into the water reservoir again dominate the borehole sites. The reluctance of users to switch to the new facilities can, however, also be explained by the improved opportunities provided by the new type of water reservoirs for controlling the numbers of users. As the possibilities to cheat or evict payment falls short, so does the enthusiasm for the new water tower.

Although the problems related to water management admittedly have a pemchant to the technical side, it is obvious that the inability to find solution to these often rather banal problems points to more deep-lying layers in the social and political webs surrounding the institutional set up of the well-committees.

In her attempt to understand the processes behind the often rather unsuccessful attempts to involve local populations in natural resource management Frances Cleaver (2003) notes a significant lack of interest for existing local institutions. Indeed, her complaint is not that the conventional water management models are void of institutional issues or considerations, but rather that these mainstream resource management models exhibit a disturbing blindness towards the existing social and institutional contexts (Cleaver 2003:15). Inspired by the theorems of institutional theory (notably Ostrom, 1988, Berkes and Farvar 1987 or Runge 1986), great faith is put in the creation of new formal institutions, "which must work in a formal and transparent way to work effectively" (Ostrom from Cleaver 2003:12). Such new and better institutions can, it is held, be actively 'crafted' by resource users and policy-makers working on a common goal. Focusing on formal structures such as clear boundaries, transparency and equal representation,

---

[45] This was the original goal of the Early Warning Systems.

[46] For instance Barkedji and Velingara where Japanese donors have made new drillings equipped with a tall water tower to increase water pressure.

the new institutions are presumed to be able to develop efficient management instruments through which codification and written rules will sanction and facilitate good resource management. Evidently, homogeneity of the group is considered a precondition for efficient local institutions to emerge, as community members who share a common culture, knowledge of the resources and knowledge of resource rules will be able to design institutional arrangements well matched to their situations and problems. If these conditions are met, community members are likely to be able to enforce the impartial and rigorous sanction against non-cooperators which is needed (Ostrom 1987, 1990).

But in this "crafting" of new institutions, as it is called, a number of misconceptions and misunderstandings are made which may turn out to obscure rather than elucidate the relational nature of local communities and hence also obscure an understanding of the local basis of collective action (Cleaver 2003: 15). A first reservation relates to a problematic understanding of the notion of community and of boundaries: that there is only one community in a certain location and that co-determinacy exists between natural, social and administrative boundaries, underlying commonality of interest (Cleaver 2003:13). To this adds an assumption that communities are capable of everything when sufficiently motivated (although nothing is done to improve their skills) and that people will find it in their rightful interest to participate (see Runge 1986:624-25)

Incentives for collective action also tend to vary immensely between different members of community. Rural producers usually employ a whole range of different strategies when pursuing a livelihood. In grazing lands herders usually have limited incentives to co-operate. Grazing strategies are dictated by a large variety of factors, such as availability of herding labour, herd size and composition of species. Also household characteristics and the relative importance of livestock production and remittances as income sources ((Leach, 1991:15) may impact on the strategies employed in the individual household unit. To this adds that benefits derived from the commons rarely are equally distributed. On the contrary, the asymmetrical benefits from the commons tend to be underwritten by local power structures. The poorer segment of society, who may be those who are most dependent on resources held in common, often lack a power base within the community from which to assert control. Marginal groups may therefore find their specific interests submerged by a community focus. While the discourse of traditional property rights may privilege certain indigenous or "tribal" groups, other groups such as mobile pastoralists or migrants inhabiting marginal areas with little or no community cohesion are neglected (Li, 1996:505). Indeeed, incentives for collective action often vary widely between different members of a community, reason for which greater competition, rather than enhancing collective action may result (Lawry 1990:9).

Also in relation to the professional career of the individual users the model usually conceived in mainstream institutional theory has turned out to be a fragile one. As stressed by Cleaver (2003:19) the positions of the individual users may change many times during a life course – the water user, the decision maker manager and the beneficiary are not always manifested in the same individual. Differently placed persons may reap different costs and variable benefits from particular institutional arrangements and making common standards may not necessarily enhance equality. In many situations people simply find it more advantageous not to participate – making it easier for him or her to cheat or to access water through relationships. Finally reference to community may be used as a definition of inclusion as well as of exclusion. Notions such as responsibility, ownership and social cohesion are not necessarily compatible with notions of equity and rights of particular individuals.

While incentives for individuals to participate in local management arrangements tend to be exaggerated, problems related to the, often weak, structures of local authority designated to enforce rules, or to the role of leaders as catalyst in initiating co-operation, tend to be omitted. Generally speaking, centralised control has not been a common attribute of pastoral societies in Sub-Saharan Africa where independent, opportunistic decision-making is essential to successful livestock production. Instead most pastoral societies are characterised by high degrees of individual autonomy where no individual can tell any other members of his community how he should handle his animals. As a result, local institutions will therefore often turn out to be unable to generate sufficient sanction locally to enforce rules and restrictions of action. (Lawry, 1989:10)

The role of culture as a sort of glue with adaptive value acting to strengthen the crafting of these new institutions while ensuring that ecological and social systems remain in equilibrium is likewise problematic. Indeed the notion reflects an instrumentalist approach where crafting of better institutions "is seen as an evolutionary process of developing the optimal institution for the job at hand". In such a perspoective culture and social structure become the raw material to be build upon and improve while the institutional resource bank from which arrangements can be drawn to reduce the 'social overhead costs' of co-operation in resource management. It reflects a functional and static conceptualisation of culture and tradition with roots back to structural functionalism and cultural ecology of the 1940's and 1950's, where social structure and institutions such as traditional authority were seen as maintaining this functional adaptation: often over and above the consciousness of community members (Leach et al., 1997:10 and Ortner, 1984:133).

The new institutions are furthermore established as if they functioned in an institutional vacuum. With their focus on formalisation and functionalism - suggesting a movement from weak traditional institutions to strong modern ones, they reflect a certain evolutionism - but also blindness to the historical and social context. Crafting of new institutions suggests that specific institutions are developed for particular functions and continue to work as single purpose institutions. But as stressed by Mearns (1995:6) they are much more than that. They are often based on kin-ship relations and co-residence and may have religious, ritual or other cultural dimensions. Often, the single individual will participate in a multiplicity of institutional relation at the same time. Obviously such multiple belongingness of individuals in social environments require that we take account of the embedded social context of natural resource management, rather than treating it as an activity in isolation (Peters 1994). The functional perception ignores that in reality, many interactions take place between people outside organisations and it overlooks that many interactions of daily life tend to be more important in shaping cooperation than those created as part of a public negotiation.

Local institutions for the management of water and grazing land are obviously deeply embedded in social relations not least because they are in charge of managing some of the most crucial aspects of pastoral livelihoods. Their management depends on a number of grey areas and ambiguities regarding rights of access, compliance with rules, on a continued process of negotiation between all users, on principles for conflict avoidance and on a large amount of decision making taking place through the practical adaptation of customs and norms and the stimulus of everyday interactions. Too narrow a focus on establishment of new formalised mechanisms for participation may evidently obscure the actual activities undertaken by community members through other well established, familiar and locally adapted channels

The indeterminacy of social formations

Just as the natural environment of Sub-Saharan Africa can be characterised by its unstableness and irregularity, so can the social environment. African societies are characterised by flexibility, mobility and a very broad resource base where producers shift between preferred resources as a reaction to internal and external change, adopting more mobile or less sedentary lifestyles accordingly (Niemeijer, 1996:98) Considering the porosity of African societies, it may therefore turn out to be difficult to distinguish 'members' of a community from the outsiders from which they are supposed to protect their resources.

The sharp distinctions drawn by many researchers and policy makers between 'interest groups' - defined according to unambiguous and sectoral locations - as well as the sharp division between public and private have little empirical relevance in Africa, because the public and private sectors are interwoven, intermeshed and even indistinguishable (Gibbon from Berry, 1994). Mapping and delimitation of community spheres are therefore not neutral. Rather they provide a perfect means for re-interpretation and re-alignment of local spheres of resource control vis-à-vis other villagers as well as foreigners. Indeed, multiple interests are at stake even in the definition and interpretation of who is a legitimate member or user of the resources and who is not. This becomes all the more serious as these competitions are articulated in terms of competing representations of community itself

But the inclination to reduce human organisation and consciousness to mechanisms for preserving equilibrium tends denies actors any conscious agency. Clearly, rules do not automatically determine peoples' behaviour and in many situations, people chose or may be forced to by-pass the rules. Such action - or non-action - may be important ways of challenging legal rules in order for people to gain command over commodities. These, so-called 'unruly social practices'[47], may contribute to challenge existing legitimacy, thus challenging prevailing power positions. To gain a more complete picture of the dynamics of institutional change, it is necessary to distinguish between institutional rules and peoples' behaviour and to clarify the relations between them. This implies studying tactics and strategies, not merely the rules of the game.

---

[47] This notion was developed by Thompson, 1971 and further elaborated by for example Scott, 1976 and 1985 and Gore, 1993 who have provided a substantial critique of the structuralist position.

Attention could instead be given to how dynamics change over time and on how, and with what consequences, sets of rules influencing patterns of interaction between resource users change. This could open for an understanding of change as resulting not solely from external intervention but also from the active manipulation by local agents of rights to resources.

Fitting social dynamics into the study of common property: Negotiated development

As emphasised above, models based on dualisms - such as private versus communal, individual versus society, self-interest versus altruism – typically fail to understand the paradoxes and conflicts of Africa's grazing lands. Such insights may more readily be acquired if the interpretative framework incorporates the historical processes, the social organisation and the structures of meaning (Peters, 1987:174). Such a perspective, stressing the need for seeing resource use as the subject of ongoing struggles, has been developed by a number of authors[48] who adopt a critical, culturally informed analysis of African rural development. These authors may be classified under the heading of negotiated development.

Central to the framework is an emphasis on human agency or praxis i.e the creative ways in which cultural ideas are adapted to new conditions and how culturally informed practices in turn, structure daily life and shape and reshape institutions at various levels. Point of departure is taken in how distinctions such as gender, class, age, origin among others, shape the practices of differently situated and positioned actors within contradictory social relations (Roseberry, 1989:10). Hence, concepts such as community are examined as political associations formed through processes of imagination and cultural creation - as the generation of meaning in contexts of unequal power (Roseberry, 1989:14). In line with the 'chaos theories', the negotiated development approach stresses multi-linearity and resilience. If one feature changes adjustments occur in the whole system. Hence, the negotiation process results in certain changes which have expected and unexpected effects requiring analysis. In other words:

---

[48] This comprises a large group of rather different contributions concerned with studies of agrarian change (Berry, Guyer, Carney and Watts, etc), local politics (for example Peters, Goheen), customary law (Sally Falk Moore, Michael Chanock etc) and ecology and society, (Leach, Mearns, Fairhead, Scoones, Shipton). Many of these have published in "Africa": the Journal of the International African Institute.

"negotiation is a metaphor that emphasises openness of interaction as far as outcome is concerned" (Sepällä, 1996:85).

The concept of negotiated development itself refers to a situation where different groups come into contact with each other and try to lay claim to a specific issue. What is of interest is that, in this process of negotiation, old social groups tend to be recomposed or new ones created. Likewise people's perceptions of the object of negotiation may change, just as the social relationships between the negotiating parties are changed during the process of negotiation (Sepällä, 1996:84). The actual object for negotiations may in fact be placed in the periphery of the analysis. What matters are the social groups and their perceptions. And, since different groups have different perspectives, their negotiation must necessarily entail contradictions and conflicts (ibid).

The embeddedness of social institutions

The innumerable movement to local frontiers, which are characteristic for the continent of Africa, have forced displaced Africans to face the problem of forging new social orders in the midst of an effective institutional vacuum. African societies therefore tend to be porous and to have mechanisms which allow individuals or groups to modify their identity and to transgress ethnic boundaries.

In consequence of low population densities and the high levels of mobility an important structuring principle is the rights of the first-comer. As will be shown below, being the first-comers gave certain rights of seniority, as it gave one the rights to show the place to those who came later. A hierarchy was established where first-comers in principle could claim superiority over newcomers (Kopytoff, 1987: 31). This relationship nonetheless remains fluid as the principle of precedence -which ties first-comers to late-comers in to a chain of hierarchy- in itself represents a paradox, as no one can ever claim to be really the first (as shall be seen in the Ferlo case). Many examples may be found of immigrant founders who took over local political systems and remoulded them to their own purpose by skilful political manoeuvring.

Consistent with these mobile and flexible features, Kopytoff also identifies a relative indifference among Africans to rootedness in physical space and a lack of permanent attachment to a particular geographical place. "African space is, above all, a social space" he claims, their roots being primarily conceived in a kin group, in ancestors and in genealogical position (Kopytoff, 1987:22).

Because abundance of land allowed Africans to secure their livelihood by mobile and extensive exploitation of the land, through shifting cultivation or pastoralism African societies have usually faced a shortage of people rather than of land. The political consequence of this has, according to Goody (1971:30) been that chieftainship has tended to be over people rather than over land; and these the leader had to attract as well as restrain. The drive to acquire adherents and dependents and to make alliances and keep them attached to one-self as a kind of political and social 'capital' is, according to Goody, characteristic of African political processes. Like Kopytoff, Goody emphasises the social space rather than geographic control and stresses the general lack of a rigid rootedness in physical space.

The search for adherents as a source of power is also stressed by Peters, Goheen and Berry. In many African societies, a person's status and influence depends directly on the ability to mobilise a following. And if access to resources and opportunities depends on one's ability to negotiate over property rights, production or exchange and influence is enhanced by followers, then it is not necessarily advantageous to exclude people from social networks, even if these networks also serve as channels of access to resources (Berry, 1993:15). Consequently, people may be more interested in keeping options open than in cutting them off, a factor which might explain the relative reluctance or lack of incentives for excluding foreigners found in many settings. Frequently, interests are ambiguous and give rise, as will be shown in the Ferlo case below, to both exclusive and inclusive strategies of social mobilisation and resource control.

With this indeterminacy in mind, it should be obvious that it is not possible to explain the fundamental features of an existing social order from what can be seen here and now. Nor is it possible to treat the workings of a system as isolated in space and time. Such simplifications do not relate the actual realities of social life and therefore are not meaningful. Quite on the contrary, it is precisely many of the features presented above that have provided some of the constants on which on-going social relations rest and on which any new social relations are built (Kopytoff, 1987:39). This fundamental indeterminacy of African social formations is stressed by Peters, Goheen and Berry who emphasise that the social construction of economic life must be seen as a creative process, whose end is not given beforehand. The social construction of economic life can take many forms. These forms are not necessarily successful, depending among other things on the ability to create some rudimentary order in competing claims and rights.

The embeddedness of commons

Contrary to those who conceive of resource management institutions as single purpose, well-defined rule-making authorities, the negotiated development view stresses the need to see institutions as socially and politically embedded, emphasising their contingent and indeterminate character. Hence, institutions are seen as regularised rules of behaviour that emerge from the underlying structures or sets of 'rules in use'.

Arguing for the embeddedness of a commons helps to avoid falling into the polemic extremes of the transformation view which, according to Peters: "casts its lot with the individual actor, the social realm being at best but a context in necessary opposition to the individual's self-interest or the "models of an idealised past". It also avoids the extreme of the preservation view that casts its individual as non-actors, only a figure inscribed in the hidden logic of an eco-cultural system" (Peters, 1987:178).

Understanding commons as socially embedded means emphasising the interdependence of decision-makers. By looking at the structures of relations, the distinctions between groups and the shared or competing meaning and value attributed to a particular commons and its use it becomes possible to avoid the unattached, autonomous and asocial individual on the one side. On the other side, it also becomes possible to avoid the view of the undifferentiated, homogeneous and harmonious community. In doing this, the contemporary situation of the commons may be described not by absence of links between the individual herder and the group, but rather as a result of competing rights and multiple claims to legitimate use. Such rights are, as will be discussed in further detail below, not only embedded in specific historical sets of political and economic structures, but also in cultural systems of meanings, symbols and values (ibid).

Rather than existing as a fixed framework, the negotiated development view perceives rules as being constantly made and remade through peoples' practices. In order to discern how, for example, rights of access and control over resources changes over time, an understanding of 'rules in use' based on analysis of peoples, regular everyday practices is required. Such a conception stresses difference and the appreciation of power relations. (ibid.:27) To "trace peoples multiple, sometimes contradictory and ambivalent actions and experiences" as proposed by Berry (1994:33) may therefore turn out to be a fruitful way to gain insight both into the dynamics of institutional structure and of the fluidity and complexity of institutionalised rules and practices.

Power, wealth and meaning

Central to contemporary discussions of agrarian change is the investigation of how land use is shaped by the dynamics of resource access, use and control; and of relating this to questions of social form and process. Disputes and negotiations about land are not only about particular tracts of lands, but are just as much about the very meanings of the lands itself and of the customs and conventions by which humans relate to it. Hence, three perspectives are sought integrated: the political, the economic and the cultural. This, according to Shipton and Goheen (1992:397), means bearing in mind three kinds of human ambitions: Power, wealth and meaning - and looking for the linkages between them[49]. This perspective highlights that people use land for many purposes: not just to produce the material conditions for survival and enrichment, but also to gain control over others and define personal and social identities. Shipton and Goheen propose an analysis of changes in resource access and control to start by posing three simple questions:

1). What does land mean, to whom? This question stresses the heterogeneity of the user groups as well as the different use made of resources by different groups. Not all groups perceive the land in the same way. Resources that are valuable for some are not important for others, just as the groups of users may vary according to seasons. Thus, on the same piece of land, people may hold different rights to different resources in different seasons[50].

The categorisation of land and its resource may also be the subject of different interpretations. For transhumant herders, the routes traversing a certain piece of land may be more important than the actual

---

[49] This is analogous to the three primary roads to social analysis suggested by Sally Falk Moore: via relations, via resources, and via 'representations' (Moore, 1986:9).

[50] These hierarchical and multi-usage dimensions of tenure have been dealt extensively with by Bruce (1988a and 1988b).

grazing potential, just as farmers may be less attached to a particular piece of land than to the right to farm in an area. Likewise people may be less attached to fixed points on the ground but rather understand their rights "as elastic spaces on a rubber map"[51] , defined in relation to other kin and neighbours (Shipton and Goheen, 1992:309). The meanings attributed to land therefore vary as part of the struggle for control: as, for example, when fallow lands or lands with absentee owners are, for purposes of contestation, classified as vacant by other potential claimants.

2). What kinds of social affiliations affect land use and control? As mentioned above, rural Africans do not generally hold land as individuals and power over land is largely a function of membership in social networks. Hence it remains contested and negotiable. As described above in discussing the indeterminacy of social formations, the social networks through which people pursue access to resources and opportunities have not been consolidated into closed corporations which act to exclude outsiders, as suggested by the transformation and preservation approaches. Instead they continue to operate as arenas for individual accumulation and mobility. For, in order to gain sufficient authority to enforce exclusive rights, it is crucial to expand the number of supporters. As stressed by Berry (1994:104), authority rests partly on inclusionary strategies which are undermined when authority is used for exclusive ends.

The existence of networks based on both inclusive and exclusive strategies does not preclude differential access to resources. On the contrary, the question of who gets the power to interpret and define the meaning, not just of the land *per se,* but also of the group itself, is central. How people gain influence on decisions regarding resource allocation and resource distribution must be understood as the outcome of negotiations between different social actors involving power relations and debates over meaning, rather than the result of fixed moral rules encoded in law (Leach et al. 1997:23).

In relation to this it is also important to stress how transformation of land in terms of, for example, the ongoing process of privatisation of the Botswana range is as much the result of the manipulations of the 'commoners' themselves, as a result of outside interference as proposed by the preservation view. Rather than treating state

---

[51] This classic example is provided by Bohannan from Tiv. For a more 'poetic' exposé see Chatwins account on the Australian aboriginals in "Songlines". See also Ingold, T. 1986: "The appropriation of nature" for a discussion of territoriality and movement.

interventions as obtrusive, Berry and co. stress that the presence of the state has been intrusive rather than hegemonic, and that rural producers have entered negotiations with their own agenda, and have had the power to manipulate the outcome or partially withdraw from social processes which they perceive as unfavourable (Berry 1993:48). In their interrelations with the state, rural dwellers often 'straddle' between formal and informal institutions in an effort to diversify their options and maintain flexibility in the face of uncertain opportunities and constraints. According to Berry, the result of this is neither effective state control over the countryside, nor an uncaptured peasantry. Rather it is a situation of multiple linkages between farmers and states which affect patterns of resource allocation and agricultural performance partly by encouraging mobility and diversification of networks and income sources (Berry 1993:66).

In such structurally unequal relationships power can always be contested. Hence, people do not passively submit themselves to external interventions in terms of projects, plans and regulations. Rather they acquire or pick up the current discourses and transform them so as to fit into their own interests and goals. Obviously some will be in a better position than others to present local problems in such a way as to reflect their own resource priorities. It is therefore also important to focus on differentiation as such claims not always are identical to those of the rest of the community.

3). Who controls the terminology? Struggles over meanings are, as stated by Berry (1988:66), as much a part of the process of resource allocation as are the struggles over surplus or the labour process. In the context of struggles over resources, multiple conflicting discourses arise and different visions of community are articulated. Such representations are important as they form part of what may be termed the practical political economy through which different parties defend their interests and advance their claims (Li, 1996:503).

Hence, processes of transformation commonly involve contestation and revision of the meaning of key terms such as property and community. Images of community, for example, are central to questions of resource access at the local level: not because of guaranteed rights provided by rules and traditions (as proposed by Runge) but because it provides a "culturally available point of leverage in ongoing processes of negotiation" i.e. a vocabulary of legitimisation (Li, 1996: 509).

Returning to the issue of boundaries, a lucid example of such (re)interpretations or 'struggles over meanings' is given by Pauline Peters when showing how the administrative requirement of a minimum distance of five miles between boreholes has led to the interpretation, that an area of approximately five square miles belongs to each borehole. Indeed, technical processes of measuring and mapping of areas surrounding the boreholes tend to give support to the notion among borehole owners that a right to land is as much as a right to the water that has been allocated to borehole owners. (Peters 1996:111) As will be shown below, similar processes can be observed in Senegal.

4. POST DROUGHT MIGRATION AND TECHNOLOGICAL INNOVATIONS.

Yerim Sow, Barkedji: "The drought enabled herders to get acquainted with new pastures"

In March 1989, when I first met Yerim Sow and his family, they were living in a temporary camp north of the borehole at Velingara. The family had no hut and their scattered belongings were either attached to the branches of the few small acacia trees encircling the camp or placed on a rack made out of branches in order to keep them out of reach of the lambs and kid who were toddling peacefully around the camp. The family had stayed in this camp less than a week. Before that they had camped at two other localities at a distance of around one kilometre from one another, three months at the first camp and one month at the second. Because of the frequent movements, the wife had not yet begun the arduous work of constructing a grass-hut. There were just some mats in the shade of a few scattered trees.

Although moving throughout the year, camping in the area around the deep well at Velingara was unusual for Yerim Sow and his family. They normally restricted their area of movement to the north of the Barkedji borehole. In the year 1989, however, the gazetted forest of Barkedji-Dodji had been ravaged by large bush-fires and the family had preferred to move 40 kilometres further south, where pastures were still to be found. Before the rains started again in June-July, the family was likely to move their camp another few times before returning to their usual wet season encampment in the Barkedji-Dodji forest. The frequent movements of the camp were part of the dry season mobility pattern which the family had pursued since its arrival in the area following the droughts.

Yerim Sow and his family originate from Ganina, some 50 kilometres south of the Senegal River Valley. Here the herding system had been fairly sedentarised. In years with plentiful rains animals could be watered throughout the year at shallow wells. In other years they were taken up to the Senegal River. When the deep well of Ganina was constructed in 1969, movements were restricted to occasional visits to the salt licks near Lac de Guiers.

When the first drought hit in 1973, the family moved south to Velingara, where they stayed at different locations until the rains resumed and they were able to return to Ganina. But as expressed by Yerim: "The drought enabled herders to get acquainted to new pastures". Already in the dry season of 1975 the family decided to spend the dry season in Barkedji. The next year the rains failed and the family stayed in the south and did not come back to Ganina before the rainy season of 1977. In the following years transhumance was not possible.

With the second drought 1983/84, Yerim's son moved south with the sheep and goats while Yerim stayed back with the cattle. But when the son returned in the rainy season, the pastures were so poor that the family decided to move south with the entire herd. From then on they restricted their normal radius of movement to the forest of Barkedji-Dodji, oscillating between a wet season camp located besides a large pond approximately 20 kilometres north of the borehole of Barkedji and several temporary dry season camps closer to the water point. Every year, at the end of the dry season, the family goes on a shorter trip southwards "to meet the rains" i.e. to move some 20-40 km's southwards where the rains have set in earlier to ensure fresh fodder as early as possible and to "shorten e dry season". They usually return to the wet season camp within a few weeks, but such late return makes it difficult to embark on any agricultural activities.

The family consists of Yerim, a tall and bony elderly man whose working abilities were seriously reduced by an accident with his horse-cart in 1988, his wife, their only son, his wife and their 4 children aged 1 to 10 years. There is also a niece, who undertakes part of the herding and the water transportation. The family has a serious shortage of manpower and, usually, a salaried herdsman is engaged. This is however a rather unstable workforce since, according to Yerim, such hired herders often run off, sometimes with a few animals, leaving the rest to roam around unguarded in the forest. Due to shortage of manpower, Yerim has not undertaken longer transhumance trips in the last 7-8 years.

In contrast to most of his kin, Yerim spent even the dry year of 1991-92 in the Barkedji-Dodji forest. Due to lack of manpower, the family had waited too long to move. The animals got sick and weak. Moving them would have resulted in considerable losses. Instead the family invested all their manpower in limiting the energy losses of the animals. As an alternative to sending the animals on the long trip to the borehole, they were watered either at shallow wells[52] where small amounts of water is "fished"

---

[52] *Bulli* in Fulani and *céanes* in French, are holes of 2-3 meters dug into humid depressions. Interlacing branches usually reinforces the brinks.

out of the dry river bed with a 2 litre can tied to a stick - like a fishing rod - or by bringing water out to the camp from the deep well by donkey cart. This very time-consuming watering method obviously reduced the amount of time the animals could spend grazing. The heavy labour input required by this system was however partly compensated for by the absence of other herds competing for the meagre fodder resources in the area. Nonetheless, losses during the dry season of 1991 were considerable. But according to the estimations of the head of households, they would have been far greater had they left while the animals were weak. Sparing the ewes for the long trip to the well also limited the number of abortions.

In spite of very serious difficulties during the years I visited them, the family has, nonetheless, fared well. As mentioned in chapter 1, it is impossible to get an accurate picture of the number of animals owned by the family before and after the drought. Nonetheless herd development between 1989 and 1996 appeared to be reasonably successful. In this period the herd increased from approximately 500 head of small stock and 44 head of cattle to approximately 900 sheep and goats and 120 head of cattle.

When Yerim first settled in the Forest of Barkedji-Dodji, he made a courtesy visit to the neighbouring village of Belkagne to inform the village chief of his settlement in the bush some 10 kilometres east of the village. According to Yerim, this was taken badly by the village chief and initiated a relationship of perpetual disputes between them. The village chief had no authority to keep the newcomers out of the area. On the contrary, the newcomers could back their rights of occupancy under the law on the National Domain which stipulates the rights of any Senegalese to settle in areas under state ownership. Over the years Yerim has invested quite a lot of effort (as well as sheep) in maintaining good relations to shifting *sous-préfets*, the administrative officers in charge of the area. Nonetheless, the status of his 'village' and its location within the boundaries of the gazetted forest is a matter of constant effort. Yerim's settling in the forest of Barkedji-Dodji soon attracted a number of other herders from the Fuuta, the majority of who were his kin. Being the first 'permanent' occupant of this bush area, he acquired status as a 'village chief' for the scattered group of newcomers of his kin group, a position which was later recognised more or less officially by the local administration. This recognition was, as will be discussed in chapter 5, not without its contradictions.

Bathil Ba, Ranerou: "The Firstcomers don't want us here; they are just waiting for an occasion to get rid of us"

When the drought hit in 1973 Bathil Ba lost his entire herd, which was said to be of moderate size. Bathil, however, had married the daughter of a very rich herder who was able to advance her part of her future inheritance to provide the means for the survival of the family. The exact size of this remittance is not known to the author.

Bathil had left the area of Kasskass in the *Waalo* shortly after the drought had set in, but returned to Kasskass where he combined livestock rearing with flood recession and rainfed agriculture. By 1977 he left the *waalo* and spent the following twelve years moving around the deep-wells of Djagueli, Louggere Tioli and Ranerou on the southern fringe of the Ferlo. At the time of our first encounter, he had limited his movements to the vicinities of the deep-well of Ranerou, moving seasonally between different camps in the area. At a certain moment Bathil Ba had even taken-up cultivation, an occupation which was later given up due to meagre results and shortage of manpower.

In 1989 we estimated his herd (formally belonging to his wife) at 500 head of smallstock, primarily sheep, and 40 head of cattle. In 1996, on our last visit, the number of sheep had increased to around 1200. In 1989 Bathil went on a pilgrimage to Mecca, a symbolic action apt also to display his prosperity to his neighbours and kin.

Apart from his temporary venture into agriculture, Bathil has no occupation besides keeping his livestock. On some occasions, however, he is consulted for possessing certain *'connaissances peuls'*, a quality which presumably is testified by his current prosperity. In spite of having left the *waalo* more than 20 years ago he still holds rights to his lands on the flood plains near KassKass, a claim which he recently attempted to renew[53], as the land was to be included in an irrigation project.

Bathil has a relatively large family which, apart from his wife, consists of 4 daughters and 3 sons of which the eldest (twins) were 13 years old at the time of our first encounter. Bathil employs 2-3 salaried herders whom he treats well and so they stay with him longer than is the case in

---

[53] He tried to get his sons and daughters registered as rightful owners of the land. It is not known whether the attempt was successful.

other families. Although he normally restricts his movements to the area around the well at Barkedji, he had no major problems in moving 100 km's south to Loumbi Aly Thedy near Payar when the rain failed in 1990/91. But the trip was hard and expensive, both in animal losses and in bribes and watering fees at foreign wells.

Although he has been in the area for almost 15 years, Bathil does not have very warm relations with the leading group of herders in Ranerou. On several occasions he has been brought to court after having been involved in fights with members of the well committee in Ranerou who have tried to limit the access of foreign herds to the drinking troughs.

Some introductory remarks

The two cases cited above are representative for many of those herders who were forced to move southwards. Characteristic for these herders was that they gave up a fairly sedentarised lifestyle, often involving important agricultural activities in the Senegal River Valley. Most of the herders started out with a period with no fixed abode, but after a while they limited their radius of activities in years of 'normal' precipitation to the vicinity of a single borehole. Characteristic of these herders is that a high degree of mobility is maintained during the dry season.

Another particular trait of these herders is the specialisation in smallstock, notably sheep. Based on very elaborate cost-benefit analyses a variety of strategies are employed to ensure high reproduction rates. First of all, considerable amounts of labour is invested in sheep rearing, a strategy which has proven to be extremely successful. Distinctive for this group is furthermore that they consider themselves, and are considered by the indigenous population, as outsiders. Hence, they may be forced to employ other means than the insiders to gain their rightful access to resources. In short, the movement into these new areas has provided new opportunities as well as new constraints.

Perceiving drought in a more open-ended perspective

Senegal, and particularly the Ferlo, are drought-prone areas. Droughts occur relatively frequently, although with varying strength. As mentioned in the introduction, it is not fruitful to perceive of drought and drought-related migration only in terms of crisis and socio-economic decline. Instead a more open-ended approach must be adopted. In this approach drought may be comprehended as an opportunity for experimentation and change, both in production patterns and in social relations i.e. understanding drought as a revelatory crisis.

As droughts vary in strength and effect, it may be useful to distinguish between droughts acting as 'watershed events' and drought acting more as 'events of articulation'[54]. The severe droughts of 1972/73 and 1983/84, were watershed events, where changes in meaning and practice reached a point where it became obvious that pre-drought production patterns would not return once the rains resumed. In contrast to this, the dry years of 1991/93 had more the character of an 'event of articulation', in which opportunities for questioning existing power structures and of adjusting them to the new emerging order were enhanced.

The present chapter deals with the profound effects, which the two large droughts of 1972/73 and 1983/84 had on the production systems in the Ferlo. It is therefore primarily concerned with the watershed effects of the drought in terms of the changing practices of herd and pasture management. The changing structures of authority over land, which this has entailed will be treated in depth in the following chapter. Here the processes of political adjustment are uncovered through an analysis of drought conceived of as an event of articulation.

The aim here is to analyse the effects that the arrival of a large group of herders had on the production systems in the southern fringe of the Ferlo. Surprisingly little has been written on the profound but largely unexpected changes which the herding systems of the Ferlo region have undergone during the last twenty years. Data material for the analysis is therefore mainly based on case material, collected in the Ferlo between 1989 and 1995. This comprises both in-depth interviews with a large number of herders and with representatives from the state administration and the extension services, and more quantitative data such as questionnaire surveys and mapping exercises. The data is examined in order to reveal the logics of the new herding strategies put into effect by the intruding herders and to analyse the impact of this on the resource management system of the area[55]. Throughout the analysis, these findings will be confronted with the

---

[54] See Sally Falk Moore's distinction between events with diagnostic qualities and events of articulation (Moore 1994:365). See also chapter 3.

[55] As the objective here is to analyse the effects of the drought-related migration on the access and control over the natural resources in the Ferlo, rather than to document the

myths and narratives discussed above: notably the perception of degradation and productive decline as the necessary outcomes of drought and increased population pressure, the understanding of range degradation as resulting from external intervention in an otherwise stable environment, and the image of pastoral societies as 'traditional" and unable to adapt to the new conditions unless helped by external interventions.

The local context

Before passing to the recent history of post-drought migration and rehabilitation, it may be useful to briefly recall a few features of the history of the Ferlo region that are relevant for this assignment. Pastoral rangelands, such as the Ferlo region, are often analysed in terms of their economic, political and social marginalisation. This is illustrated through the continuous loss of rangelands due to insecurity of tenure and agricultural encroachment and the neglect of productive investment in infrastructure by the state. Continual loss of rangelands and insecurity of tenure are also characteristic of the situation in the Ferlo. Nonetheless, productive opportunities in the Ferlo have expanded tremendously during the last 40 years. In fact, the recent history of the Ferlo region is best understood as a simultaneous process of diminution and enlargement. The physical diminution is the result of a continuous squeeze on the pastoral zone from agricultural encroachment. At the same time, however, the digging of wells and improved conditions for mobility have provided new production opportunities, enlarging, so to speak, the pastoral area from within. This situation has profoundly altered the relations between the wetlands of the Senegal River Basin, the *waalo*, and the dry hinterlands, the *jeeri*. In this way, even the early history of the region dismisses any stableness of the environment or inability to adapt to new conditions.

Landscape as a largely anthropogenic creation

As mentioned in the introduction mainstream approaches to natural resource management often perceive of the environment as being largely in equilibrium. According to this view relatively stable conditions outside the system would allow the internal processes of the system to equilibrate and regulate system structures and dynamics.

---

functioning of the new herd management strategies, not all this material is presented here.

According to the records of the early French explorers, the Ferlo region was, by the end of the last century, covered with dense forest. According to the chronicle of Lieutenant Monteil of his exploratory journey in the Ferlo in 1879, the Ferlo was a forest so dense that it in places was impossible to advance without first burning off the bush. (Monteil in Pouillon, 1990). Furthermore, large mammals such as elephants, girafs and crocodiles could be found in the area.

Today the Ferlo is characterised by open grasslands. Fine-leaved annual grasses such as *Schoenfeldia grasilis, Cenchrus biflorus, Dactyloctenium aegyptium* and *Aristida mutabilis* are the main components of the herbaceous layer in most of the area. To the south and east some taller grasses such as *Pennisetum pedicellatum* become more common (Hanan et al., 1991:175). Tree cover canopy is less than 5% in the north, increasing to 15-20% in the south and south east (Marks and Faye, 1990), as the soil structure changes from sandy soils overlying stabilised dunes in the north and west to gravelly rock and laterite plateaux in the south and east (Hanan et al. ibid.). Wildlife is reduced to a number of antilopes and jackals while, in rare cases, a solitary ostrich may be observed. This situation has often been interpreted as a sign of severe degradation, due to increased dissecation of the climate combined with the effects of overgrazing (see for example Touré, 1986 and Barral, 1982).

According to recent findings, this biological structure is not the outcome of recent degradation, as presumed in current development discourse. Rather, it results from a long term construction/modification of the landscape conditioned by human intervention, sometimes the active outcome of management sometimes unintended consequences. In the Ferlo, as in the rest of the western Sahel, "the mixing of animals and plant species of the desert and savanna eco-zones have been, in part, the result of long centuries of human land use practices whereby livestock herding and agricultural practices have produced a derived natural environment" (Webb, 1995:3).

Indeed the recent forest cover of the region seems to be a largely anthropogenic creation. When the first colonial administrators arrived in the area by the turn of the century, large clearings were frequently interspersed with the wooded landscape. Along the River Valleys of the Bounoum and the Ferlo, forest cover was largely replaced by fields, a visible sign of the grain export to the desert economies of the North (Freudenberger, 1992:84,85).

The pastoral Fulani also contributed to the change in the landscape. Livestock grazing and field crop cultivation by herders transformed the tree cover from one in which broad-leafed trees (*Sclerocarya birrea* and *Pterocarpus lucens*) dominated to one where hardy, short-leaved species such as *Acacia raddiana* and *Balanites aegyptiaca* were more prominent (Benoit, 1988:106; Freudenberger, 1992:98). The dense stands of *Acacia senegal*, so appreciated by the colonial administrators for their valuable production of gum arabic, are not reminiscences of pristine vegetation but result from this "humanisation" of the area by its pastoral population. In the same way, fires designed to clear the grasslands and forests of disease vectors such as ticks and at controlling the population of wild animals encouraged the development of fire-tolerant tree and grass species. In many cases these species proved more palatable for livestock than the previous vegetation.

Hence, pre-drought Ferlo was far from the image of a pristine or virgin forest, which had been depleted within recent history through the invasion of unprecedented numbers of livestock. It was an environment already moulded and transformed by human intervention. And albeit "disturbed" by human intervention, these transformations contributed largely, not to degrade but to improve the productive potential of the area. Nonetheless, human intervention in the interior of the Ferlo was, until the end of the 1950's, limited to a few months during the rainy season. This situation was completely altered when the colonial administration started its drilling programme in the pastoral Ferlo.

The borehole revolution

Access to water has been the structuring element in the history of the Ferlo. Until the 1950's, the area was largely inaccessible during the dry season due to lack of water. Only a few artisan wells existed, and the vast areas of the interior Ferlo was exploited only occasionally by black Maures engaged in the collection of gum arabic.

Map 7:
Installation of the first boreholes of the Ferlo.

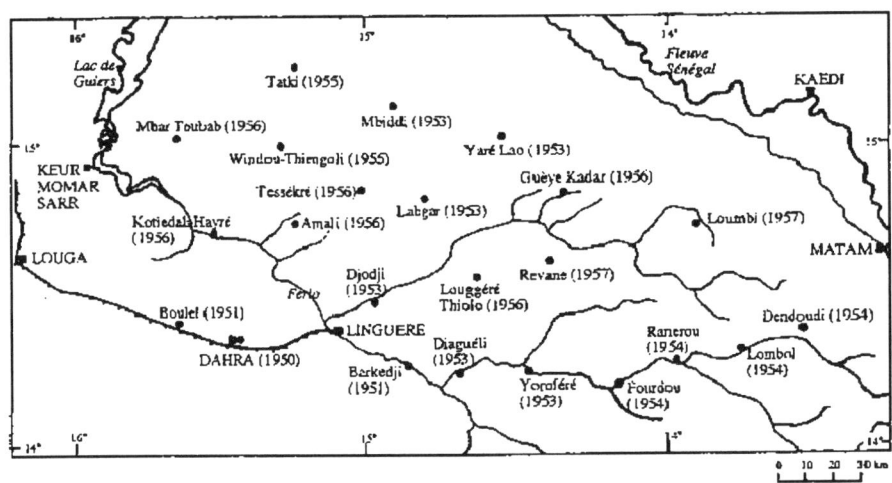

Source: Touré and Arpaillange, 1986.

In 1937 a large fossil acquifer was discovered covering most of Northern Senegal. In order to exploit this enormous water potential, a large drilling programme was launched by the French colonial administration. By the end of the 1950's a network of boreholes had been established. Each of these boreholes was equipped with a diesel pump enabling water to be pumped from the aquifer 80-400 metres beneath the pastoral zone (Freudenberger, 1992:175,176). This opened the area for all-year grazing.

The aim of the colonial administration was first of all to improve pastoral production. Once permanent water sources were accessible herds would no longer be forced to return to the river during the dry season but could exploit the rich pastures of the Ferlo even after the surface water ponds had dried out. Over the next ten years large numbers of Fulani gave up their annual transhumance journeys and settled in the vicinities of the boreholes. The intensified use of the vast pastures of the *jeeri*, combined with improved veterinary services, allowed for considerable increases both in average herd size and in the total number of livestock in the region (Mathieu, Niasse and Vincke, 1986:227; Richter, 1991:12).

Map 8.
Dry season movements in northern Ferlo before installation of the boreholes

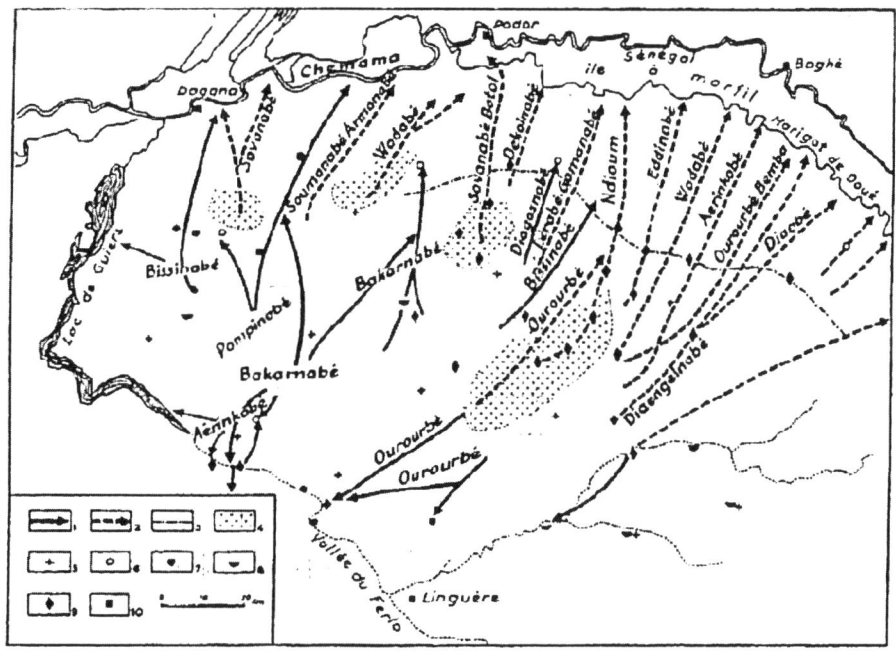

1. Pastoral movements; 2 Movements by herders who are cultivating the Waalo; 3. Southern limit of dry season grazing of waalo herds; 4. Areas occupied mainly by herders cultivating the waalo; 5. Borehole;7. Well; 8. Artisan shallow well *(céane)*; 9. Wet season Fulani camp; 10. Village or agglomeration

I. Sedentarised Fulani and Toucouleur; II. Sedentarised Fulani (HaboBe); III. Sedentarised Fulani (JenguelBe) IV. Fulani of the central Valleys; V. Fulani of northern Ferlo.

Source: Grenier, 1960.

The success of the drilling programme was spectacular. Within a few years the system of seasonal migration had been completely transformed by the new opportunities. Separated by a interval of only 7 years, the surveys of Bonnet-Dupeyron (1950) and Ph. Grenier (1957) show a significant difference in transhumance activities before and after the installation of the boreholes (see map below).

Map 9. Current main axes of transhumance

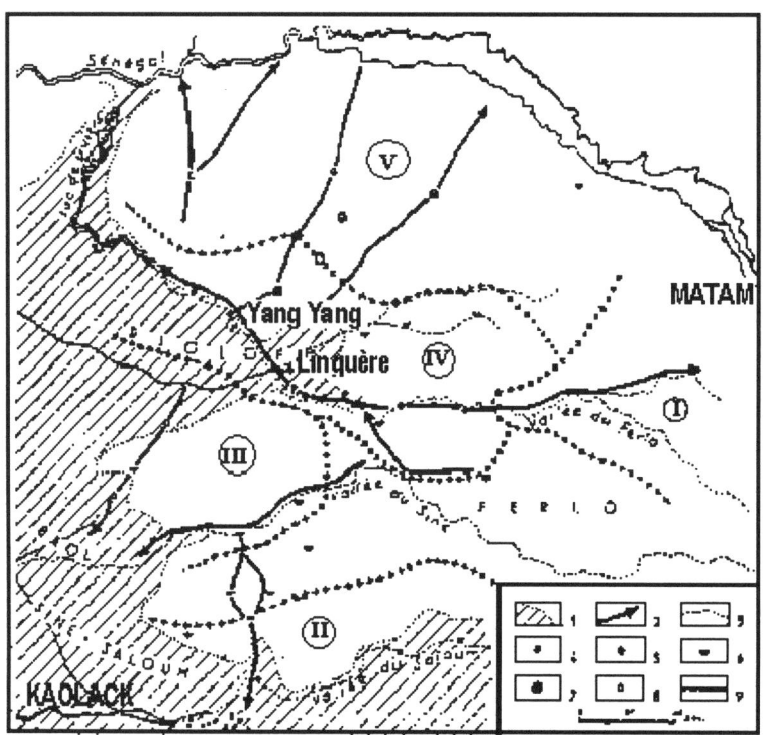

1. Area where sedentary Fulanis, Wolof and Serer are dominant. 2. Principal migration routes. 3. Dry Valleys, 4. Sedentary Village. 5. Fulani camp. 6. Artisan Well *(Céane)*, 7. Pond, 8. Well, 9. Railroad.

I. Sedentarised Fulani of the East and Toucouleurs. II. Sedentarised Fulani of the south and HaboBés. III. JengelBe Fulani. IV. Fulani of the Central Valleys. Fulani of the North.

Source: Grenier 1960.

While 60% of the heads of households interrogated in 1950 declared that they regularly sent their animals to the *waalo* pastures, 52% of those households who had formerly practised transhumance declared they had abandoned this practice between 1952 and 1962. Abandonment of the binary transhumance practices was further accelerated, in the following years, not the least in response to the rain-deficits and droughts from 1968 and onwards. By 1975 Barral (1982:44) notes that only 3% of the herders in the area were still keeping up their previous transhumance schemes[56].

---

[56] i.e. 22% of those previously practising annual *waalo-jeeri* movements of their herds (ibid).

Movements on the southern fringe of the Ferlo were altered also by the construction of the boreholes, although in a less spectacular manner. According to Barral (1982:51), 40% of the households used to carry out regular movements towards the Djoloff and the Ferlo Valley prior to the establishment of the boreholes. Between 1952 and 1962, 52% of these households had given up tranhumance on a regular basis and by 1978 only 10% of the livestock was undertaking regular transhumance movements.

As transhumance movements were largely abandoned, the tight relations previously connecting the pastoral and the agricultural zones tended to evaporate. A pure 'pastoral area' was created, freed from the perpetual confrontations between farmers and herders. Herding was now reduced to simple surveillance as herds no longer would be trespassing into the flood recession fields. Likewise, the labour inputs required for watering were greatly reduced at the mechanized boreholes which were equipped with watering troughs (Pouillon, 1994:180; Touré, 1990; Barral, 1982).

Nonetheless, the construction of the boreholes did not give way to a full sedentarisation of the herders nor to a concentration of settlements near the boreholes. Dry season camps remained dispersed in the bush within a radius of 5-10 km from the borehole, and a system of micro-nomadisations (see Barral, 1982: 63-67) was put into effect. This involved regular movements between the dry season camp within reach of the borehole and wet season camps installed further away in the bush in the vicinities of rain water ponds where water was free and readily accessible. According to Pouillon (1990:181), the dispersion of camps also had a political dimension, as it limited tensions between the heterogeneous selections of clan groups who had been attracted by the borehole. As can be seen on the map of the settlements around the Velingara borehole (map 11), a certain tendency may be traced of settling according to clan groups. This structure, which is far from absolute, may also be read out of the selections of village chiefs. These are often not only representatives of a particular area (*section* in the local French vernacular) but frequently also represent a particular sub-fraction (FafaBe, DiawBe, WodaaBe etc).

In consequence of this dispersion of settlement, the villages or groupings of houses in the vicinities of the borehole are usually occupied primarily by Mauritanian shopkeepers, by state employed technical, by administrative personnel, or by Wolof farmers i.e. people with no or limited herd ownership.

It remains important to stress, that although patterns of

transhumance movements have changed in character, mobility has preserved its importance. The highly variable rainfall, the frequent bush fires and the recurrent breakdown of the borehole pumps make transhumance an indispensable exit option in an environment characterised by variability and unpredictability. In fact, mobility was greatly eased through the construction of boreholes, as compared to the former hazardous and risky transhumance across territories marked by absence of accessible water sources. With boreholes within reasonable reach it now became possible to reach distant pastures without significant increases of animal energy loss.

There can be no doubt that herders took full advantage of the new opportunities created by the wells[57]. Once more interesting production opportunities were created, the binary system structured around flood recession agriculture and dry season grazing in the *waalo* and wet season grazing in the *jeeri* hinterlands was quickly abandoned by a majority of herders. Instead herders adapted to the new system and moulded it in such a way as to best suit their own advantages. Such adaptive capacities obviously contradict any assumptions that herding systems should be stagnant and unable to change.

But contrary to the expectations of the planners, herders preserved a mobile lifestyle, moving between the distant wet season camp and a dry season camp within reasonable reach of the watering facilities.

Boreholes and environmental degradation

As described above, it has been common to attribute to the boreholes a detrimental effect on the vegetation around them. Le Houérou (1977: 25-30), for example, states that they have lead to the destruction of pastures within a radius of 15 to 30 km around them. Such destruction has been termed 'desert patches' by more alarmist researchers such as Rapp (1976) and Glantz (1977).

The idea that boreholes lead to destruction of the vegetation was

---

[57] Obviously the new opportunities also carried with them new constraints such as the new diseases, notably botulism, which very significantly is labelled 'la maladie des forages' by the local population. These illnesses can to a large extent be attributed to the mineral deficiencies of both water and pastures of the Ferlo River (Müller, 1989; Pouillon, 1990:1982). This issue is, however, not within the scope of the present study.

seriously challenged in a study carried out in 1987 by researchers from The Centre de Suivi Ecologique in Dakar (Hanan et al. 1991). Using a satellite image derived map of biomass production to measure east and west transects at twenty selected deep-wells in northern Ferlo, the researchers showed that patterns of changes of production were variable across the individual well-area. It was, however, not possible to establish a relation between changes in productivity and distance to the well. The variations occurring were frequently related to factors other than grazing. This indicates that the deep wells of the Ferlo have not caused the formation of desert patches (at the limits of resolution used (1.1 km)). In no case did production alongside a well decline to near zero, although for just over half of the transects a significant relationship existed between distance and production. This corresponds with the findings of Valenza from 1981 showing that herbaceous vegetation is primarily dependent on rainfall and that grazing has little effect. Although it is common at the end of the dry season to observe large areas of bare ground around some of the deep wells, these are the effect of 9 months of livestock grazing and trampling en route to the drinking point. According to Hanan et al. the desert patch prescription does not apply to this phenomenon as total productivity during the rainy season appears to be little affected. Hence, nothing seems to indicate that the establishment of boreholes increased desertification in the Ferlo.

The findings of this study confirm the hypothesis of researchers within the 'new ecology' framework. They stress that it is rainfall rather than grazing that determines biomass production in non-equilibrium environments.

Boreholes and agricultural encroachment

Originally, the aim of the borehole programme was primarily to facilitate the transport of livestock by hoof to the urban markets and to provide meat to the booming peanut economy (Freudenberger, 1992:177). The grandiose character of the colonial vision is well illustrated by the following quote:

"We recognised straight away that the deep boreholes were the dream technology which would permit all the animal trails in the sylvo-pastoral zone of the Sahel to be bordered by modern, well-equipped drinking troughs. One can imagine the borehole as destined to satisfy the water needs of these transhumance herds in much the same way that train

station cafeterias or drink stands meet the needs of rail travellers"[58].

Boreholes constructed between 1942 and 1951 met this objective. By the early 1950s, however, new options emerged. In fact, the opening up of a new all-season pastoral space turned out to provide an unexpected solution to a difficult structural crisis. For, together with a significant increase in the number of livestock due to the improved veterinary services and favourable weather conditions throughout the 1950s and 1960s, the groundnut economy in the south was putting increased pressure on the pastoral zones and conflicts between FulBe and Wolof were increasing dramatically.

Through the borehole development scheme, the colonial administration hoped to persuade herders to settle in the proximity of the boreholes and leave land further south to cultivators. The idea was to establish a sort of "pastoral sanctuary" where herders could graze their animals freely. Around the borehole it was envisaged that economic growth poles would form. In the optimistic view of the colonial administrator Grosmaire, it was envisaged that:

"By attaching life to the region as a result of water availability, the boreholes will enable a whole geographic area to be opened for modern economic activities and call forth all manners of human enterprise" [59].

The suggestion of a specialised (but also significantly reduced) pastoral area was promoted under the heading "zone sylvo-pastorale" (Pouillon, 1990:180). As will be shown later on, this merely verbal distinction between an agricultural and a pastoral zone did not effectively halt the expansion of the groundnut economy.

Agricultural encroachment on the southern part of the dry hinterlands, the Ferlo, goes back to the turn of the century when a cash economy emerged, based on production and sale of groundnut for the colonial market. The expansion of peanut production into the inhospitable and remote areas of Senegal's interior was largely undertaken by disciples of the Islamic brotherhood of the Mourides[60]. Through a social, economic and

---

[58] Grosmaire 1957 in: Eléments de Politique Sylvo-pastorale au Sahel du Sénégal Fasicule 15 p. 41, here quoted in Freudenberger's translation 1992:177).

[59] Ibid. :179

[60] The Mouride brotherhood is one of the three major Sufi sects in Senegal. It is built on

religious organisation of pioneer farming communities, the so-called *daara*[61] they were able to resist the hostile pastoral population of the area and clear vast areas for groundnut production. The methods used by Mouride disciples to get control over Fulani grazing land were often extremely aggressive, frequently involving the expulsion and destruction of Fulani settlements[62].

Before the creation of the boreholes, the expansion of groundnut production northwards from the central peanut basin into the case area in the "cercle"[63] of Linguère was relatively unimportant. Competition between Wolof and Fulani in terms of land and other natural resources was limited to the key areas around the dry river valleys. According to Santoir (1983:43), the increased contact to Wolof farmers even provoked a phenomenon of assimilation. Many Fulani's residing in the area took up groundnut production, and some even converted to Mouridism. The increasing importance of farming also entailed higher levels of sedentarisation. The effects of Mouride expansion were therefore not only detrimental or one-sided.

Nonetheless, the creation of boreholes in the beginning of the 1950s increased conflicts between herders and farmers, notably in the southern part of the Barkedji arrondissement (Thiel, Linde, Gassane). In spite of their designation by the colonial administration as "pastoral deep-wells" (as opposed to agricultural or mixed wells further south), they were soon invaded by Mouride *talibé* who, together with other Wolof farmers, started clearing large tracts of land in a completely anarchistic manner. Numerous conflicts can be listed about conflict over land being illicitly cleared by Wolof farmer and about animals captured and beaten by the

---

the spiritual allegiance to a local Muslim spiritual leader, the marabout, but also implies a number of reciprocal responsibilities between the marabout and the *talibé*, his disciple. The Mouride brotherhood has been described among others by Cruise O'Brien, D., 1971 "The Mourides of Senegal" and 1975, "Saints and Politicians'.

[61] *Daara* are pioneer villages of young single, male disciples (*talibé*) of a Mouride saint *(marabout)*.

[62] In the case of Kaël in 1914, the creation of a *daara* implied the expulsion and destruction of 8 Fulani settlements (J. de Bevert, 1937: "L'exode d'une race" Rev. Outre-Mer, here from Santoir 1983:43).

[63] The colonial *cercle* was more or less equivalent to the contemporary *prefecture*.

talibé.[64]

Faced with the anarchistic expansion of the Mourides, a number of gazetted forests and "sylvo-pastoral reserves" were created by the colonial administration during the 1950s. Within the limits of these reserves cash-crop production was formally prohibited. But due to the increasing political weight of the Mourides within the administration, the many cases where these restrictions were ignored did not lead to any legal proceeding. And in several cases, the administration has even taken to declassifying large areas of forest in order to satisfy the demands of the Mouride saints[65].

While the opening of the boreholes in the south lead to a process of 'Wolofisation' of the villages where the Fulani to a large degree moved out to avoid conflicts and the persecutions of the powerful Mourides[66], it is interesting to note that, in some cases, opening the boreholes, such as Barkedji, had the opposite effect: of marginalising the Wolof vis-à-vis the Fulani.

Before the construction of the borehole, Barkedji was a Wolof village, in fact the western-most Wolof agglomeration in an otherwise Fulani pastoral area. The drilling of the borehole attracted large concentrations of herds during the dry season, creating problems of

---

[64] See also Weicker, 1983.

[65] A prominent example from 1951 is the borehole of Deali, where the Mourides exerted very strong pressure to be attributed a large piece of land near the newly opened borehole. Within 3 days around 1200 ha of land was cleared by Mouride disciples, leaving paralysed the administration who did not dare to protest against the seizure of land and who preferred to close their eyes to the violent injustices carried out by the *talibé*. In total 8250 hectares of hitherto classified land were attributed to the marabouts in 1962. Between 1965 and 1980 more land was attributed to the various Mouride marabouts. By 1980 only 49.275 hectares of the formerly 75.900 hectares constituting the gazetted forest remained classified. Also other forests in the Département of Linguere (forest of Boulel) or Département of Kaffrine (Kassas, Delbi and later Mbégué) have been partly declassified in order to satisfy the demands of the Mouride saints. (Archives de la Direction des Eaux et Forêts, Dakar). Notably the declassification of 45.000 hectares in the forest of Mbégué (also called Khelkom) in 1991 gave way to furious protests by herders and environmentalists. (See Schoonmaker Freudenberger 1991.)

[66] Santoir's survey of the borehole of Linde, south of Barkedji, shows that within 10 years the Wolof population had quadroupled while the Fulani population decreased from 130 Fulani inhabitants of a total of 250 to only 58 persons out of a total of 612 inhabitants in 1979 Santoir, 1983:57-66).

cohabitation between Fulani herders and Wolof farmers. As a result, the Wolof population stagnated between 1953 and 1957 when which it started to decrease (Santoir, 1983:72). In order to avoid conflicts with the herders, farmers increasingly moved their fields away from the borehole towards the east. The "liberated space" was largely taken over by Fulani immigrants. This process was further enhanced as the Fulani in 1961, due to their the increased political importance, were able to establish a regulation prohibiting all cultivation within a radius of 1 km of the borehole. Today the village is divided into a Wolof part and a Fulani part of approximately equal size. But, due to the numerous Fulani settled in the surrounding bush, it is the Fulani that constitute the dominant political force in the area. In spite of having a majority in the Rural Council since its establishment in 1976, the Fulani have, nevertheless, been unable to control the anarchistic clearing of rangelands by Wolof farmers. This process has become even more important since 1975, when Mouride disciples started entering the area in search of land for organisation of new *daara* (ibid.: 80).

The actual amount of land currently converted from pastures to farmland is difficult to evaluate as fields are spread throughout the range and often not registered properly by the rural councils in charge of land registration[67]. In several cases, the large tracts of land attributed to the Mouride marabouts are not put under hoe. In other cases, the *daara* expand over the boundaries of what is attributed to them. In addition, many individual fields are cultivated by Wolof newcomers. In some cases, this land is cultivated illegally while in other cases it is attributed to them by the rural councils. In reality, it is not so much the actual plot under cultivation that poses problems but rather the aggressive attitude of the Mouride disciples. In order to avoid having their animals impounded or beaten, herders tend to evade vast areas in the vicinities of the *daara*'s. The scattering of fields over a large area, therefore represents a bigger problem than what can be read out of the actual acreage under cultivation.

Faced with this sort of problem, herders dispose of few means to defend their pastures from agricultural encroachment. The legal framework is strongly biased in favour of agricultural production[68], and the state and

---

[67] According to the registrations of the rural council of Velingara 13.040 hectares of land were attributed to the Mouride *daara*s between 1984 and 1990. Even in an arrondissement as vast as Velingara (261.170 hectares) this is a considerable portion. Unfortunately, reliable figures from the communauté rurale of Barkedji were not avaliable, but they are considerably lower.

[68] The legal framework will be discussed in more detail below.

the rural councils are generally unwilling or unable to confront the Mouride expansion[69]. Nonetheless, more resistance has been demonstrated by the new rural councils elected in 1991. On a few occasions, they have managed to either refuse or postpone further land allocations to Mouride saints. Recently, councillors of certain localities where Mouride expansion is particularly threatening have also started attributing very large tracts of lands (between 10 and 20 km^2) to themselves and their "allies" in order to create a buffer zone vis-à-vis the expansion of *daara*[70]. The consequences of these 'spontaneous privatisations' in terms of rights of exclusion are yet to be seen. But it is noteworthy that, in spite of their obvious discrepancies with the legal framework governing land attribution, they have, so to speak, been *de facto* accepted by the state administration in the area, and have contributed to block, at least temporarily, Mouride expansion in the area.

Post-drought Ferlo as a porous and dynamic formation

As can be seen from the above, the area into which the "drought refugees" from the North migrated was characterised not by stable and homogeneous communities but by perpetual population movements in a very porous social environment. The period leading up to the droughts had provided a number of new opportunities which were readily seized by the Fulani population: such as the venture into groundnut production by the Fulani *JengelBe* in the southern fringe of the Ferlo or the extremely rapid adjustment of herders to the post-borehole situation in terms of new patterns of mobility and increased market integration, to mention a few of the most important examples.

As will be shown below these so-called stagnant herders have been able to face profound changes such as the perpetual squeeze on grazing lands from the agricultural encroachment in the south and the expansion of irrigation. At several occasions herders have managed to restrict agricultural encroachment, proving to be less politically marginalised than often anticipated.

---

[69] The cases of Déali and Mbégué discussed in note 65 are examples of this.

[70] For a discussion of this phenomenon, see Juul, 1993.

The effects of drought: expansion of irrigation and out-migration

Irrigation along the Senegal River has been a major policy option in Senegal even before independence. Nonetheless, the effects of irrigation on the herding system of Northern Senegal were relatively negligible. With the creation of the SAED[71] in 1965, the para-statal in charge of promoting irrigated agriculture along the river, the state hoped to attain two goals: 1) to reduce the country's food deficit, and 2) to mobilise the population of the Valley in order to improve their standard of living. Due to bureaucratic inefficiency, soaring costs and unresolved technical problems related to irrigation, the production results obtained were, until 1972, very poor. It was first in connection with the drought periods of 1972/73 and 1983/84 that considerable investments were made to expand both large-scale and small-scale irrigation schemes along the river.

The year 1968 marked the end of a period distinguished by particularly favourable conditions for pastoralism. In the following 20 years, annual precipitation rates in the *waalo* and the adjacent *jeeri* were very poor and reached a nadir during the two great Sahelian droughts[72]. The combination of failing rains and absence of proper flooding over several years severely affected both pastures and flood recession agriculture. The *waalo* practically lost its importance as dry season or drought refuge[73], and the on-going process of differentiation was further accelerated.

One of the reasons why the drought of 1972/73 hit particularly hard was the increased sedentarity. This had been prompted by generally favourable climatic conditions and in particular by the improved watering situation in the *jeeri*. By 1970 75% of the FulBe *JerjerBe*[74] of the Valley

---

[71] Societé d'Aménagement et d'Exploitation des terres du Delta du fleuve Sénégal et des vallées du fleuve Sénégal et de la Falémé.

[72] In Dagana, Podor and Matam the mean annual precipitations from 1970 to 1987 were 192 mm, 178 mm, and 299 mm respectively as compared to 317 mm, 317 mm, and 518 mm between 1918 and 1969. (Profil de l'Environnement,1990:4).

[73] In Vidou Thiengoly, an area traditionally closely connected with the *waalo*, only the poorest herders, possessing small numbers of sheep and goats sought refuge in the waalo during the 72/73 drought. (Richter, 1991:23) In general the survival rate for these animals was low.

[74] *FulBe JerjerBe* are the Fulani settled on the sandy dunes, *jeeri*, bordering the Valley wetlands, the *waalo* .In contrast the *FulBe WawalBe* are those who have retained property

were sedentary the entire year in proximity to the borehole (Santoir, 1994:242) while those cultivating in the *waalo* limited annual migration to a few family members with perhaps some sheep and goats. This hampered former risk management strategies based on mobility and herd dispersion.

When the drought struck, most herders therefore remained in their wet season camps and waited until the end of the rainy season before they finally abandoned the most drought ridden zone and moved southward. By that time the animals were already extremely weak and therefore less able to endure the long trip and to adapt to new fodder regimes. They were also far more vulnerable to animal diseases encountered in the south (Santoir, 1977 cited by Santoir, 1994:243). Although 60 % of the herds and 40 % of the families ended up having left the Valley to seek refuge in the Peanut Basin, herd losses were considerable. Santoir estimates that around 60% of the cattle of the Senegal River Valley was lost during the drought[75] and that by 1973 more than 1/4 of Fulani households had no cattle left[76]. In general, those families who left early and went farthest south were the ones to endure the least losses.

Many of those Fulani who had suffered too heavy losses to continue making a livelihood solely from pastoral production were left with little alternative than to opt for an irrigated plot[77]. *Waalo* cultivation, which had previously provided an important supplement to pastoral production, had diminished significantly due to the limited flooding. It was therefore primarily in the irrigated fields that herders could hope to produce sufficient agricultural surplus to prevent further sale of animals and to ensure their annual cereal consumption. Also a large number of Wolof and Toucouleur farmers were mobilised. From 1975 to 1988 the area under irrigation increased from 9,000 ha to 35,000 ha (Seck, 1991:18.). In this period, village schemes funded and operated either by the SAED, by various external donors and NGO's or by the villagers themselves mushroomed

---

rights in the *waalo*. They have in general preserved an agro-pastoral lifestyle cultivating both flood recession crops (primarily sorghum) in the *waalo* and millet on rainfed *jeeri* land.

[75] Tourrand (1989:4) estimates losses in the Senegal River Delta for each of the two drought periods to 50% of the cattle population and 30% of the smallstock population

[76] Santoir (1979:6). Unfortunately no figures are given for smallstock.

[77] The degree of impoverishment of Fulani cultivating in the irrigated schemes is indicated in a survey made by Santoir in the Nianga scheme near Podor. From a total of 62 Fulani households cultivating in the scheme only 15 possessed cattle (Santoir, 1979:14).

along the Valley. As part of the privatisation efforts of the state, peasant organisations were now granted legal recognition and credit facilities. These efforts resulted in the conversion of another 20,000 ha into irrigated fields between 1988 and 1992. This massive mobilisation of producers in search of alternative subsistence contributed to make the period from 1975 to 1988 the peak expansion period of the SAED.

Not all destitute herders, however, were able to gain access to land in the irrigated schemes. A large group of those Fulani living in the numerous villages along the *Waalo* road are now earning their living as occasional workers in the rice fields during harvest, sometimes in combination with limited rainfed millet and sorghum cultivation on *jeeri* land.

Paradoxically, it was the government policy of increasing food security that provided the most important obstacles to livestock rearing in the *waalo* which until then had been an important element of the agricultural economy of the area[78]. First of all, the development of irrigation is taking place in the depressions which used to contain some of the best pastureland. Secondly, access to the river has become increasingly difficult as few cattle tracks have been laid out and even fewer respected. It has therefore become very difficult to avoid animals trespassing into irrigated fields and the exorbitant fines make it a hazardous undertaking to keep large herds in the vicinities of irrigation schemes. Thirdly, the dikes hamper the filling of ponds which used to provide fresh water in those areas where the aquifers are salty (Santoir, 1983:151). As a result the majority of herds are now kept all year round in the *jeeri* at distances of 30 to 40 km from the rice fields.

Apart from the spatial constraints, labour demands of pastoralism have also proved difficult to fit into the demands of irrigated agriculture. Whereas labour inputs in flood recession agriculture are low and fall outside the peak periods of pastoral production, labour requirements in irrigation are considerable in terms of sowing, weeding, and timely application of insecticides and fertilisers, etc. If these activities are not carried out in accordance with the agreed schedule, farmers risk being expelled from the irrigation scheme. Many herders lack sufficient manpower to split the family into two units during the cultivation season.

---

[78] In this sense it is yet another example of the cases highlighted by Galaty and Bonte (1992) of development policies aiming at diversifying income source contributing to the undermining of otherwise relatively 'sane' production systems.

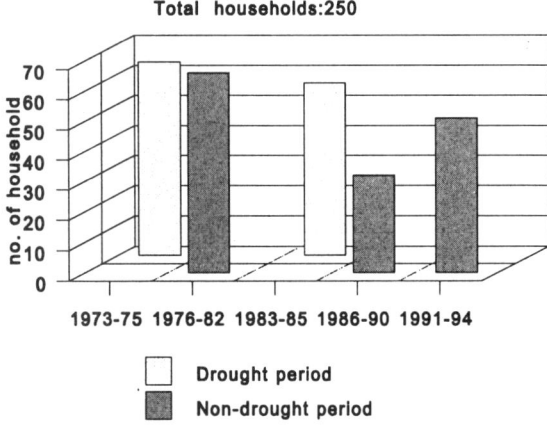

They therefore show poor agricultural (and pastoral) results as they are forced to be constantly moving between their herd in the *jeeri* and their agricultural production in the *waalo* (interview with Santoir, April 1994)[79].

With the drought of 1983/84, the increasing split escalated between Fulani involved in irrigation and Fulani maintaining a pastoral lifestyle. On the one hand, Fulani in areas such as the Lower Delta, hitherto relatively untouched by the expansion of irrigation schemes, started demanding the transformation of certain grazing areas into rice fields (Tourrand, 1989:5). On the other hand, Fulani with important numbers of animals remaining in the area started moving southward to save their animals. These movements took place on a far larger scale than had been the case in 1972/73.

While the 'skewed' development of the irrigation process is well described in the literature on Senegal (see the articles in Crousse, Mathieu and Seck, 1991 as well as Schmitz, 1986a; 1986b; Tourrand and Jamin, 1986; Jamin, 1986 etc), few scholars have dealt with the fate of pastoral production along the river (Santoir, 1982, 1983 and Tourrand, 1994) and even fewer with the fate of these migrants once they left the Senegal River Valley. It is the latter process that the rest of this chapter will deal with.

---

[79] As the rains improved after 1984 many farmers in fact abandoned their irrigated plots to take up rainfed and flood recession agriculture which is less demanding in terms of labour and financial investment.

The Egge-egge in the Linguere-Matam area

The principal reception area for drought migration has been the southern fringe of the Ferlo, mainly along the axis Linguere/Matam. This does not, however imply that the herders have settled; rather they have installed a more or less permanent wet season camp. During the dry season they continue to depart on transhumance trips of shorter or longer range depending on the availability of pastures. Referring to their mobile lifestyle or their zone of origin, they are called either "egge-egge", which in FulBe means "those who are always on the move"[80]. They are also called" FuutankoBe" referring to the Fuuta area which includes both the *waalo* and the northern fringe of the *jeeri*.

As could be seen from the two cases cited in the introduction of this chapter, settlement in the new area did not occur in a single blow. The large majority of herders moved back to the *waalo* once the rains had resumed after the first drought. Only in the second drought did they settle on a more permanent basis in the south (the example of Yerim Sow). A smaller group continued to roam without fixed settlement around the deep-wells along the Matam/Linguere axis (see Bathil Ba). By the end of the 1980s also this group had become relatively settled.

The chart below[81] shows that a large group of herders (25.6%) claim to have departed definitively from the Senegal River Valley in connection with the first drought (i.e. between 1973 and 1975). A group of almost similar size (26.4%) claims to have arrived in the intermediate period of 7 years between 1976 and 1982. The second drought of 1983/84 precipitated the settlement of another 32 households (12,4%). Most surprising is, however, the important number of households which have settled after 1986 when more normal precipitation patterns had resumed. Although on a more moderate scale this migration process is still ongoing. Significant for this last 'wave' of migration is that it is made up of herders who have only recently managed to build up a herd sufficiently large to be

---

[80] According to Cheick Ba 1986, the term "egge-egge" comes from "eggol", exceptional nomadisations, usually caused by drought. Their hesitant movements often lead to permanent change of the area of residence.(Ba, 1986 p.137).

[81] Data for the chart was collected in October 1994. 5 boreholes are comprised in the sample (Barkedji, Djagueli, Yonofere, Fourdou, and Ranérou). The boreholes of Naoré and Velingara are not included.

able to resume a purely pastoral production strategy. Once this is accomplished they move to join their more prosperous kin in the south, in the hope of replicating their success story.

Obviously the two short drought periods account for a far most important influx (note that the time intervals of the 'x' axis in the chart are not equal). 38% of all resettlements within a period of 20 years took place during the 4 years of heavy drought. Nonetheless, the important resettlement taking place in the intermediate periods may be attributed to at least three factors: a). that precipitation in the intermediate years remained very low, b) that the expansion of irrigation creating increasingly difficult conditions for livestock production in the valley and was an equally important incentive for out-migration and c) that some herders who had lost a lot of livestock could not move immediately, but had to wait until their herds were sufficiently reconstituted. Finally, d) the rain deficit in the Valley between 1991 and 1993 also prompted some herders to leave the more drought prone pastures of northern Senegal for good.

To estimate the number of herders involved in the post-drought migration process is a hazardous endeavour. First of all, it was impossible for the
researcher to cover all boreholes in the vast Ferlo region. No official statistics are available on these population movements. Local administrators have no means of evaluating their real number, as very few of the immigrants are registered residents, and tax payers, in the area of settlement. What is clear is that the largest contingents may be found around the deep wells between Linguere and Matam in the arrondissements of Barkedji and Ranerou (see map 1). FuutankoBe herders are also well represented at several boreholes further south.

In order to get a more accurate picture of the actual number of FuutankoBe immigrants present in the Southern Ferlo, a field survey was carried out in October 1994 around the 7 boreholes where FuutankoBe presence, according to local sources, was most prominent.

Table 1.
Distribution of indigenous and FuutankoBe households around 7 deep-wells of southern Ferlo, October 1994.

	Indigenous		FuutankoBe		Total households
Barkedji	241	(83%)	51	(17%)	292
Naoré	36	(29%)	87	(71%)	123
Velingara	154	(81%)	37	(19%)	191
Diagueli	146	(61%)	93	(39%)	239
Yonoféré	60	(41%)	86	(59%)	146
Fourdou	56	(64%)	31	(36%)	87
Ranérou	127	(85%)	22	(15%)	149
TOTAL	820	(67%)	407	(33%)	1227

This survey revealed a FuutankoBe population far larger than expected[82]. It turned out that the number of immigrants at certain deep-wells even exceeded the indigenous population (see table 1). On average, they constituted 1/3 of the total population or user group around a deep well.

---

[82] It is important to stress the indicative character of this population and herd property survey. In order to cover a relatively large geographical area, the data was collected through interviews with representatives from the well committees at 7 selected boreholes and (in the cases where such lists existed) consultation with the list of users. At each borehole the data was verified with both FuutankoBe and sedentary herders, and whenever possible with the village chiefs/sub-clan leaders representing the existing groups. The sampling unit was the gallé, the Fulani household or family unit, at which level decisions about herd management are made. These households are usually nuclear families eventually with the presence of old parents. They may however vary considerably in size as several adult sons in some cases remain together and manage their animals as a single herd. This obviously makes the data less reliable when assessing the pressure of the newcomers vis à vis the local population.

The large majority (60%) of the FuutankoBe herders comes from a relatively small area in the arrondissements[83] of Kass-Kass and Salde[84]. At the boreholes located in the western-most part of the area of incursion one also finds immigrants coming from the western parts of the *waalo* and northern *jeeri* (from the arrondissements of Ndioum, Thile Boubacar and Mbane).

Despite the individualistic decision-making that all herders profess, it is, at least in some periods of the year, possible to distinguish a tendency to cluster according to kin/clan (see maps p. 116-118 on distribution of Fulani clans around the borehole of Velingara). When questioned on this subject, herders admit that it is easier to settle in areas where some relatives may be found.

"During my transhumance trip I have mainly settled near my kin. It's in order to be close to people I can trust, that I chose this particular itinerary" (Herder from Mbiddi, on transhumance near Loumbi Aly Thedy Feb. 1993).

In certain cases large groups of herders from the same area and clan appear to have moved more or less simultaneously thus creating one or several new "villages" in the area of settlement (as was the case of Yerim Sow). The most spectacular cases of "villagisation" are found in Diagueli and in Barkedji. No less than 68 UururBe Daka households have left the small village of Bano from 1973 onwards to settle in the UururBe Daka settlement called Fidjiti near the Djagueli borehole. Even in 1994 new households were still joining. From the area of Namarel 22 households of the UururBe Ndioum subclan broke away in 1973 to establish two new villages in the south of Barkedji.

If one considers the important scale of this immigration wave and, not the least, its impact on the production systems both in the area of

---

[83] An *arrondissement* is the intermediate administrative level in Senegal constituted by 2 or 3 *communautés rurales* and headed by a centrally appointed civil servant, the *sous-préfet*. Higher administrative levels are the *département* and the *region*.

[84] 170 of the egge-egge households registered in the survey, originate from the areas of Madina Ndiatebe (28), Gollere (35), Meri (6), Mboumba (7), Haire Lao(6), Boki Diallobe(6) and Louggue Foulbe (6), all located within a distance of 25 km along the tar road running alongside the Valley. The village of Bano located 20 km south of Gollere, in the *jeeri*, contributes with the largest share (68 households). 8 households originate from Yare Lao (50 km south-east of Gollere).

out-migration and in the area of reception, it is surprising what little notice it has received. Until recently the phenomenon, and especially its extension, was almost unknown to the Senegalese administration, especially at higher levels. Indeed FuutankoBe herders tend to be perceived as a tiny minority by state administrators who become aware of their existence mainly in cases of dispute and open conflict.

Apart from the obvious problems related to monitoring of such a fluid population, one reason for such a blind spot to emerge, is that the process of 're-pastoralisation' carried out by the post-drought migrants, for many state administrators, represents a 'regression' from the higher state of sedentarised agro-pastoralism, which does not fit within the models received during their education.

Uneven herd distribution

The extent of this migration and its impact on the existing production systems becomes all the more spectacular if one looks at the distribution of animals among sedentary[85] and FuutankoBe households. Such differences in herd ownership were investigated as part of the survey of October 1994[86].

---

[85] The term "sedentary" is used to describe those Fulani agro-pastoralists (FerlankoBe, SannaraaBe, JaawBe, FafaBe, HaabooBe and YalaBe) that were present in the area before the arrival of the FuutankoBe migrants. Wolof and Maure households are likewise included in this group. It is important to stress, however, that the term sedentary does not exclude annual migrations between wet and dry season camps, nor exceptional nomadisations prompted by drought, breakdown of the deep-well or other types of calamities. Although some exceptions are found within the group, these households are predominantly agro-pastoral with limited possibilities of mobility on a larger scale. For the sake of variation the terms "indigenous" or "first-comers" have equally been used for this group.

[86] If collection of accurate data on population movements is difficult, data collection on herd ownership is even worse, being both extremely time-consuming and full of pitfalls and inaccuracies. Hence I have chosen to present data of a more indicative character, but to refrain from further "fudging, cooking and manipulating" in order not to conceal the inherent validity problems of the data material. (see Polly Hill (1986:30-50)). In order to cover a relatively large geographical area, the data was collected through interviews with representatives of the well committees at 5 selected boreholes. At each borehole the data was verified with both FuutankoBe and sedentary herders, and, whenever possible, with the village chiefs/sub-clan leaders representing the existing groups. As the focus of the research presented here is on FuutankoBe migration rather than on the actual herd development, or grazing pressure, the informants were asked to

The survey reveals a rather skewed distribution of cattle and smallstock ownership. Indeed, the first impression of the situation at the boreholes is, that not only have the local population in the south of the Ferlo endured the reception of a very large number of foreign herders, but they have also been 'invaded' by foreign animals. But as will be shown later on,

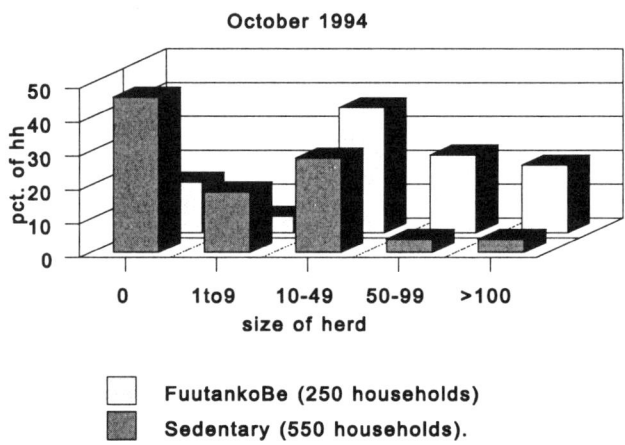

this development is not quite as conflictive as could be anticipated.

Not surprisingly, households possessing no animals at all (135 households or 15%[87]) are found entirely among sedentary households[88]. Destitute FuutankoBes herders have little reason to remain in the southern rangelands. Among both sedentary and newcomers, households are found who do not have cattle. However, the number is more significant among sedentary households where 46% have no cattle as compared to 15% among FuutankoBe.

---

give only rough indications of the sizes of the herds using the deep well on a regular basis. These were grouped in 5 categories. Finally, the survey was only carried out at 5 boreholes.due to ongoing conflicts at certain boreholes. Evidently, a number of pitfalls persist. As we have not collected data on family sizes it is not possible to control to what extent the very large herds correlate with very large families and thus with several owners of equal status i.e. not wives or children. One could suspect this to be the case with some of the very large herds of smallstock of several thousand heads.

[87] Data from Velingara and Naore are not included in these figures.

[88] Including both Wolof and Fulani.

In contrast, the large herds of over 50 heads are owned almost exclusively by newcomers (8% by sedentary against 43% by FuutankoBe). The uneven distribution of livestock is even more pronounced when looking at sheep and goats, which constitute the core of FuutankoBe herding strategies. Consequently the very large herds of smallstock (>300 heads) are almost entirely owned by FuutankoBe households. By contrast, sedentary herders own the small herds between 1 and 49 heads. However 12% of the sedentary households dispose of herds of 50 to 99 heads (i.e. a herd of quite significant value).

With this uneven herd ownership in mind, it is not surprising that FuutankoBe herd owners often are referred to as *Jaarga* i.e. very rich herd owners. Nonetheless the survey reveal exhibits a certain differentiation within the FuutankoBe group. According to the survey 15% (or 37 households) of the FuutankoBe households possess only smallstock. Of these, 14 own less than 50 sheep. Part of these households consists of former WodaaBe captives living near Barkedji.

The picture revealed by the survey fits well with a previous mapping exercise carried out around the deep-well of Velingara in 1991[89]. In that case (Juul, 1991b) it was found that, of the 109 pastoral camps located within a distance of 2-20 km from the deep well[90], 41 households were established after 1973, the majority indicating 1984 as the year of settlement. A large majority of these households originated from the Senegal River Valley[91].

---

[89] This mapping exercise, carried out by my patient assistant, a local guide and myself, was made before the existence of GPS (Global Positioning System) was put to our knowledge. The location of each camp was measured by means of a car and a compass, driving in as straight a course as possible from the point of departure (the borehole). For obvious reasons this method does not give very exact locations. The method was however reliable enough to prove the initial hypothesis that it is the most livestock-rich herders who live farthest away from the borehole. It turned out to be extremely time- and diesel consuming, reason for which we refrained from repeating it at the 6 other wells as initially planned.

[90] While included in the 1994 survey, the central village of Velingara inhabited almost exclusively by Wolof farmers was excluded in the 1991 survey. This gives the 1991 survey a bias towards pastoral producers.

[91] Mainly Gollere, Ndioum, Haire Lao, Kass Kass in the Middle Senegal River Valley and in a few cases from Tessekre, Amali and Ganina in the north western Ferlo. A few FafaBe households had arrived from Ndiayene Fuuta in the north-eastern Ferlo.

The 1991 survey (see below) showed a similarly uneven distribution of animals between FuutankoBes and sedentary. While households settled in the area prior to 1973 owned a total of 560 heads of cattle and 1107 sheep or goats, the "newcomers" owned a total of 2092

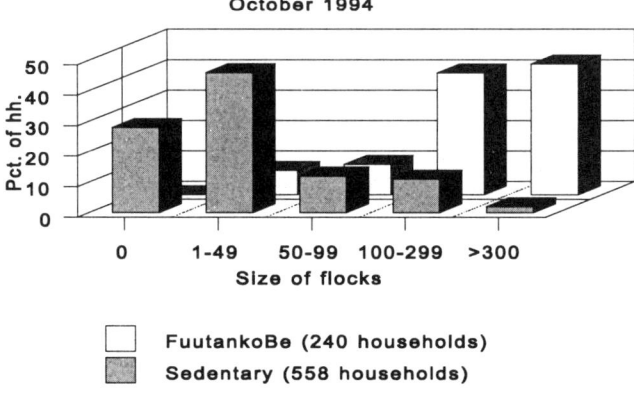

heads of cattle and 5029 heads of smallstock. Only 6 of the households present in the area before 1973 disposed of herds of more than 30 cattle, while none had flocks of smallstock of more than 100 head. All the large herds of smallstock were owned by herders from the Senegal River who had specialised in this type of pastoralism[92]. On the basis of these, still quite unreliable answers, a very tentative average may be calculated according to which average herd size among sedentary households is 8 heads of cattle and 16 smallstock, while among the newcomers the average is 51 heads of cattle and 122 sheep and goats.

More important, however, is the correlation of the two findings of the surveys. The 1994 survey revealed that, contrary to what was to be expected, it is the newcomer population that posses the bulk of livestock in the area. This prosperity (especially in sheep and goats) is closely interconnected with the findings of the 1991 survey, showing that those

---

[92] The herd sizes expressed in the 1991 census seem surprisingly modest compared to other egge-egge households encountered in the area. Most of the "newcomers" interviewed from 1989 to 1994 on migration patterns indicate ownership of flocks of sheep and goats ranging up to 400, 700 or even 1000 heads. Such herd sizes have also been confirmed by the well committees as well as by the veterinary doctors in the area and they tally with the 1994 survey.

herders who lived farthest away from the borehole also tended to be the most livestock-rich.

It also turned out that the most distant camps were those belonging to FuutankoBe herders. Hence far from being a sign of marginalisation, the 'distant' location of FuutankoBe camps is a conscious strategy by resourceful and speculative herders who strive to be as close as possible to the pastures.

But in order for this strategy to be viable, the key problem related to watering had to be solved. And it is here that a simple technological device, the tractor inner tube, proves to be the most important single factor for the highly successful herd management strategy of the newcomers.

Map 10
Distribution of households around Velingara borehole, Oct. 1991

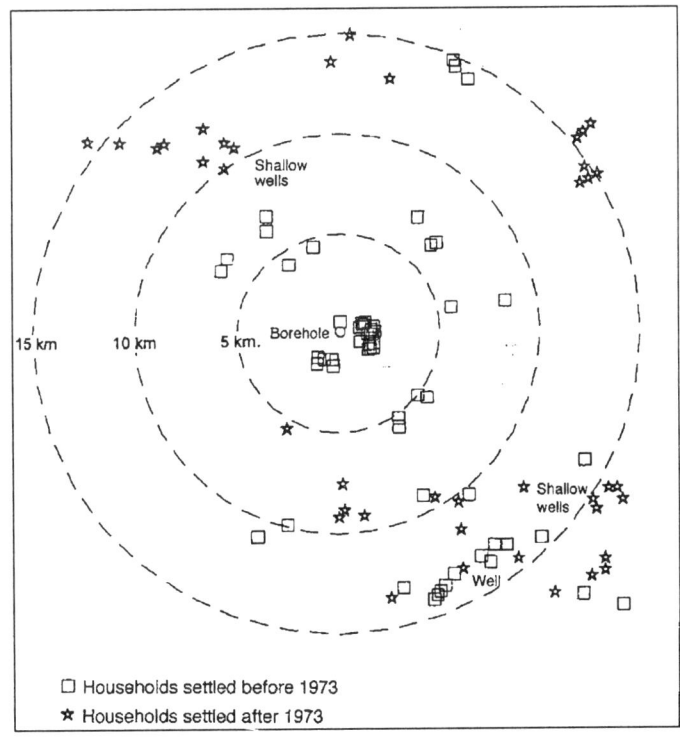

Map 11
Distribution of households by clan groups.
Velingara 1990.

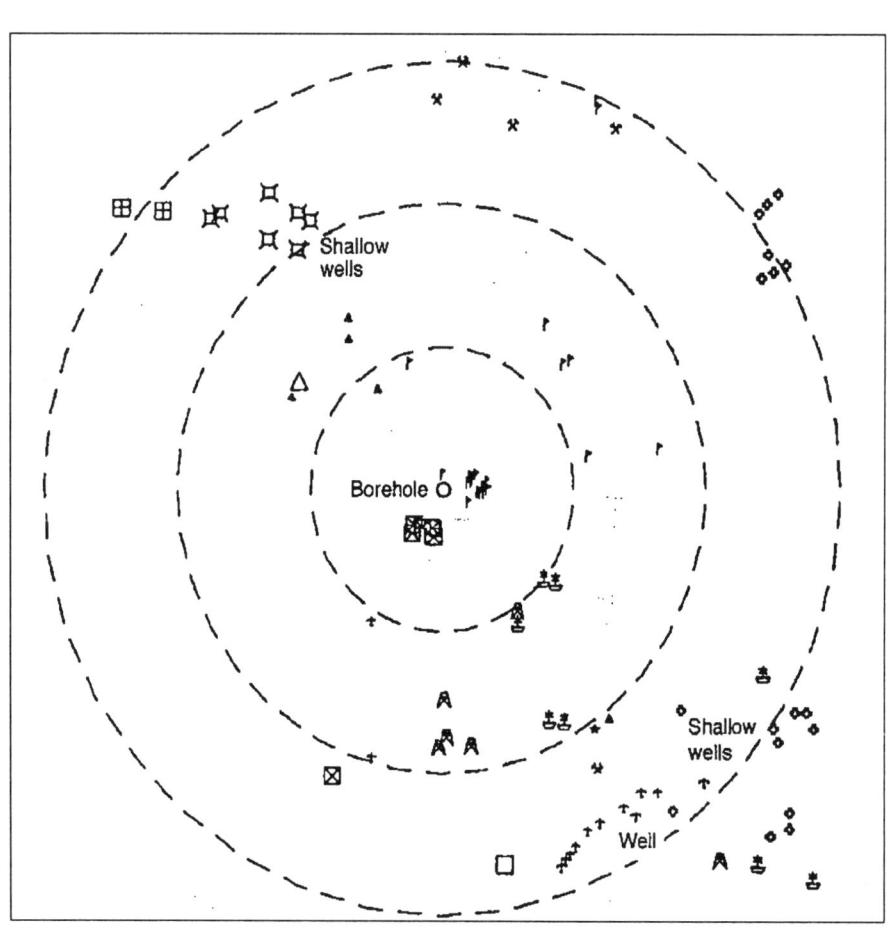

FuutankoBes:
- ◊ UrurBe
- ¤ BissinaaBe
- △ AerinkoBe
- ✷ Other FuutankoBe

"Locals":
- ⊠ YalalBe
- ≛ FerlankoBe
- ᴀ FafaBe
- ᛏ HaaboBe
- ▲ SanraBe
- ᵣ DjawBe
- ☐ Maures
- ✶ LawBe (artisan c

Map 12
Distribution of cattle and smallstock around the borehole of Velingara, 1990.

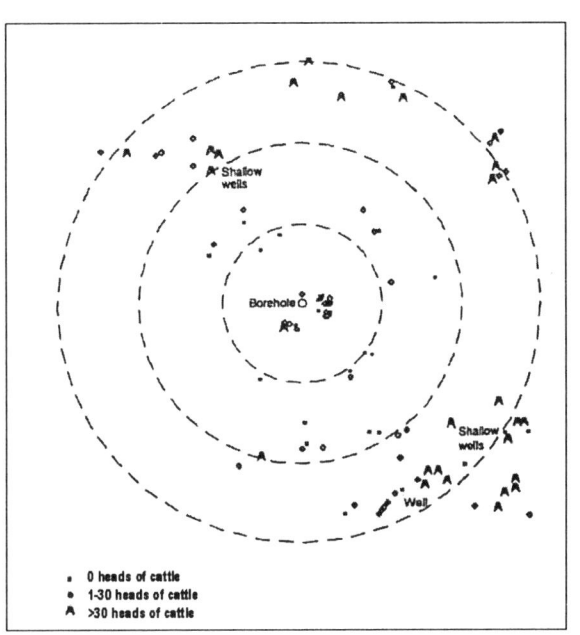

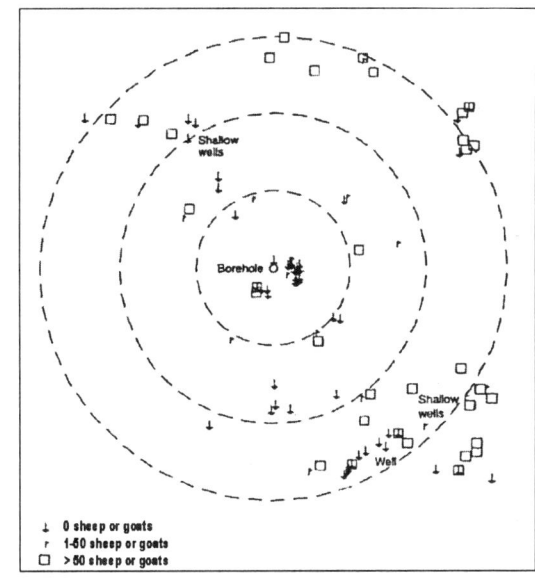

The inner tube and the donkey cart

The invention of a new way of transporting water over long distances by recycling the huge tractor-type inner tubes from bulldozers and other heavy machinery from the irrigation schemes into huge water containers in fact provided for a minor revolution in the range management systems of northern Senegal.

As mentioned in the introduction, the ground water table in most parts of the Ferlo region is several hundred meters below surface. The pastoral space is therefore structured above all, by the boreholes placed at a distance of approximately 30 kilometres from each other. These deep wells occupy a central position in pastoral resource management.

In the extensive Sahelian livestock systems, a major difficulty during the dry season consists in simultaneously ensuring optimal fodder conditions while limiting energy losses related to watering. For as the dry season progresses, the distance between the watering point and the fresh and untrampled pastures increases. If cattle are grazed further than 15 to 20 kilometres away from the well too much energy is spent on getting to the water. For sheep and goats the maximum distance is considerably shorter.

Among the indigenous herders of the Ferlo region, the dry season strategy consists in approaching the camps to within 5 or 6 kilometres from the deep well once the natural pools have dried out. The animals are then grazed in a centrifugal movement reaching pastures still farther away as the dry season progresses. With this system energy losses by the end of the dry season are significant.

By means of the tractor inner tube, herders from the Senegal River Valley are able to attack the problem in a radically different manner. While the adult animals may continue to water at the borehole every second day, the ingenuity of the new system consists in sparing the youngest and the sick animals from the long and constraining trip to the well. For when lain on a donkey cart, these tubes can transport large quantities of water over long distances, enabling the weakest part of the herd to be watered at the camp. This considerably reduces energy losses. The younger animals that graze in the vicinities of the camp have easy access to fresh pastures and the herd is ensured optimal fodder conditions. This situation is maintained by frequent movements of the camp during the dry season (see the case of Yerim Sow[146]). In this way the newcomers are able to live closer to the fresh and untrampled pastures, at a distance of up to 20 kilometres from the wells.

The radius of pastures accessible to the herds is now considerably enlarged as compared to the "centrifugal grazing strategy"[147] employed by the more sedentarised households. The result is a considerable decrease in mortality[148] and an increase in reproduction rates and other parameters of herd productivity. For these reasons the tube is often referred to as "the secret of the Fulani".

According to my informants, the 'invention, was rather accidental:

"It was Harouna Mody Ciro from Gollere, who invented the tube for water transportation. During the drought he was forced to go very far away to get fodder and every day he brought with him a 4 litre can to carry water. One day the can fell off the cart and broke and he was forced to use a tube he incidentally carried with him to conserve the remaining water. People had told him that the tubes were poisonous, but the experience showed him that they weren't. From then on, he started experimenting with still larger tubes". (Herder Fourdou Feb. 93).

It is indeed ironic that it is a spill-over effect of the irrigation process, itself a major factor in evicting herders from the Valley, that constitutes the key factor in this new and highly productive herd management system. Nevertheless, the use of rubber from inner tubes is in itself no new invention. Rubber is used in many pastoral societies for making different utensils such as soft buckets for drawing water from wells, strings for different sorts of attachment, shoes etc. The use of inner tubes for water transport was, for example, observed by the author in Mauritania in 1986, where car inner tubes were cut and attached at both ends and lain over

---

[146] Seasonal movements along the same gradient from the borehole are carried out by most of the herders interviewed, however the frequency varies considerable according to precipitation and pastures as well as availability of labour, size of herds and as herders repeatedly stress: the "devotion of the herder"

[147] See L'Hoste, Ph. and P. Milleville 1986.

[148] Not being a veterinarian I have not been able to verify these statements in a scientific manner.

a donkey-back to carry quantities of around 40 litres of water from the well to the household. Similarly, expansion of grazing lands through regular use of donkeys to carry water for young livestock and human consumption has been described by Jacobs (1980:287) as one of the management techniques employed by the pastoral Masai to conserve and improve their pastures. Nonetheless, the transformation "waste" tubes from the irrigation schemes into containers suited to transport large quantities (300, 600 or even 1000 litres[149]) of water on donkey carts to camps located 15 to 20 km from the borehole, seems to be peculiar to northern Senegal.

The 'triumph of the tube' relied on a number of contingent factors among which the most important precondition was the diffusion of horse and donkey carts among herders. During the seventies attempts to introduce carts had been made as part of the general attempt to mechanise the agricultural sector. Results had nonetheless been meagre and by the beginning of the eighties the number of pastoral households with access to a cart was extremely limited[150] (Santoir, 1982:30).

Between 1975 and 1991, however, the number of carts increased tenfold (Santoir, 1994:251) from one carriage per 24 households to a carriage and a horse for almost every second household. This booming period coincided with the massive migration of the FuutankoBe herders. For these herders the carts became a sine qua non for the development of new herding strategies. As we shall se further on, the cart-and-tube system was promptly picked up by the local herders.

What makes the development even more extraordinary is that these rather substantial investments[151] were made during a period

---

[149]Thebaud 1994 registered 3 sizes of tubes around the borehole of Widou Thiengoly, 200, 400 and 600 litres. I have observed larger tubes at several occasions but they are less popular as they are difficult to handle and require many donkeys to pull. Furthermore they are difficult to get hold of.

[150] In 1982 Santoir (1982:30) states that Fulani herders rarely dispose of horse or donkey carriages. According to a survey made by Berot-Inard and Di Meo in the mid-eighties only 1 out of 5 Fulani households in Labgar, where the main centre of SODESP is located, disposed of a cart. SODESP (Societé de Développement de l'Elevage dans la zone Sylvo-Pastorale) the para-statal in charge of livestock development in northern Senegal was the main distributor of carts.

[151] In 1998 the local blacksmith of Barkedji indicated to sell a locally produced cart at 75.000 F CFA. Factory produced carts are considerably more expensive.

characterised by serious drought and largely without external assistance (ibid). From 1983 onwards, private traders in the area report a rapidly growing interest in carts and tubes. Today there is a flourishing market for used inner tubes as well as second hand tires and spare parts for carts. Local manufacturers, mechanics and specialists in vulcanisation are present in every village, having a borehole.

At present most pastoral households dispose of at least one, but often two or three, carts[152]. According to our questionnaire survey of April 1995, the average number of carts is 1.88 for sedentary households, while it is 2.39 for FuutankoBe[153].

The carts are pulled either by horse or by donkey. When used for the transportation of water, 2-4 donkeys usually pull the cart. The number of carts exceeds the number of tubes, indicating that the carts are used for multiple purposes. Besides transport of water, they are used for travelling. In case of transhumance they carry young and older members of the family, luggage, poultry, water and sometimes industrial feed concentrates to ensure proper feeding of the animals. With the carts herders are now able to transport the new-born lambs or sick animals otherwise unable to accomplish the voyage[154]. As can be seen from the quotation below, this development is not necessarily an advantage for the local population.

"The transhumants are useful; there is no reason to limit their number. If they are close to you, they may offer you some animals and if they leave they will give you the new-born lambs, who cannot survive such a trip". (President of the well-committee, Loumbi Sanrabe 1989)

---

[152] The questionnaire survey comprised 53 households and showed that 32 % of the sample dispose of 1 cart, 34% of 2 and 21% of 3 carts. Three households claimed to own between 7 and 9 carts while only one family claimed to posses none.

[153] These findings are more or less equivalent to those found by Thebaud in 1994 in Bouteyni (in north-western Ferlo). According to Thebaud pastoral households (*galles*) in Bouteyni disposed of an average of 1,62 carts. 18 of the 33 households included by Thebaud had at least one cart while the richest households disposed of 3 to 6. (Thebaud, 1994:24). In some parts of eastern Ferlo (Loumbi Sanrabe and Dendoudi, a large group of the poorest households do not to dispose of any means of transport.

[154] For unknown reasons Berod-Inard and Di Meo (p.101) claim that the carts rarely are used for transport during transhumance. This statement does not correspond with the findings of the present author. On the contrary, donkey and horse carts play a crucial role in maintaining mobility.

As to the number of tubes, 43 % of households indicate that they dispose of 1 tube[155]. Herders possessing more than 1 tube are found mainly among the newcomers. The average number of tubes per household is 1.8 among sedentary households and 2.28 among FuutankoBe. This obviously does not indicate anything about the size and capacities of the individual household.

The number of daily trips varies seasonally as watering needs increase significantly by the end of the dry season. As camps are placed as far as 15 km from the borehole the women, usually those in charge of supplying water, easily spend 7 to 8 hours a day fetching water[156]. By the end of the dry season it is not unusual that several women in a camp are fully occupied with water transportation. It is usually those households located farthest away that dispose of the largest number of tubes.

From cattle to sheep

The full extent of the utility of the new water transportation technique is perhaps best understood when it is linked to the development by the FuutankoBe herders of a highly specialised herding system based on the raising of sheep rather than on cattle.

Herders as well as researchers have a long tradition for considering cattle as the superior and most valuable part of the herd. According to Fulani herders "it's the cow that constitutes the only real prosperity" (Bonfiglioli et Diallo, 1988). In fact, many surveys hardly take into account other species (see for example Barral, 1981; Fayole, 1974; Lhoste et Milleville, 1986). The general assumption is that smallstock is raised mainly to limit off-take on the cattle herd. Because of their shorter

---

[155] 2 households indicated not to posses any tubes, but due to the selection of respondents (only 1/3 was local sedentary households) this is not necessarily very representative.

[156] A measurement of time consumption for filling of tubes was carried out by the team of Thebaud at the borehole of Widou Thiengoly in April 94, (Thebaud, 1994 p.25). According to them, queuing at the water source and filling of the tube amounted for approximately one hour. Unfortunately the study does not comprise the time spent travelling the long distances to and from the camp and the boreholes is by far the most time consuming. According to my findings it is not unusual to spend more than 2 hours each way if the camp is located more than 15 km away. To this adds time spent doing the shopping, the laundry as well as time spent on renewing social contacts.

reproduction cycle[157] they provide a means of restoring (cattle) herds after drought or diseases, as surplus head of smallstock may be exchanged for heifers. Once the herd was reconstructed, smallstock is likely to lose its importance and be limited to a few animals kept for slaughtering at festive occasions.

Since the drought periods of 1972/73 and 1983/84, smallstock, notably sheep, has acquired considerable importance and is given a dominant role in many herds in the Ferlo[158]. This may largely be attributed to the influence of the FuutankoBe herders.

Even before the drought, the agro-pastoral Fulani from the *waalo* tended to put more emphasis on the rearing of smallstock than did their relatives in the *jeeri*[159]. But when moving southward in the aftermath of the drought the rehabilitation strategies of the FuutankoBe herders were centred primarily on the sheep. This was a way of adjusting herd composition to suit the new and more difficult ecological conditions since a large part of fodder requirements of sheep and goats can be met through browsing on tree products that are less affected by failing rains. Contrary to what might have been expected, this strategy was not abandoned once precipitation resumed more normal standards after 1988.

Indeed, the rearing of sheep has proved to be an extremely viable strategy. Due to the higher drought resistance and shorter reproduction cycle of sheep, herders originating from the Fuuta area were able to recover their losses very quickly and today most of them dispose of flocks far beyond their pre-drought size[160]. Among FuutankoBe herders residing in the

---

[157] According to Projet Sénégalo-Allemand d'Amenagement et de Reboisement Sylvopastoral de la zone Nord (P.S.A.) in Widou Thiengoly the fertility rate in traditional herding systems in the Ferlo is 32 % (of reproductive females) for cattle, 82% for sheep and 100 % for goats (PSA: 1991 annex 21) Off-take of smallstock for meat for sheep is made at the age of 9 to 15 months, while for cattle it is between 3 and 4 years (Wilson, 1988.)

[158] The growing importance of smallstock has been reported by Bonfiglioli et Diallo 1988, A.T. Diop 1991 and Thebaud 1994.

[159] According to a survey made by Santoir in 1978 the mean herd held by WalwalBe (FuutankoBe) households consisted of 18 heads of cattle and 69 heads of smallstock, while JerjerBe households would have 39.2 heads of cattle and 34 heads of smallstock (Santoir 1982 p.4). Variations between households were, however, considerable.

[298] Unfortunately no studies of flock sizes before 1972/73 seem to be available. Studies on

southern part of the Ferlo region it is not unusual to see herds of 400 to 700 or even 1000 sheep and goats.

Table 2 shows the distribution of those 101 households (43% of the October 1994 sample) possessing more than 300 heads of smallstock:

Size:	300	400	500	600	700	800	900	1000	2000	> 3000
No.	41	22	6	10	4	5	0	7	4	2

This shift in herd composition was only possible due to the improved watering and grazing conditions facilitated by the tube and the donkey cart which enabled herders to keep far larger flocks of sheep than had been possible before. But while the tube and cart system contribute to limit the energy losses of the animals, it is important to stress that the new system of water transport is extremely labour demanding and leaves little time for supplementary income activities. Also in terms of labour investment, the new system challenges conventional wisdom on pastoral herd management.

Drought recovery through specialisation instead of diversification

According to most accounts on drought recovery in pastoral societies, the principal remedy for herd reconstitution is to limit off-take on the herd through the creation of alternative income sources[161]. The primary

---

herd composition in the Senegal River Valley after 1975 report of average flocks of smallstock of 30,9 (Blanc SEDES 1975, downstream of the Valley) 40,6 (Santoir 1975, Mbane and Thille Boubacar) 21,3 (ibid Matam 1979) and 35,1(ibid. Senegal River Basin 1979) pr. household. Tourrand and Direction de L'Elevage estimate drought losses for smallstock in the 2 drought periods to be between 30% and 50% (Tourrand 1989 p.4. and data from DIREL Statistics unit).

[161] See for example Dahl, G., 1979 on the Waso Borana, Bonfiglioli et Diallo, 1988 on the Senegalese Fulani subgroup, the FerlankoBe.

strategy for risk management consists in diversifying into other economic activities (cropping, wage labour, collection and sale of wood or fruits gathered in the bush, etc.). With income generated from other sources, grains and other necessities can be purchased without selling off animals. In successful cases, surplus income might also be used to purchase livestock to ensure faster reproduction of the herd. As mentioned above, smallstock in such a model is regarded mainly as an intermediate category, which is later to be exchanged for cattle (see for example Richter, 1991:22).

Although effective, especially in cases where little livestock is left or where families have sufficient manpower available, the diversification strategy has its disadvantages. It often involves at least a seasonal limitation on mobility to give time to cultivate, to build up a clientele, or to create a network of people who might help in specific ways. As stated by Khazanov (1983:19) "even limited agricultural production exercises a considerable influence on many aspects of the life of semi-nomads, for example on herd composition, routes and prevalence of pastoral migration".

Increased emphasis on agriculture limits mobility particularly in periods critical for herding such as the end of the dry season where water and pastures are scarcest and labour requirements highest. At a certain stage of the herd's reproduction, the herder is therefore faced with a choice. He can choose to limit weight losses at the end of the dry season by migrating to more remote areas with fodder resources remaining and later continue southward "to meet the rains"[162]. Alternatively he can stay at home and prepare the fields for a new agricultural season. This choice is conditioned on the one hand by the availability of labour (to enable successful diversification) and on the other hand by the size of the herd and its ability to cater for the consumption needs of the family.

Even though the FuutankoBe herders were agro-pastoralists before moving southward, the majority of those remaining in the southern Ferlo seem to have opted for increased specialisation. Hence, supplementary income-generating activities besides pastoralism are rare. Instead of reconstruction through restriction of off-takes, as in the diversification model, the strategy of FuutankoBe herders aims at keeping reproduction

---

[162] i.e. moving to areas where the rains have started and new grasses have come up.

rates as high as possible by ensuring optimum fodder availability throughout the year. This is ensured through increased mobility.

According to herders it was the wish to "spare the lives of their animals" that determined this choice of strategy. Obviously, other factors are equally at play, such as limited labour availability due to nuclearisation[163] of households, or the fact of being "foreigners" lacking the necessary social network to get access to alternative sources of income. But first and foremost, it is the size of the remaining herds that determines the number of alternatives[164].

"It's only three years ago that I started to go on transhumance regularly. It has a good effect on the general shape of the herd. Before I couldn't leave because I was in charge of my old folks. Now the size of my flock forces me to move" (Transhumant, Well of Belel Touffle Feb. 1993).

For contrary to the description by Lattimore (1967, cited from Khazanov, 1983:70) of "the poor nomad being the true nomad", mobility was and is not a real option as a survival strategy for the most impoverished herders. Only richer herders dispose of sufficient animals to depend solely on the herd. Poorer herders are forced to seek supplementary sources of subsistence, often involving sedentarisation. Such "forced" sedentarisation needs not, however, be permanent. Once the herd has reached a certain level, other activities may be abandoned and mobility resumed. This seems to have been the case for many (younger) households who have left the Fuuta area after 1990 (see also Niemeijer, 1996).

---

[163] Since the advent of the boreholes there has been a radical shift in the extent to which labour is a critical factor of production. At present most households consist only of the nuclear family, the average number of people pr. household being 8,3 (Sutter, 1983 p.200).

[164] Although it does not fit into the idealised picture of the specialised herder that the FuutankoBe herders like to make of themselves, more herders than anticipated have turned out to cultivate, though not in a very systematic manner. The survey from April 1995 showed that many of the poorer FuutankoBe households had some agricultural activities. However, this was the case of only 1 of the households possessing more than 300 heads of smallstock. This fits with the case-story told in the introduction to the chapter of Bathil Ba, who maintained some cultivation while waiting for his flock to grow to a suitable size to provide for the entire income of the family.

Changing herding strategies

The turn towards breeding of sheep has a number of consequences for the herding strategies adopted and the amount of labour invested in livestock herding. For although herds are still mixed it is now the sheep rather than the cows that determine the herding and production strategy.

In herds based primarily on cattle, the principal production goal among Fulani herders is to ensure constitution and growth of their herd, and to increase milk yields (Niamir, 1990:20). Although rearing of sheep is compatible with a milk-oriented strategy (Thebaud, 1994:24)[165] it is meat production and commercial sale that constitute the essence of the system. Owing to their inferior market value, goats are normally a smaller part of the herd. Being good milk producers they act primarily as support animals, providing milk for the young lambs in the dry season when milk production from ewes tends to run short[166]. Cattle are kept for milk production and as savings. They are mainly sold to cover large expenditures such as purchasing of horses or donkey carts, vehicles or machinery or to pay for a pilgrimage to Mecca[167].

Since the establishment of the boreholes labour demands for cattle rearing have been fairly limited. Due to the safe environment[168] and the reduced mobility the herd is normally not guarded (see Touré, 1990) except during the agricultural season to prevent them from straying into

---

[165] In many families a large part of the milk consumed is ewe and goat milk. The high content of milk fat makes ewe milk very good for production of butter which is highly esteemed in the local "cuisine" and an important source of income for women during the rainy season.

[166] An important task of the women and young children is to ensure that the lambs that do not get sufficient milk from their mother can suckle a goat. Considering that many flocks have large numbers of lambs, this is in certain periods very time-consuming.

[167] This is of course a function of the general economic standing of the family. Poorer households may be forced to sell even reproductive females to ensure family subsistence (see Sutter, 1987).

[168] In order to limit the number of predators attacking cattle in the Ferlo, the colonial administration carried out a strychnine campaign between 1950 and 1955 (Touré and Arpaillange, 1986:41). Considering the extremely limited number of predators (apart from jackals) inhabiting the area at present, it is likely to have been quite efficient.

cultivated fields. During the dry season cattle is only chased off in a specific direction by the herder. In the evening the milking cows will return by themselves to the camp. After milking the herder might chase them off for night grazing. With regards to watering, the cattle herd is also able to move unguarded to the borehole. Here the herder is present to ensure proper watering and to avoid mixing with foreign herds. Most herders also visit the pastures regularly. Finally the herder controls fodder quality once in a while by examining the dung and the general state of the animals. This is used as an indicator for when a change of pastures is needed.

In the traditional sedentary management system, the rearing of sheep and goats has normally consisted in having a few heads grazing freely in the vicinity of the camp, sometimes under the supervision of the youngest members of the household[169]. As a result, production results have generally been poor, and mortality among smallstock high[170].

In contrast to this system, labour inputs in FuutankoBe flocks are considerable. First of all, herding of the flock is carried out either by several adolescent boys and/or adult herders already well initiated into herding practices. Furthermore, the animals are subject to intensive care. Suitable pastures and fodder are carefully selected[171] in order to ensure proper feeding. Intense surveillance is carried out both on the trip to the deep well and to the pastures. This contributes to reduce losses due to attacks from predators. Also the number of animals lost in the bush is diminished. Finally large flocks are split into several units, often separating goats and sheep while the youngest animals are kept near the encampment and herded by the women or the youngest members of the family. This allows a more careful selection of the pastures most suited to each category of animals

But if mobility increases so does labour requirements. During transhumance also cattle must be closely guarded to avoid straying and

---

[169] From the age of 5 children take care of the youngest animals kept in the vicinity of the encampment. From the age of 9 to 10 years they have the full responsibility of taking the sheep, goats and calves to the pastures. At the age of 12, they are considered able to take care of the cattle herd (Ba, 1986 p.142).

[170] According to ISRA, 1992, mortality rates for new-born lambs (between 0 and 1 year) were 17% in the Louga Region in Northern Senegal.

[171] A good herder is supposed to ensure a varied diet to his animals by ensuring access to different types of grasses and by leading them to low grounds where they can browse on tree foliage and where pods from certain tree species can be provided through shaking of the tree (see Thebaud, 1994).

losses due to theft and predation (Sutter, 1987:212). They need to be guided to the new pastures until the animals are familiar with the routes and can find way on their own.

All this makes the system very demanding in terms of labour requirements and skills. In the many cases where herders make use of hired labour they often complain of difficulties in ensuring proper care of the herd by the hired staff. The often quite mediocre salaries paid to the hired labour contribute to make hiring such herdsmen a risky business. In the course of the fieldwork many stories were told of animals that were lost or abandoned in the bush. In some cases the hired herdsman had fled his post leaving most of the flock unguarded while bringing a smaller part of the flock with him to sell to the first buyer. In other cases theft and sale of smallstock was the work of adolescent sons unable to convince the head of households of the need for pocket money.

Increased mobility and new grazing techniques

As mentioned earlier, the high survival and reproduction rate of FuutankoBe herds is closely related to the higher mobility and the enlargement of the range of accessible pastures, both of which were facilitated by the new means of water transportation.

Pastoral mobility covers a range of different practices. It may therefore be useful to distinguish between "migration" and "micro-nomadisation". Migration normally refers to longer nomadisation, mostly inter-seasonal. In many cases, it is related to a shortage situation in the area of out-migration.

In contrast to this, the term micro-nomadisation is used to describe the short-range movements between a dry season camp close to the borehole and a wet season camp located away in areas where surface water sources can be exploited. Both newcomers and the locals carry out such annual movements between dry and wet season camps. The main purpose is to move the animals away from the fields to avoid straying. Another objective is to reduce individual watering expenditures and to preserve the pastures closer to the deep well for the beginning of the dry season (Sutter, 1987:197). In the current context micro-nomadisations also refers to the frequent movements of camps within the range of the same borehole carried out during the dry season by the majority of FuutankoBe herders.

Nomadisations over longer distances are, in principle, kept to a minimum. In years where rains and pastures are relatively abundant, most herders with moderate herd sizes prefer to remain in the vicinities of a single borehole. In years where fodder is insufficient, nomadisation over longer distances is employed. Although inherent in the pastoral lifestyle, it is obvious that nomadisation is a risky undertaking, involving considerable obstacles for both family and herd. The individual decision to stay or move is therefore a calculated assessment based on a number of parameters. The most important are herd size and labour availability, access to markets for live animals and milk and disposal of sufficient technology. The advantage of limiting weight losses through nomadisation must be balanced against the considerable constraints related to moving animals into areas to which they are not acquainted and where the number of predators makes unguarded night pasturing of cattle more or less impossible. Finally, migration over long distances practically inhibits engagement in agriculture or other supplementary activities. The complex nature of the cost-benefit analysis carried out by the individual herder certainly contradicts any assumption of economic and technological stagnation among Senegalese herders.

Lately, the number of herders migrating regularly over longer distances has increased considerably. This can partly be attributed to failing rains, especially in the northern parts of the Ferlo as was the case in 1991 and 1992. In that period the boreholes in the south were practically swamped by drought-ridden herders from the north. However, the number of migrations carried out even in relatively good years, together with the considerable length of the journeys, show that risks related to transhumance has diminished along with the spread of donkey carts and inner tubes. As stated by one herder:

"Many things have changed for pastoralism since 1973. This is due to the arrival of the donkey carts, the water inner tubes and the industrial feed concentrates[172]. All three ease mobility".

---

[172] The use of agro-industrial by-products and feed concentrates to supplement the poor pastures in the end of the dry season is another example of herders "unwrapping" of selected project interventions. Feed concentrates were originally promoted by various livestock projects as a means to improve milk production and increase fertility. It is now widely used by herders. In most cases, however, it is not applied systematically but is given mainly to weak and sick animals. In a survey carried out in 1989 by the author in collaboration with O. Touré, 58% of the herders indicated that they used agro-industrial by-products and feed concentrates. Only 15%, however, indicated that they used more than 50.000 CFA (i.e. 250 French Francs pr. year) for the purpose.

It's difficult to make an exact evaluation of how transhumance patterns change, as peoples' decisions depend on a wide range of factors, from rainfall patterns to the age of family members. In our survey of 1995, we tried to investigate mobility patterns from 1988 and onwards. During 1988 and 1989 (years of good rains) the large majority (83 and 81%) of herders stayed at the same borehole all year round. In 1990 (rain deficit year in the north) 13% had moved. As the rain deficit continued in the year 1991, the number of nomadising herders increased slightly to 17%. This upward trend continued in 1992: Here the number of households going on longer transhumance trips increased to 21%, a trend which was similar in 1993 (21%). What was remarkable, however, was that in 1994, when rains had been normal all over the country, as many as 23% spent the dry season in the pastures of the Saluum[173].

The tendency to move more and earlier was also expressed during interviews with herders, notably among those from Djagueli:

"Before I stayed put in Djagueli, for I have seen that it's here that the animals develop. All those who have many sheep now go on transhumance every year. It's not possible for all the animals to stay in Djagueli all year round. There isn't enough of neither water nor pastures. And more and more transhumants arrive. If we stay in Djagueli in the dry season the flock will not grow, and the lambs will die" (FuutankoBe from Djagueli on his way to the Saluum, 1994).

Nonetheless, nomadising continues to be a strenuous endeavour, where people easily walk 30 km a day, and up 2-300 km in total to reach the pastures in the south.

What is most tough about nomadising is walking long distances. When the lambs are transported on the carts, you have to do the distance by foot yourself. Besides, watering is too expensive. Animals have to be looked after at night so you have to stay awake and be on guard. What is tough is also that before installing yourself at a borehole you have to negotiate with the borehole committee." (FuutankoBe herder from Ranerou on

---

[173] A methodological problem arises, when trying to access mobility in the area of out-migration. In fact the number of households is likely to have been larger than what is revealed, as some already might have left in April when the survey was made.

transhumance in the Saluum, January 1992).

But also with regard to comfort, the FuutankoBe herders have been innovative. By the end of the fieldwork period, the growing popularity of large tarpaulin cloths from trucks became apparent. This turned out to be yet another sign of the increased importance of mobility. Being the owner of such a tarpaulin cloth enhances possibilities for mobility during the rainy season. One is no longer forced to return (or send some of the women) to the wet season camp before the rains start to collect dry grass to repair the old and damaged grass huts or to construct new ones. Now shelter can be found by making a sort of tent by draping the tarpaulin over one or two of the carts. As construction of huts is a time consuming and meticulous work[174] this means sparing important manpower in the most intensive labour period of the year. This new practice is also important as it enhances the possibilities of short-term mobility, 'to meet the rains'. This practice, carried out regularly by a majority[175] of the newcomers, considerably improved the productive conditions of the animals.

Apparently the new practice gained momentum after the Mauritania/Senegal crisis of 1989 where tarpaulin cloths were distributed among the refugees to serve as tents. Due to the size of the investment (between 50.000 and 250.000 F CFA) they are, however, not within reach of all herders[176]. As was the case with Yerim Sow and his family, most herders continue to endure many rainy nights without shelter during their transhumance trips.

Apart from movements directly related to drought or the breakdown of borehole pumps, mobility generally aims at reducing weight losses during the dry season. It is especially the search for *Zornia glochidiata*[177], a

---

[174] According to the women interviewed the construction takes between 1 week and 10 days, as it has to fit into their other tasks related to household and herd.

[175] 78% of the newcomers, according to the 1995 survey.

[176] Only 21% of the herders comprised in the 1995 survey indicated to posesss such a "tent". Apart from one case, they were all FuutankoBe households. 1 family claimed to possess 5 pieces.

[177] *Zornia glochidiata* has spread on the Sahelian pastures of Senegal since the beginning of the seventies. Its proliferation was by some researchers (Barral 1982, Santoir 1983: 80) considered as a sign of range degradation. Herders were equally hesitant to use the pastures, as the young shoots can be toxic (Thebaud: 28). At present *zornia* is cited unanimously by herders as one of the best types of forage for sheep. Another valued

leguminous plant that is particularly appetising for smallstock, which motivates herders to extensive nomadisation. FuutankoBe herders may travel several hundred kilometres south of their usual zone of interest to reach areas with large stands of *zornia*.

"I take my flock of sheep and goats to the Saluum every year in the dry season. My cattle herd stays with my brother back home in Ganina where the pastures for cattle is better. For the smallstock it is good to leave to get access to zornia and to browse the tree foliage. But it's important to be back for the rainy season. If not, your animals will not reproduce properly". (Transhumant herder from Ganina, April 1995).

Marketing strategies

Obviously the considerable increase in labour input in the new small- stock based herding systems is motivated not only by the higher reproduction rates of sheep amnd goats. It is also caused by the substantial rise in market value of notably sheep, which has been experienced during the last one or two decades[178]. According to calculations made by Tyc (1994:43) the financial productivity of sheep is estimated at around 5,000 CFA pr. animal pr. year as compared to 9,400 CFA pr. cattle and 2.500 CFA pr. goat[179]. However, due to the higher reproduction rate of sheep, a herder disposing of few heads of cattle but an important flock of sheep is better off than a herder with a majority of cattle (Thebaud, 1994:19). Other producers have confirmed this:

---

species is *Borreria radiata/Borreria stachydea*.

[178] In 1992 mean prices for adult males (The most expensive category) registered on Senegalese markets was 368 F CFA per live kg for bulls, while adult rams were sold at an average of 712 F CFA/live kg. Young females (cheapest categories) were sold for 322 F CFA/live kg (calves) and 570 F CFA (sheep) Source DIREL annual report 1992.

[179] These figures relate only to meat production. If milk production is added a calculation of financial productivity gives:
15.740 CFA for cattle (28 kg of meat at 335 CFA/kg and 53 kg of milk a 120 CFA /kg)
5.824 CFA for sheep (11,2 kg of meat at 520 CFA/kg and 4,4 kg milk a 120 CFA kg)
2.144 CFA for goats (6,4 kg of meat at 335 CFA/kg and 7,9 kg milk a 120 CFA/kg).
If calculated in terms of Tropical Livestock Unit (TLU) i.e. a ruminant of 250 kg, the financial productivity of 19.675 CFA for cattle, 60.495 for sheep and 38.650 CFA for goats (Tyc, 1994:43-44).

"One is better off with 10 cows and 100 smallstock than with a cattle herd of 50". (Herder from Mbiddi, 1989).
"With 100 head of smallstock you can have 30-40 lambs every year". (Wolof Peasant, Dodji Sept. 89.)

"If you sell two sheep you can buy one heifer, with three a cow" (Tessekre 1989).

In addition, small stock is easier to commercialise, especially at village level, and they are, in contrast to cattle, usually paid for in cash. Furthermore, the revenues from sale of one or two heads of small stock tend to fit better with the cash needs of the head of household, who is under considerable pressure from his family members if a large animal is sold and large quantities of unspent cash is available. As stated by one herder:

"The sheep is closer to the mouth. You can slaughter it if you have visitors and sell it if you have needs".

Finally, commercialisation of rams for religious feasts is a rapidly growing market. There were particularly favourable marketing conditions after the 1989 crisis in the relations with Mauritania, which led to important reductions in import from this important producer[180]. Prices of rams skyrocket on the eve of Tabaski and the prices of a big ram in the Tabaski season will easily reach three times that of an adult female.

Making a good "Operation Tabaski" may be extremely lucrative but is also a gamble. During 1990 and 1991, many herders were seriously trapped when rumours of prices up to 50,000 F CFA per ram where reported from Dakar. Around the boreholes, the air was thick with rumours of enormous profits made overnight. The case of one particularly rich and entrepreneurial herder who had been able to sell 4 million CFA worth of rams in order to buy a 4-wheel-drive truck for public transportation (taxi-brousse) particularly intrigued many herders. Many local producers therefore rushed to buy up large quantities of rams to supplement their own produce and to hire trucks to transport large flocks of rams to the capital. Here fodder had to be purchased just as the instalment and surveillance of the animals had to be paid for. Supply, however, quickly exceeded demand and many herders were forced, at considerable loss, to move their animals

---

[180] In 1988 the annual demand for rams at Tabaski was estimated to 320.000 heads. It is estimated that local production is sufficient to cover demands in Senegal.

back to the Ferlo again. In fact, 25% of the rams available on the market in 1991 were not sold[181]. Nonetheless, it seemed that pastoralists were increasingly learning how to carry out the operation[182] and many of those interviewed indicated the intention to group their rams in order to sell them at favourable prices on the eve of Tabaski.

This is another sign of pastoralists being extremely speculative in their herd management and marketing strategies. Rather than autarchic, herders must be characterised as fully market integrated and adapted to the new opportunities offered by the expanding market. This rapid switch from cattle to sheep-production conveys a quite different picture of the entrepreneurial and market-oriented herder than the one created by the cattle-complex narrative.

The new herding strategies and the orthodoxy of overgrazing

Inspired by the success of the FuutankoBe herders and the new and interesting market opportunities, the original inhabitants in the Linguère and Matam area are now beginning to copy the FuutankoBe herding strategy. As a result, the livestock population, the stock composition and the geographical distribution of the herd have been substantially modified during the last two decades.

The growing importance of sheep and goats in the southern part of the Ferlo has resulted in an increase of 162% in the smallstock population in the Département of Linguère from the pre-drought level in 1971 (286.000) to 1993 (751.200)[183]. Part of this boom may be attributed to a transfer of animals from the north to the southern fringe of the Ferlo. According to Santoir (1994:233), the density of smallstock in the south has increased five times between 1970 and 1990 (from a density pr. km^2 of 8 to

---

[181] See ISRA, 1992: Groupe de Travail sur l'autosuffisance en moutons de Tabaski au Sénégal, Mars 1992.

[182] At the end of my fieldwork in spring 1995 I witnessed how one (very well organised) family was able successfully to carry out the transfer and commercialisation of several hundred rams in Dakar during an interval of only two days before the Tabaski feast.

[183] Source: National Department for Livestock (Direction de l'Elevage, DIREL Dakar (unpublished). Unfortunately movements within the *Département* of Matam are difficult to measure, as the *Département* comprises both the area of departure and the area of reception.

a density/km² of 41 in 1990) This is in contrast to a far more moderate development in the North from 24.5 in 1970 to 34.4 in 1990.

The same tendency may be observed for cattle, although in a less spectacular manner. Here the increase is from 10 head of cattle/km² in 1970 to 12.4 heads of cattle/km² in 1988. In the North development has been directly negative, from 20.2 heads pr. km² to 12,7 in 1988.

As a result of this development, herd composition has altered significantly after the drought. According to Santoir (1994:234), cattle exceeded smallstock in numbers in the northern half of Senegal until 1968. In 1994, one finds 35 heads of cattle to 100 heads of smallstock in Senegal north of the Gambia[184]. Preference is given to sheep rather than goats, the relation between the two species being approximately 1 to 2.3 (Tyc, 1994:8).

According to mainstream range management orthodoxies such rapid increase in the number of grazing animals inevitably leads to overgrazing, range degradation and ultimately to desertification, not the least in an area, as the Ferlo (and further to the South, the Saluum), where rangelands have been severely diminished through the perpetual process of agricultural encroachment.

Contrary to these widely shared orthodoxies, the increased number of animals browsing on the range does not seem to limit the amount of pasture available. In fact, migrants and sedentary herders alike recognise the positive impact of migrant herds contributing not only to open up new lands for pasture but also to improve the quality of the range.

The logic of this statement is the following: In order to find pastures which have not been trampled, the egge-egge herders usually settle far away from other herders and in considerable distance from the borehole. Consequently, they often penetrate into areas formerly dominated by dense bush vegetation[185]. According to the herders, browsing sheep in such areas

---

[184] Measurements at local level confirm this tendency. In 1982 Sutter measures a ratio of 1 head of cattle to 1,1 head of small stock in Gueye Kadar in the eastern Ferlo. Recent figures from a census made in Bouteyni (Northwestern Ferlo) show a herd distribution significantly in favour of sheep with a cattle/smallstock ratio of 1 to 3,7 (i.e. 2,8 sheep and 0.9 goat) Thebaud 1994 p.16.) Data from the systematic reconnaissance flights of 1992 on the Linguere department display a ratio of 1 head of cattle to 2,8 small ruminants in 1992 (215.022 heads of cattle to 602.297 heads of smallstock (CSE 1992).

[185] The movements into dense bush areas are likely to have a negative impact on the

tends to clear the bush so that high quality pastures can come up with the next rains.

"The egge-egge who came in 1983/84 contributed to the formation of large stands of Zornia in the bush areas of Velingara. The areas where they settled in great numbers are where you now find zornia in large quantities. These species are highly appreciated by smallstock". (Agropastoralist, Velingara, Feb. 1993).

The results of a study carried out by Carl Bro Int. in Koungheul in 1988 point in the same direction. Here the most frequent answer given by the local (sedentary) population when asked to compare conditions of pasture before and after the drought was that pastures were much better now. The herders attributed this to the reduced number of trees leaving more space for pasture[186] (Carl Bro Inc., 1988:10.6).

Research during 9 years in the GTZ project of Widou Thiengoly in the northern Ferlo confirms these statements. Contrary to the expected impact, regeneration of pastures turned out to be lower in the fenced areas where grazing pressure was controlled and reduced than it was in the areas subject to "normal" grazing. In years of consecutive good rainfalls (such as 1988, 1989 and 1990) controlled low grazing proved directly harmful to pastures. The explanation seems to be the following: When the range is not grazed sufficiently, the grass left over from last year will bend when the rain starts. When such grass covers the ground, proper germination of graminaceous and leguminous species is hampered (Tluczykont, 1991:41). Quality and stability of pastures in the controlled and enclosed plots thus proved to diminish significantly during 3 successive years of good rainfalls. Some of the most drought resistant and nourishing graminaceous and leguminous plants tended to disappear to give way to other graminaceous species browsed only in the rainy season and with little or no nutritious value as fodder reserve for the dry season (for example *Schoenefeldia gracilis*). This was apparently an effect of hardening soils due to limited trampling[187].

---

habitat of wild animals. This problem is, however, not the scope of the present article.

[186] In the report, this answer was ascribed to a lack of consciousness of the scarce fodder resources.

[187] A reduction of the reserve of seeds from drought resistant species led to an almost total loss of primary production the first dry year after a cycle of years with good precipitation (e.g. 1990). It is not known how long the recolonisation of pioneer species takes. (S.

At present nothing seems to indicate that the increased number of animals grazing in the southern part of the Ferlo is leading to range deterioration. On the contrary, the new water transportation techniques enable herders to disperse their camps in the bush, spread their animals over a larger area and exploit formerly under-used pastures. Range deterioration is therefore likely to be insignificant in comparison with agro-pastoral and more sedentarised production systems where animals are concentrated around the village.

Competition for natural resources and conflicts over access

As mentioned the introduction of cart and inner tube has provided a substantial boost to the pastoral production systems of the Ferlo. Nonetheless, the increased mobility it engendered has also given rise to increased competition and conflicts over water and grazing resources, both in the area of "inception" and in the areas targeted during the transhumance trips in the area.

Many villages experience genuine invasions of foreign herders in the dry season. This is particularly the case of those located in the narrow tract of land through which all transhumants going to the Saluum[188] have to pass; between on the one side the Ferlo Boundou, where wells are too distant to one another to provide a transhumance route, and on the other side the fenced area of the huge state owned fattening ranch, the Ranch of Doli (see map 5).

Conflicts can be ascribed to differences in range management practices. As part of a risk management strategy farmers and agro-pastoralists in the Southern Ferlo have tended to put more emphasis on livestock during the last two decades. Consequently, the number of cattle found in the southern half of Senegal now exceeds that of the traditional cattle breeding areas in the north (Santoir, 1994:232)[189]. Where herders on

---

Miehe: Inventaire et suivi de la vegetation dans les parcelles pastorales a Widou Thiengoly 1988-90).

[188] The area described as the "Saluum" by the herders is the area from Velingara and Thiel to the Kaolack-Tambacounda road (Ribo, Payar, Loumbi, Koungheul and Tambacounda Nord).

[189] In general cattle densities per square kilometre in the dry season are highest in the most

transhumance from the North formerly represented an opportunity for the farmers to get their fields manured, most farmers now possess at least some animals themselves. As former ethnic specialisations disappear, reciprocal arrangements such as manure contracts lose importance and the general environment becomes more hostile to receiving transhumant herders. The following statements by herders in the area confirm these changes:

"Before, herders on transhumance were well received. You were even given part of the groundnut harvest if you would let the animals manure their fields" (FuutankoBe herder Fourdou, 1993).

"Transhumance is more difficult now. There is more jealousy and competition than in 83/84. At that time, people in the south were agriculturalists and hunters rather than herders. It's now, that they have started copying on the newcomers and have large herds of smallstock themselves, that the problems arise".(Transhumant herder from Mbiddi interviewed in Loumbi Aly Tedy, 1993).

The changing herd composition has further added to the problem as FuutankoBe herders today rarely accept leaving their animals on the fields to graze the stubble. Contrary to the past, when cattle dominated the transhumant herds, today's herds of predominantly smallstock need other types of fodder than what can be found on and in the direct vicinities of the fields. As the range of daily movements for smallstock is shorter than it is for cattle, the disadvantages are substantial of settling on fields located in proximity to the borehole. Herders are now more attracted to living in the bush rather than close to areas of agricultural production.

The FuutankoBe strategy of dispersing their camps in the bush impacts on the range management strategies employed by indigenous households. As mentioned above indigenous herds are usually grazing in a centrifugal motion from a fixed dry-season camp located close to the borehole (Sutter, 1987:197). As the dry season progresses, animals frequent still more distant pastures. With the installation of FuutankoBe camps in the

---

densely populated area, in central Senegal, the so-called Peanut Basin (departments of Diourbel, M'Backe, Mbour and Kaolack (respectively 27, 29, 30 and 26 head of cattle per square km.)). For smallstock the Peanut Basin also provided the highest densities in the dry season of 1989/90. The highest densities were found in Bambey Diourbel and M'Backe (respectively 34, 33 and 29 heads per square km.)(CSE doc. NT 91-02 1991). Sedentary farmers own a large part of these animals.

bush the animals of the autochtionous herders are likely to reach pastures already grazed and trampled by the FuutankoBe herds. The obvious result is that the FuutankoBe herds tend to be in much better shape than the "local" animals. To the more sedentarised indigenous populations the FuutankoBe micro-nomadisations is unfair competition. It has therefore contributed to hostility and jealousy towards the newcomers.

At some boreholes indigenous herders have tried to control access to pastures by forcing newcomers to install their dry season camps at the same distance from the deep well as their own camps and preferably on their fields in order to take advantage of the manure. But such settlements are incompatible with their herding strategies and FuutankoBe herders have generally refused, pleading the free use rights to the range affirmed in the 1964-law code.

Where well committees have managed to enforce this 'controlled settlement' it has in fact turned out to be a double-edged sword as it implies a considerable limitation of the radius of pastures grazed. Once the accessible radius of grazing is devoured, the FuutankoBe herders move on leaving the sedentarised population to cross vast areas denuded of herbaceous vegetation before reaching adequate pastures. In such cases, otherwise settled agro-pastoralists may be forced to get on the move once the fodder reserves in the area of residence are exhausted. Such forced migrations often involve considerable constraints as many agro-pastoralists do not dispose of sufficient manpower nor of the necessary equipment in terms of donkey carts and inner tubes. They also risk facing considerable losses in revenue, as they are unable to pursue their usual supplementary income generating activities.

As can be seen from the following quotation, disconcertion among the local population with regards to the possibilities of regulating access is great:

"It ought to be a task for the Rural Council to monitor the installation of foreign herders. It would be good to install them at the same level as the firstcomers instead of letting them settle scattered in the bush. This has been tried for instance in the village of MalemBa in the Saluum. However, even there it ended up being an expensive experience for the firstcomers. For once the pastures was devoured, the newcomers went elsewhere leaving the local animals in very poor conditions. The best solution would be to have more rains. But as it is, the best is maybe the way it works now, where newcomers settle where they want. In that way the most

densely populated areas are spared and they leave once the pastures are exterminated. (Agro-pastoralist, Velingara, Feb. 1993).

Such forced transhumances may also be prompted by the breakdown of the borehole motor pump. Due to the old age of the majority of the motor pumps, the constant pumping to supply sufficient water for the large number of animals results in overheating of the motor and to frequent breakdowns. In such situations all herders are forced to migrate to neighbouring pumps for shorter or longer periods. Such forced migration can be very strenuous especially for small herd owners, who may easily lose a large part of the lambs under such a trip[190].

The large number of foreign herders scattered over the bush also represents an inconvenience with regards to the supplementary activities of the sedentary population, such as the collection of gum arabic. This contributes to create a climate of distrust:

"Transhumants do not fit well with the collection of gum arabic. They will not refrain from settling in those areas where the gum producing acacias are located. This year I hardly harvested any gum. Production was generally low, but on top of that a large part was eaten by foreign goats on transhumance in the area, while the owners of the goats collected another part. Everybody knows that the transhumant herders sell gum, we just haven't caught anyone selling it, yet. They are in conspiracy with the gum traders." (Sedentary agro-pastoralist, Ranerou, January 1992).

Finally the population increase created by the influx of foreign herds inevitably contributes to inflate the number of cases of animals straying in the cultivated fields:

"When the egge-egge arrive during the cultivation season, there are many cases of field damages. Herders do not respect the cultivation zones, but it's also because people make their fields all over the pastures. There is no system of regulation and no text on the basis of which a regulation could be made. I think it would be a good idea if foreign herders could be chased away during the cultivation season. At that time neither watering nor pastures pose any problem. But it is not good to chase away

---

[190] As an example: one respondent claimed to have lost 20 lambs and kid during one month were he had to move to another well (Loumbi Sanrabe, May 1990). Other interviews revealed similar losses.

everyone. That would be to transgress the traditional solidarity among Fulani." (Agro-pastoralist, Thiargny, Febr. 1993).

The question of field damages is a very serious issue during the rainy season. In the areas of predominantly pastoral production, field damages are usually negotiated directly between the offender and the field owner. In many cases, especially if the plants were still small, the field owner is likely 'to forgive'. Otherwise compensation is paid based on an estimation of the value of the harvest lost. Only in those cases where the two parties are unable to reach a mutual understanding is it likely for the authorities, i.e. the village chief or ultimately the sous-prefet and the extension officers to become involved in the conflict settlement. Nonetheless, the problems increase the further one moves south and agriculture gains momentum.

There is no regulation of the location of transhumant camps. Everybody settles where he wants. Once the pastures are devoured, the herders are forced to buy animal fodder. Here 20% are Wolof cultivators. There are problems of animals destroying the fields, but at least the farmers get a compensation for what has been destroyed. The inconveniences related to the arrival of FuutankoBe herders are felt more by the [local] *Fulani population who gets no compensation for the increased competition on pastures. However, it's also the Fulani who have harvested the advantages of copying on the new system".* (President of the well committee, Ribo 1993).

Adaptation to new opportunities

"Certain local people make a profit on the transhumants. They serve as their hosts [diategui], they help them to water the animals and take care of part of their herds. Some people are favourable towards the newcomers, others are against. The shopkeepers are always in favour." (Veterinary assistant, Velingara, February 1993.)

As underscored in the two quotations above, the arrival of the egge-egge has not only brought conflict, but also new prosperity to at least some of the local inhabitants. First of all many agro-pastoralists involved in trading livestock or consumer goods have been able to extract considerable benefits from their enlarged clientele. Agro-pastoralists are able to barter their surplus grains with FuutankoBe herders for either milk or animals on favourable conditions. Finally, the arrival of large groups of rich transhumant herders provides a considerable boost to the weekly markets in the areas of reception.

The new herding strategies developed by the FuutankoBe herders have also given rise to innovations within the indigenous herding systems. The raising of smallstock is gaining momentum among the indigenous populations and more labour is invested in surveillance of the flocks. (As could be seen in table 3, 25% of indigenous herders now possess flocks of smallstock of more than 50 head while a large group possesses even more). In order to make better use of the available pastures many of these herders have also started to move their camps farther out in the bush in the dry season. Finally, the practice of micro-nomadisation during the dry season is being taken up, even by agro-pastoralists in the south.

"The habits of the local population have changed a lot since the people from the Fuuta arrived. Before, they had little livestock, maybe 2 cows and 2 sheep, which were not guarded. After they saw the well kept herds of the newcomers, they bought a cart and installed themselves in the bush. Some are even starting to move southwards during the dry season." (FuutankoBe herder, Fourdou, February 93).

The innovations brought about by the FuutankoBe herders in terms of increased productivity and easier access to otherwise unexploited pastures although improved conditions for water transport and mobility has brought about new opportunities as well as new constraints to the producers of the Ferlo region. The change of emphasis towards smallstock has turned out to be more difficult to combine with agricultural production than cattle raising. In April 1993, members of the well committee of Loumbi Aly Tedy explained:

"It is the smallstock that provokes problems. Before we had mainly cows and maybe 5 heads of smallstock besides. But since the droughts of 72/73 and 83/84 we started having both small and large stock. Now we are forced to do as the FuutankoBe. We are forced to live in the bush and to transport water. Now we have more beasts but they are not in good shape and give less milk. In general the sedentary Fulani have 5 times as many animals as before. Add to this the animals belonging to transhumants. No wonder the pump has difficulties".

Their colleagues from Ribo added:

"It is mainly the ways in which the herds are managed which has changed. Now people live out in the bush and have increased surveillance of the animals. It is difficult to combine this form of herding with manuring of fields. Animals get thin if they are attached when competition on pastures is high as now. It is no longer possible to convince migrating herders of making manuring contracts. They want to ensure the well-being of their animals."

The shift in herd composition and intensification of herding practices pose a number of problems for agro-pastoral producers. Previously, animals were herded during the rainy season, or were kept together in a village herd which was moved to another area to avoid trespassing into the fields. Now the individual agro-pastoralist has too many animals to leave supervision of the flock to a village herder. Instead he is forced to find labour for this task within his own household. As was in the case of the agro-pastoral systems in the *waalo*, this may create bottlenecks in peak productive periods. Instead of creating closer linkages between the agricultural and pastoral activities by increasing yields through manuring and fattening of animals on farm by-products, some households appear to be 'delinking' these activities. Animals are fed almost entirely on fodder from the bush and are kept at considerable distances from the fields. Hence, it is the opposite process of the much-praised intensification through 'on-farm' livestock-crop integration which is at stake. It should however be kept in mind that use of manure has never been very developed in these areas, where population densities are low and land still readily available. In many cases manuring has mainly been applied to the fields of the village chief.

The different distribution of workloads between the sexes among southern Fulani clans also complicates adaptation to the new system. Among the nomadic clans from the north such as the FuutankoBe, fetching of water and building of new huts (a considerable task during longer transhumance journeys) is the task of women. Among the southern clans more devoted to agro-pastoral activities, these tasks, which increase considerably in the new herding system, are supposed to be carried out by men. Such a re-organisation of the labour division between sexes, may not necessarily be an advantage to the women.

"It's only the last 3 years that the local HaaboBe herders have started nomadising to get closer to the pastures. But it's very hard. Among us, the HaaboBe, all work related to the herd is the men's' job, fetching

water, milking, and even making huts. With the FuutankoBe much of this is the task of the women. With the new system, even our women will have to change". (HaaboBe agro-pastoralist, Loumbi Aly Thedy, Senegal Oriental. Feb. 1993.

The drought as a watershed effect

The profound changes which post-drought migration had on the production systems in the area of reception justifies treating this period as a watershed event. Through the movement southward and the transformation of their herding systems, the 'drought victims' managed to improve their livelihood significantly and to limit their vulnerability against future calamities.

The arrival of the large number of drought refugees from the Fuuta area profoundly altered the social relations in the area of reception. The newcomers quickly installed themselves as an economically more consolidated group than the firstcomers. They managed to take advantage of the new opportunities offered by the drought, as expressed in the citation of Yerim Sow: "the drought enabled herders to get acquainted to new pastures". By means of technological innovation, the herders who were evicted from the Senegal River Valley by the effects of drought and proliferation of irrigated agriculture, proved not to be passive 'victims' of the drought but rather active agents engaged in examining and taking advantage of the new possibilities offered.

Although conflictive in many ways, the reception of a large group of foreign herders also proved to be advantageous to the local population, who were able to copy on the improved herding systems put into effect by the newcomers. So, to return to the views of Solway, there can be no doubt that changes in practices and in meanings have arrived to a point where it is unlikely that a return to a situation 'before drought' is on the agenda for any of the two parties.

Characterising the post-drought situation in Senegal as a watershed event does not imply any inclination towards interpreting the changes in terms of an epochal change. Rather than establishing the drought as a sort of fictive reference-point, which relates traditional and harmonious pre-drought societies with current post-drought turmoil, the notion of watershed event implies the recognition of a turbulent past. As could be seen in the brief historical introduction of the Ferlo, also the past is characterised by many turbulent events, such as the introduction of boreholes or agricultural encroachment. All of these have contributed to alter the production systems and the prevailing social relations. Similarly, the shifting climatic conditions (in terms of increasing or decreasing aridity) have been followed by adjustments or modifications of the production patterns.

But as shown above, development in the region has often taken courses that where different from what was anticipated. The expansion of groundnut production did not entirely squeeze out the herders from the southern Ferlo. For some it even provided an opening towards new production opportunities. The herders did not become entirely sedentarised once the boreholes enabled them to stay year round in their wet season camps. As was the case with the boreholes, originally devised as 'cafeteria stands' along the cattle marketing routes, or the industrial fodder packages geared towards fattening selected animals, herders have been swift to adopt these innovations as part of a general risk-reducing strategy. Nonetheless, this adoption has not taken place uncritically as herders have been quick to 'unwrap' the technology or opportunities provided to select those parts of the 'package' which fitted into their general aims of enhancing the productivity of their herds. This process of unwrapping could also be observed in the recycling of tubes and tarpaulin cloths.

By the same token, producers have proved to be able to adapt quickly both to shifting ecological regimes and to the changing demands of the market. This flexibility and adaptation of course strongly repudiates any reference to pastoral production systems as being timeless, conservative and autarchic, as conveyed in the narrative of the cattle complex.

The way in which the herders have adapted their herd management system to the changing ecological conditions also gives a somewhat more dynamic picture of the relation between the herder and his environment than the image of pastoralists as holders of the one and only form of resource exploitation in balance with the 'harsh and fragile' ecological environment of semi-arid lands, as presented by many 'environmentalists'. Rather than deducting the systems of production from the nature of the environment, it seems more fruitful to look at the many different kinds of adaptation, which are put into work by the resource users. For as stated in the introduction, many interdependent influences determine the particular outcome of a process of adaptation. It is therefore necessary to stress multi-causality and the interaction of many different factors in order to understand the processes generating human action.

As emphasised by the 'new ecology' and chaos theories, non-equilibrium systems are profoundly affected by changes external to them (such as drought) and continually controlled by the unexpected. Therefore constancy of behaviour becomes less important than the persistence of relationships. Instead of focusing on drought as a rupture of old practices it becomes important to look at the ability of the system to adapt. And as could be seen above, the potential for resilience and adaptation of both ecosystems and production systems in the Sale have shown to be significant, making any reference to the fragility of the eco-system utterly misleading.

The success story of the FuutankoBe herders was largely unpredictable. An analysis of the process through a crisis scenario in which ends are given beforehand therefore makes little sense. As has been shown above, the situation of pastoralism in Northern Senegal cannot be analysed only as a function of the perpetual encroachment of the area through agricultural expansion. Due to technological innovations, mainly in terms of improved water transportation, more animals are now able to survive on a smaller area. In most years, they even become fat enough to ensure high reproduction rates. Although important pastoral key resources were lost as irrigation expanded in the *waalo*, herders have shown a remarkable ability to adapt to the new conditions. The pastoral area has so to say been 'enlarged from within' as new production opportunities have been seized by a large number of herders. Greater mobility as well as increased use of industrial fodder, mineral supplements and veterinary medicine have provided at least partial compensation for the resources lost and have rendered herders less vulnerable to future droughts. As a result, the large majority of FuutankoBe herders indicate that they have become richer than they were before the drought forced them to migrate southward, a trend which is also admitted by a number of sedentarised herders. In contrast to the development in a number of other Sahelian countries, herd ownership has not been transferred to absentee herd owners but has been kept in the hands of highly skilled and specialised producers with in-depth knowledge of their environment.

The arrival of a substantial number of transhumant herders as well as the generally increased mobility present a number of disadvantages for the more sedentarised segment of the Fulani society. But it has also created new opportunities, which have been apprehended by the most dynamic layers of sedentary farmer communities. While it remains important to document the increased pressure on resources due to loss of rangelands to mainly agricultural production, it is equally important not to underestimate the ability of pastoral societies to adapt through technological innovations. As stated by Leo Strooschnijder:

"The production level that can be reached and the number of people that can be fed without destroying the natural resource base is everywhere more a function of production technology than of the renewable resources."(Strooschnijder, 1994:6.)

In view of the important changes taking place in post drought pastoral society it appears useless to continue discussions on basis of a scenario according to which pastoral societies are growing increasingly vulnerable to drought (ref. Moorehead, 1991; Lane, 1994; Thebaud, 1993 and others). This is not to underestimate the less favourable effects of the present development: for instance the exfoliation of those segments of pastoral society which have been unable to accumulate sufficient livestock to participate successfully in the increased competition, or the difficulties experienced by producers more oriented towards agricultural production, or the loss of habitat for wild mammals and birds when bush steppe is transformed into pastures, etc. It is, however, important to recognise the basically healthy state of the pastoral production system and herdsmen's capacity to renew and adapt, even without outside interference. If this is omitted, blind spots affect our analyses.

In view of this, the increasing number of conflicts related to resource management should be treated as problems inherent in a highly competitive system where "modus vivendi is guided not only by mutual interest but by the balance of forces" (Khazanov, 1983:35). In these highly individualistic societies, the 'symbiotic' and 'reciprocal' relations between herder and farmer communities as well as the mutual solidarity between herders often turns out to be a simple correlation of forces whereby the stronger is guided exclusively by their own interests and needs without any considerations of the weaker. This is to some extent what is happening with the well committees where individual economic interests rather than collective ecological concerns determine the present policy. This issue will be treated in the following chapter.

5. STRATEGIES AND MANOEUVRES TO GAIN ACCESS TO AND CONTROL OVER RESSOURCES

The findings of the previous chapters clearly showed that the actual state of pastoralism in Northern Senegal is not usefully addressed in terms of a crisis scenario. Obviously, the influx of a large contingent of mobile and very specialized herders has not been taking place without conflicts, as will be shown below. This does not, however, alter the fact that in the case of Senegal, drought acting as a catalyst for technological innovation has provided for a substantial boost to the pastoral production of the Ferlo. The increased competition for resources provoked by the growth in animal and human population was to a wide extent compensated for by the new and highly mobile herd management strategies, which allowed for rising prosperity and improved risk and resource management not only among the migrating herders but also among the original agro-pastoral population. But by giving rise to a new class of very rich pastoralists of which the majority is to be found among the FuutankoBe population, the technological innovation also contributed to alter the existing social relations.

The adaptation of the new pastoral production system also brought about new exigencies in terms of realignment of political authority and of rights and control over resources. This will be the theme for the present chapter. Although successful individual economic performance may be a great help, it is seldom enough to secure access to resources. Herders also need to improve the level of control over resources in the long term. This depends on investments in social relations understood as the ability of the individual to gain influence over decisions regarding resource allocation and resource distribution. Opportunities for such political and social adjustment have to a wide extent been provided by less spectacular events in the aftermaths of the drought, such as for example the more localized drought of 1991-93.

As will be illustrated below, an immediate effect of this process of adjustment has been that conflicts between first-comers and newcomers have intensified in recent years. Since the beginning of the 1990's, it appears that the normative codes of Fulani solidarity, according to which water and pastures are open to anyone and denial of access is considered shameful, have come under particular hard pressure. On the other hand 'foreign' herders are increasingly trying to convert their newly acquired wealth into social capital in order to increase their political influence and the control exercised over the productive resources. Only a few of these struggles of political alignment erupt into open fights. Many of them tend to pass unnoticed as few of them involve the participation of local representatives of the state apparatus. Instead they are fought as struggles over meanings attributed to key statuses, principles, codes and customs, as part of a social and political manoeuvring. Such social manoeuvring is, however, often hampered by local conceptions of rights and obligations as denial of for example access to well or pastures may require rationalizations that are not shared by the population as a whole. In such situations, events such as droughts may, as will be shown below, act as pretexts for transgressing or altering previous codes of social behaviour.

In order to introduce the reader to the ways in which the process of political realignment is taking place, the chapter starts by narrating the case story of the well-committee of Naoré. This conflict is in many ways typical for the manner in which struggles over access and control over political and productive resources are taking place. It gives a good picture of the ways in which political alliances are generated across and between the different categories of users just as it illustrates how the locus of political conflict has shifted since the arrival of the 'foreign' herders. The Naoré case is in no way unique. Rather it is similar to many other conflicts or events encountered during my fieldwork. Nonetheless, it has 'unfolded' itself more thoroughly than the other cases. So in order to avoid too much confusion, this case is chosen as the prime reference in the analysis, making reference to other similar cases primarily when specific events or detail need to be highlighted.

As shown above, it is standard within the Common Property school of thought to attribute local communities the ability to generate institutional arrangements that ensure sustainable and optimal resource use. This stems from a vision of the communities as sites of consensus and sustainability. Where local resource management arrangements are less successful, this is often attributed to the obtrusive effects of state interventions, which are liable to undermine the authority of otherwise well-functioning traditional resource management institutions. Departing from the case of Naoré, the validity of this conviction is examined in order to understand the 'institutional climate' into which the migrant herders were to be inserted. First of all, the institutional framework governing the crucial resources in pastoral societies i.e. water and land will be discussed, as will the social affiliations affecting land use and control. Secondly, the extent of state powers in the Ferlo will be addressed.

After this excursion, the discussion on the political and institutional repercussions of post-drought migration will be resumed. With emphasis on the rising level of conflict observed during the third wave of migration, the dry years of 1991 to 1993, the tactics of the first-comer population vis-à-vis the migrants will be discussed, as will the reactions of the newcomers. On basis of these discussions the nature of the process of political realignment will be analysed.

An example from real life: The borehole of Naoré

During the dry seasons of 1994 the borehole of Naoré, located in the *arrondissement* of Ogo in the Matam *département* was the scene of fierce hostilities between rival groups of herders. At the height of tensions young Fulani could be seen patrolling around the borehole with drawn machetes. At several occasions the police forces from Matam were called out in order to avoid bloodshed.

The conflict arose when members of the local community sent a letter to the *sous-préfet* of Ogo to protest over the seizure of the local well-committee by herders who were foreigners to the zone. This seizure had happened in conspiracy with the President of the well-committee who during his ten years in office had held no general assembly or election to the board of the well-committee. In the course of the years, members of the original board who had withdrawn or died had simply been replaced by the president by members of his own choice. The result was, according to the critics, an over-representation of FuutankoBe herders and of Mauritanian refugees.

According to the legal framework relating to the local management of wells, the mandate of the well committee is only for 2 years after which new elections should be held. In consequence of the protest from the population, the *sous-préfet* therefore felt obliged to dissolve the old committee and appoint a new one. This was carried out at a meeting in February 1994, with the presence of 5 village chiefs (including the old president of the well-committee in his function of chef de village of Naoré central), a representative of the FuutankoBe population and a representative of the refugee population. According to the official record (*proces verbal*) the aim of the meeting was: to settle the "legitimate claims of the Senegalese users to hold leadership of the deep-well" together with the equally "legitimate claims of the transhumant and the refugee user group to participate in concordance with their share of the watering taxes"[191].

In the meeting, the *sous-préfet* took the opportunity to lament, that elections had not been held to the board of committee for 10 years and that "posts were now held by individuals with no relation to the former elected board i.e. refugee and transhumant herders". He also regretted the effects of the internal fighting between the local factions of the ruling party, PS (*Partie Socialiste*). Finally he complained of the fact that no proper accounts existed for the spendings and earnings of the well-committee and that only one tax-collector, the representative of the 'refugee' population, kept any sort of account of the watering fees collected.

Seeking a compromise, the *sous-préfet* appointed a new board whose members represented a broad mixture of the two opposing local political tendencies and of the 'settled' and 'transhumant' population: The leader of the protesters was appointed president while the son of the former president was designated as his deputy. The post of treasurer was given to a sedentary while a refugee was appointed vice-treasurer. Finally, tax-collectors were chosen in such a way as to ensure full representation of all ethnic groups and sub-groups of the area[192].

It is of interest to the case to mention that the leader of the protesters was also the local representative of tendency B of the ruling Socialist Party, while the old president represented tendency A[193] of the same party. Noteworthy is also that Naoré is one of the boreholes in the Ferlo around which the largest contingent of drought refugees from the Senegal River Valley have settled in the aftermaths of the drought. These have been joined by a large number of very rich herders originating from Mauritania who have arrived either in connection with the droughts or in relation to the Senegal-Mauritanian conflict of 1989. According to population survey carried out in 1994, the population of 'newcomers'

---

[191] As the share of the FuutankoBe herders officially was estimated to 80% of the total revenues these two claims were not easily harmonised.

[192] Wolof, Black Maures (Haratins), UrurBe, FafaBe, FerlankoBe, DiawBe etc.

[193] The system of political tendencies is described by Schmitz (1993) as a binary system, referring to the opposition between the leading faction (A) and it's inevitable opponent, tendency B. This characteristic feature of Senegalese politics will be treated more thoroughly below.

amounts to around 70% of those households using the well on a regular basis.

So when the *sous-préfet* selected the official village chiefs as representatives of the population, he actually favoured only a small faction of the actual users of the deep-well, whereas the majority of the users, including the ones providing the heaviest financial contributions, were represented by only 2 persons who, even more importantly, were grouped under the categories of "strangers" or "newcomers" and not as part of the regular user group.

The solution proposed by the *sous-préfet* was therefore perceived by the FuutankoBe as a way of excluding them, the interest of the sedentary population in controlling the well-committee being the large sums of money collected every month[194].

Far from the peaceful solution anticipated by the *sous-préfet*, the result of this meeting was a total uproar among the 'foreign' population and the mobilization of all available resources. First of all a parallel committee was established (identical with the old one). As all large taxpayers withheld their watering taxes from the official committee and instead contributed to the parallel committee, the official committee soon went broke unable as they were to deliver the services expected. Provision of water was therefore soon taken over by the rich parallel committee, leaving the new committee with no real functions. It was in the course of this operation, where the borehole was being 'protected' by youngsters armed with machetes, that the police of Matam were forced to intervene.

Secondly, a letter of protest, signed by 95 users of the well, was sent to the sous-préfect of Ogo. The protest was threefold,
a). a protest against the under-representation of the majority of the population who financed the bulk of the running costs of the well,
b). an accusation of embezzlement by the new well-committee, and
c). a protest over the measures taken by the new well-committee to raise the watering fees. Such measures taken by a minority board, it was stressed, would not be tolerated by the majority population.

---

[194] Estimated by the FuutankoBe to be around 265.000 CFA of which the sedentary herders contribute only 15.000 CFA Francs

To give further weight to the claims, important funds were raised among FuutankoBe herders, not only from Naoré but also from the neighbouring villages. This was used to finance the equipment and dispatch of delegations who could visit various influential persons on the Senegalese political scene in Dakar as for example the leading *marabouts* (saints) of the Muslim Tijanya brotherhood.

The effectiveness of these measures could soon be observed. Shortly after the dissolution of the old well-committee, a letter from the Minister of Waterworks referring to the case of Naoré appeared on the desk of the Governor of Matam. The letter stated that a majority of the population of Naoré considered the newly elected committee as illegitimate, as not all members of the user group had been present at the founding meeting and the non-sedentarised population were excluded from the election of a new board reason for which the Minister pressed for a solution to be found as quickly as possible.

Evidently, this letter was the result of contacts taken by the FuutankoBe herders, to *marabouts* from the influential Tall family to whom most of the herders from the Fuuta claim spiritual allegiance and to the influential director of the Dakar cattle market. Through these channels contacts were established to Djibo Ka, at that time Minister of Interior and a Fulani from the region. He in turn had contacted the Minister for Waterworks.

The Governor, kicking the hot potato further down in the system, ordered the Prefect of Matam to solve the problem, a task he assigned back to the *sous-préfect* of Ogo, i.e. to the same person who had originally been compelled to intervene in the conflict.

A meeting was held with the participation of the *sous-préfect* of Ogo, the UNHCR representative, the commander of the police forces of Matam, the departmental chiefs of Waterworks and of the Livestock services, the local veterinary assistants, the President of the rural council and the village chiefs. At this occasion the FuutankoBe herders complained that the "genuine" herders were not represented in the new board. They were not, they declared "ready to hand over their money to people just waiting for an opportunity to embezzle it".

In spite of the massive representation of the Senegalese administrative system, the meeting was, characterized by its lack of clear decisions. The only decision taken was a de facto approval of the dissolution of the *sous-préfect*'s new committee. A suggestion to form a provisional committee consisting of representatives of extension services was never carried out, neither were the proposed new elections to the board. The immediate effect of the meeting was therefore primarily that status quo was restored.

But despite of its apparent inertia, the incident is significant on a number of levels:

First of all, it illustrates how the influx of herders from the Fuuta region has altered the social relations between newcomers and sedentary herd-owners. Obviously, the growing amount of animals and the herd management strategies carried out by the newcomers represent a number of obstacles to the local and more sedentarised Fulani agro-pastoralists. But the Naoré case shows that it is less questions of access to the grazing resources, than efforts to gain control over key institutions such as the well-committee and, not the least, the financial resources it accumulates, that are at the heart of struggles.

Secondly, the case serves to illustrate some of the problems related to the handing over of responsibilities over the deep-wells from the state to the local communities, which took place in 1984. Contrary to the assumptions of the Common Property view, the transfer of responsibility of this vital function has resulted in poor management, frequent breakdown of the pumps and generalized misappropriation of collected funds[195]. Popular participation based on equitable representation, is not a sticking feature at any of the boreholes visited[196].

The current situation is the result of an ambiguous, fragmentary and contradictory legal framework which together with a limited (or hardly existing) control on the part of the state agencies, more or less invites to

---

[195] According to a rough estimation made in 1989 (Juul et al) taxes should largely suffice to pay for the running costs of the borehole if fees were collected for all animals using the watering facilities. Explanation for the constant deficit characterizing the vast majority of boreholes, must be found in the (clientelistic) exemption of a large part of the herd from taxing, and in misappropriation of collected funds. This results in serious obstacles for the individual herder in terms of frequent stand-stills of the pump as no funds are available to purchase diesel oil.

[196] The democratic elements of the clientelistic and patrimonial structures characterizing most management institutions will be discussed further on.

mismanagement and embezzlement. To this adds that the well-committees serve several functions at a time. They are not, as perceived by the NRM framework, institutions concerned exclusively with the management of boreholes and pumps. Rather than single-purpose institutions, these institutions play an important role in the political and social life of the village as control over watering facilities in these dry areas has turned out to be the most important means to control access to the grazing lands. With this in mind it is no wonder that the well committees are turning into prime arenas for local political struggles.

Thirdly, the Naoré case exposes part of the vast potential of resources and strategies that newcomers and locals respectively are able to mobilize in order to control access to water and grazing lands. For in spite of the ostensible remoteness of Naoré, herders are both well-informed and have strong networks that enables them quickly to get access to the central political stage of Dakar and, no less important, to get their message through.

In this context it is interesting to note, how the sedentarised herders have shown themselves adept in taking on the mode of discourse of the administration. In their appeal to the local administration of the Matam department they advocated for the legitimacy of their claims through a discourse of decentralization, stressing the distinction between the settled population[197] and 'the foreigners'. From their side, the FuutankoBe herders, of whom a large part have been present in the area for almost 20 years stressed their rights as the "genuine" herders and as (the largest) taxpayers - a tactic which made the *sous-préfect* conceive of their protestations as an attempt to install "*la loi du plus fort*" i.e. to turn the principle of one man one vote into representation according to ownership in animals[198]. Moreover, the 'newcomers' relate to the parallel discourse of the free grazing rights granted to any Senegalese according to the Rural Code *(La Loi sur le Domaine National)*. It is this justification, together with the mobilization of influential patrons, which has enabled the 'foreigners' to mobilize the support of the Minister of Interior, against the immediate interests of his own kin.

---

[197] This is justified by the *sous-préfect* because the first-comer population (presumably) have been paying for the borehole for more than 30 years.

[198] The *sous-préfet* is apparently unaware that the 'foreign' population comprise approximately 70 % of the regular users of the borehole.

Fourth, it illuminates the ways in which conflicts tend to become politicised as local strives to gain control over resources are mixed with struggles for larger political goals. This could be seen by grapples between the competing factions of the ruling party (the struggle of tendency A vs. tendency B[199]). This perspective might add another dimension to the understanding of Djibo Ka's surprising intervention. For maybe it was not only the rights of the FuutankoBe herders that was at stake, but also the maintenance of political support from the leader of Tendency A in Naoré, the president of the outgoing well-committee[200].

The partial non-application of the legal framework and the ambiguous role of the state furthermore illustrate how decisions taken at the decentralized level at any time may be overruled by decisions taken further up in the system. This ambiguity is further elucidated by the absence of clear decision-making and the relatively peaceful return to status quo. This issue will be discussed in further detail below.

Finally the event serves to show how access in spite of state ownership to both water resources and grazing remains subject to political manoeuvring. The case clearly illuminates how part of the struggles over access and control are fought as struggles over meanings attributed to crucial terms such as the definitions of "strangers" and "locals".

The issues presented above all represent crucial aspects in tenure disputes in agro-pastoral Senegal. The following section will therefore elaborate more on a number of these questions.

---

[199] Although much has been written on factionalism as a dominant feature of Senegalese politics, little has been written about the competition between political tendencies at the local level (exceptions are Blundo, 1995b; Jacob and Blundo, 1997; Schmitz, 1993 and Cruise O'Brien, 1975). My impression is that the labels A and B refer only to their status as respectively majority or minority faction. Hence tendency A in various localities may be mutually opposed. It is, however, important to note that each faction have representatives at all levels of the party hierarchy, making it very difficult to separate local politics from politics at the central level. (Schmitz, 1988:600). Nonetheless, given the fluidity of factional affiliation within PS, adherence to one tendency or the other does not provide a clear (or static) affiliation at the central level (See also Cruise O'Brien, 1975:174-177).

[200] Unfortunately this obvious connection did not occur to me during fieldwork, reason for which I did have not the opportunity to check these relationships with local connoisseurs of PS party politics.

Fluidity, flexibility, ambiguity and negotiability:
Aspects of property relations to grazing land in the Ferlo

Common Property theorists such as Ostrom and Bromley argue that "problems in rural managerial capacities stem from unclear institutional arrangements and from the absence of an authority system to give meanings to such rights" (Bromley and Cernea 1989:55) According to them, problems arise from free and unregulated access resulting from the perpetual undermining of local systems of authority and regulation by obtrusive state policies. Efforts to improve local management systems should therefore be directed at establishing more firm property rights to the group, including the rights to exclude others from use and decision making (ibid.: 15).

This diagnosis indisputably fits many of the problems revealed by the Naoré case, at least at a first sight. Obviously the local population struggles with the absence of clear rules and are constrained by the limited means they dispose of to regulate access to the well and the adjacent pastures. The question is however whether improved management may be reduced to a question of reviving traditional management institutions. Will increasing the authority and means to sanction local rights of exclusivity as proposed by the Common Property framework alone do the job? For how extensive were in fact capacities of the 'traditional' institutions involved in managing local natural resources in the Ferlo? To what extent is it possible to distinguish a clear user group and discern a distinct resource territory to defend against the intruding "foreigners"? And can struggles over access to resources in the Ferlo be reduced to a question of improving the legal framework and establishing a firm set of rules?

As mentioned above, traditional institutions or customary rights are seldom as unchanged or original as they appear. Rather redefinition of custom and invention of tradition are part of the local power struggles and are as such crucial aspects in the transformation of social and cultural systems. As could be seen in the Naoré case, redefinition of customs has been one of the means used by the local, mainly Ferlanke, population to legitimise exclusion of the FuutankoBe population from the well committee. By suggesting a strong dichotomy between 'locals' and 'strangers' the FerlankoBe population has managed to establish a 'discourse' linking up to a central assumption in the discussion of local-level resource management: that resource degradation originates in the dissolution of customary common property arrangements whose very purpose was to give rise to resource use patterns that were sustainable (Bromley and Cernea 1989).

Rather than establishing the basis for understanding ongoing struggles concerning access to and control over local resources, it seems that the focus on state intervention as the prime agent for the undermining local authority structures further contributes to the creation of 'blind spots' with regards to the intricate power struggles at play at the local level. The next section examines number of the myths relating to 'traditional' resource management in the Ferlo region. These are: a) The myth of the strong customary tenure arrangements. b) The myth of the distinct user community. c) The myth of the stable resource environment and d) The myth of the obtrusive state.

Customary regulation of access to pastures

In conformity with mainstream views on environmental degradation, range degradation in the Ferlo is often attributed to the absence of rights of exclusivity. This, it is held, hampers any attempt by local management institutions to control the access of free riders and hinders motivation to limit the number of animals grazing on the range.

As elsewhere, projects and official development policies in Senegal often take their point of departure in the narratives of the Tragedy of the Commons and the Cattle Complex blaming destruction on the contradictions between individual interest and social obligation and the irrationality of the traditional extensive herding systems[201]. In contrast to this, a number of scholars and projects have argued for the existence of customary rules and traditional authority structures in charge of regulating access to the water and grazing resources of the Ferlo region. But in the attempt to confirm herders as rational and conscious managers of their territory another narrative is created that contributes to oversee the subtleties in local decision making and to exaggerate the extent/reach of existing regulations.

---

[201] See for example the documents of "Projet d'Appui a l'Elevage" (PAPEL) Algor Thiam (1995) and SODESP (1995). Also Grenier 1960:38-40 decribes what he calls 'la boomanie des peuls', the desire to have a large personal herd, which inclines the herders to live separated from one another and incessantly to be on the move according to the seasons. Grenier underscores that this is a passion with no religious attributes:"The cow is regarded as a member of the family. The herder makes use of his livestock, he does not exploit it", as he put's it. In his work from 1987, however, Grenier states that the new lifestyles of the boreholes imply that herders are commercialising a larger part of their herd than before.

With regards to the rights over lands, it is difficult to trace any customary regulation of access to the grazing lands in the Ferlo. A majority of those professing the existence of strong resource regulating institutions draw heavily on the work of Barral from 1982[202]. In this study Barral shows how use of the pastoral space in the Ferlo was regulated through respect of the *hurum* (from arab *haram*: interdiction). This interdiction was divided between *hurum ngesse*, "interdictions of the fields", which prohibited animals to graze in the vicinities of the fields during the cultivation season and *hurum durungol*, "interdiction of the pastures", alluding to the spatial entity grazed by the individual herd within which other herders should avoid camping.

Barral stresses, that rather than a customary pastoral code, the system of *hurum ngesse* was a regulation to defend the cultivated fields while *hurum durungol* was a way of maintaining herd segregation. Nonetheless, the notion of *hurum durungol* has been used as an indication of the existence of territorial units over which the encampment exercised control. Such bounded territorial units, it is argued, have tended to be dissolved with the emergence of the boreholes and replaced by the prevailing situation of *de facto* open access. For being state owned, these boreholes conferred free and unlimited access to anyone, thereby undermining traditional means to limit the number of users to the adjacent pastures[203].

Little evidence seems to support this construction of a regularized past governed by rigid customary restrictions to pastures. Although the empirical sources to the pre-borehole tenure systems are quite limited, they do not (to my knowledge) make reference to direct rights of exclusivity on specific parts of the range. The existence of clear territorial rights is indeed questionable. For even if the different sub-clans (as shown in the maps over transhumance movements made by Bonnet Dupeyron in 1951 (see map 6) tended to direct their transhumance routes to roughly the same areas every year, settlement of camps was more a function of opportunistic calculations over water and pasture availability than regular movements to a fixed and bounded territory.

---

[202] See Touré et al., 1986:17-19 and Touré 1990:4, Diawara, 1984:72 and Malick Faye in UNSO/UNDP 1993:17 and Richter, 1991.

[203] For examples elsewhere in the Sahel see notably Thebaud, 1988:68 (Niger), and Benoit, 1984 (Burkina Faso).

This non-existence of rights over pastures among the Fulani of the Ferlo was confirmed unambiguously both in the survey carried out by Grenier in 1957 and in my own interviews from the period between 1988 and 1995. According to Grenier, pastures are the property of everyone (Grenier 1957 from Pouillon 1990:190[204]). In my own interviews, surprisingly few herders recollected to have ever heard of the notions of *hurum*. In contrast, the freedom to settle wherever one chooses turned out to be a prominent feature in herders own self-knowledge (as could be read out of the stories of Yerim and Bathil).

With regards to the present state of tenure rights, interviews carried out between 1988 and 1995 wholly confirmed the lack of property rights at present and the rights of any herder to camp and exploit pastures where and whenever he wants without asking anyone for permission to settle (see the story of Yerim Sow). This is also what can be read out of the many unsuccessful attempts to regulate the distance of transhumant settlements vis-à-vis the borehole, discussed briefly in chapter 4.

This moderation of the presumed importance of regulation generally confers with the views of for example Jeremy Swift (1988) or Lawry (1990) who underline that in areas where resource availability is characterized by spatial heterogeneity and temporal variability, independent and opportunistic decision making appears to be the most efficient response to a heterogeneous environment. Such resource management systems are more likely to be characterized by flexible arrangements, which allow transhumant herders to gain access to the crucial resources, water and pastures, over a vast area.

Regulation of access to pastures through the control over water?

But if pastures were unregulated, then what about access to water? As water primarily is a means to get access to the prosperities made up by the pastures, it has been common to regard water sources such as wells as the key customary resource management institutions of the clans (see Thébaud, 1988:51). Many scholars have therefore blamed the drilling

---

[204] See also Grenier, 1960:57. Unfortunately I have not been able to get hold of the 1957 document by Grenier. In the later works of Grenier (1960 and 1987), the statements regarding free and open acces are not so clearly expressed.

of state owned boreholes, where access was open to anyone, for undermining hitherto well-functioning resource management institutions, bounded as they were in the ability to restrict the number of users of private wells.

As in the case of the pastures it turns out to be difficult to trace any customary regulation of access to water in the case of the Ferlo. Nothing seems to indicate that either the natural ponds or the shallow wells dug into the dry riverbed of the Ferlo Valley were subject to restrictions of access before the boreholes were drilled. In fact, both Islamic law (Bonte, 1993:58) and Fulani concepts of proper 'conduite' repudiate private appropriation of water sources, even in those cases where they are dug by an individual or a group.

Hence, when the colonial administration in the late 1950's started setting up a network of publicly owned deep-wells throughout the Ferlo, they did not break up any primordial customary organization. Quite on the contrary, it was the boreholes and the new opportunities that they created, in terms of year-round settlement, which started off new, but initially rather vague, claims of territorial ownership to the areas around the well. Such tendencies of tribal appropriation were observed as early as 1956 by the French anthropologist Marguerite Dupire[205]. According to her, a certain 'nationalism' was developing around the wells as rivalling sub-clans would request to have their own deep-well because: *"the government has given a well to the UrurBe, but they have done nothing for [us] the BarkanaBe"* (Dupire, 1957:23).

At present all water resources officially belong to the state and are considered an integral part of the public domain. According to the Water Code[206] "such resources are a collective asset and their use on the national territory is subject to prior authorization and supervision". In fact, user permits are issued by the Minister of Water Resources and Land Reclamation *(Ministre de l'Hydraulique et de l'Assainissement)* their purpose being "to reconcile the interests of various categories of users, to take into account previously established rights and customs and finally, to conserve national water assets" (Ministère de l'Hydraulique et de l'Assainissement,

---

[205] Marguerite Dupire was part of Gromaires team and was in charge of studying how the boreholes affected Fulani lifestyle.

[206] Law 81.13 of March 1981, Journal Officiel de la République du Sénégal no. 4829 of April 1981 pp.411-418, (here quoted from Allisoutin, 1996:3)

from Allisoutin, 1996:3). Needless to say, very few of the users, at least in the rural areas, have ever heard of the existence of legal provisions requiring them to obtain permit to use water resources. As noted by Allisoutin, ponds do not in the mind of the rural population belong to anyone and anybody may make use of them (ibid.: 4).

With regards to the ordinary wells, which for a large part are state financed, access is not restricted. Nonetheless, more informal types of regulation may be enforced. According to my informants, foreign herders may, for example, be asked to refrain from watering their livestock until the animals of the regular users have drunk. At this moment the water level has sunk and water is more difficult to access.

Similar rules apply for privately owned wells, bearing in mind that according to the legislation access to and use of publicly owned ground water is open to anyone. The fact of being man-made (i.e. privately sponsored) does, however, attach rights of a more private character to the well. Hence, also the shallow wells dug into the dry river beds have certain rights attached to them, obliging a possible lender to provide a gift for the owner, while the annual enforcement and maintenance is left in the charge of the user. But as shown in the quotation below the actual extent of these rights remain somewhat blurred:

"A great number of transhumants have settled here. We don't know where they come from. They haven't talked with us. They water their animals at the well and at the hand-dug shallow wells [céanes]. They don't even ask for permission to use the well, in spite of it being the villagers themselves who have dug it and paid all expenses. With regards to the shallow wells everyone is free to dig one, where it is possible. But if you make use of one, which has been dug before, you ought to get the permission of the one who initially dug it. If you dig one yourself, you are free to prohibit others from using it." (Village chief, Sessoum, Velingara, Febr. 1993.)

As shown above, presumed rights and enacted realities are not always congruent, but rather the source of constant strives and redefinition. This is part of the constant realignment of power relations: In the interpretation given by the village chief, it is the local population who are holders of certain (unspecified) rights over the well, rights which are trespassed by the foreigners in their impolite behaviour *(they haven't talked to us, they haven't asked for permission)*. The response of the villagers, in this representation, is one of tolerance and indulgence towards the aggressor. Tolerance and indulgence have positive connotations. They are features often accentuated by herders and centrally placed in the Fulani code of conduct. To be tolerant is no sign of weakness, rather it is the position of the strong one, who has force to respect the codes of proper conduct and be generous (see Riesmann, 1990).

Access to land is free and unrestricted. This does not, however, imply that settlement is completely random or chaotic. For while the individual herder is free to use whatever pastures he wants, settlement into new areas will take place with due regard to a series of informal conventions on proper conducts. According to Niamir (1990:32) this 'choreography of movements' or 'passive coordination' derives from a mutual wish to avoid mixing of herds which could be the consequence of settling too close to other herders. Likewise, a wish to avoid confrontations usually inspires transhumants to refrain from settlement in zones already occupied by large numbers of herders. The following quotation may illustrate this mentality.

"If more wells are drilled it would destroy the bush. It's good for the animals to be able to move the whole day without meeting other herds. At present I'm taking advantage of the breakdown of the borehole-pump. Once the pump is repaired and herders come back, I will move another 10 km's away". (Herder from Mbiddi, on transhumance near Loumbi Aly Thedy, Febr. 1993).

In contrast to the interpretation stressing the existence of a customary regulation of access to pastures, the view expressed above underscores the individual interest in avoiding too close contact with other herders. It is the right of the individual to move away from others and to have unrestricted access to a large number of different resource regimes and not the rights of a restricted group of users to exclude others, which is at stake. The relatively low priority given to creation of rights of exclusivity to a distinct resource regime also explains why the majority of herders are extremely favourable to the drilling of more wells (in contrast to the herder quoted above). For although creation of new wells increases competition (the concern expressed by the Mbiddi herder), it still opens up new resource spaces for grazing. As will be shown below claims of exclusivity therefore often turns out to be as much a question of gaining and securing political control as of limiting the pressure on the grazing lands.

The system of 'passive coordination' which in principle gives everyone equal rights of access, does not exclude that herders generally recognize the needs of being on friendly terms with their neighbours. In many cases, settlement into a new area will therefore involve some sort of compensation to the neighbours in the area of settlement. This may be done either through manure contracts (shorter or longer periods), through temporary employment of members of the host household to draw water or through other types of relations which may constitute an advantage to the host population. Although no formalized practices exist, and herders generally are reluctant to mention such transactions, transhumant herders may in certain occasions also give away animals as gift to neighbours, village chiefs and local authorities in order to ensure good relations.

Ultimate dichotomies? Sedentary vs. mobile/indigenous vs. foreigner

If flexibility and lack of clear regulation with regards to the productive resources turns out to be not the result of undermining of well-functioning customary institutions but rather the corollary of a society characterized by a broad and flexible resource base, then the distinct user group with shared interest in a long term maintenance of a sustainable resource environment may also turn out to be difficult to identify.

As argued in the previous chapters, the productive strategies of the Ferlo population are not homogeneous and may vary considerably over time. In the Ferlo, as elsewhere in the Sahel, most producers turn out to combine a large variety of very different economic activities such as collection of gum arabic and other forest products, commercialisation of livestock or salaried work in order to pursue a living. Such activities are not necessarily linked to either agricultural or livestock production. In recent years a growing number of the herders have, for example, established themselves as shopkeepers in the borehole villages.

Often these productive activities are not either very closely linked to a specific and bounded geographical setting. In fact extensive travelling, as part of a productive strategy, is not practiced only by transhumants herders. Also apparently 'sedentarised' inhabitants of the Ferlo frequently turn out to make use of resources in other, even fairly distant, resource regimes. Some continue to cultivate seasonally in the *waalo*, other travel extensively during the dry season offering treatments on basis of their magical powers (*maraboutage*[207]), still others supplement their

---

[207] Notably SanraBe herders are considered to possess magical powers, reason for which

incomes by travelling to town or abroad as migrant workers on shorter or longer terms[208].

It is important to stress that such supplementary income-generating activities are not carried out solely by the resource-poor rural dwellers. Also large herd owners may turn out to supplement their incomes as travelling *marabouts,* livestock traders or the like. This variation in productive strategies underscores the need to substantiate the image of rural producers as having common goals and interests. Obviously, those herders who are active in commercialisation of livestock or are involved in retail trading may be only moderately interested in setting up firm rules to reduce the number of foreign herders settling in the area.

Consequently, sedentarity and mobility can neither be considered as fixed entities nor as the two opposed poles in an evolutionary process. Such dichotomies do not hold in the case of the Ferlo, where producers constantly shift between different types of production and between various degrees of sedentary lifestyle and mobility, according to their immediate constraints and abilities in constant adjustment to where it is most profitable for the moment.

"Those who left in 1973, used to be agro-pastoralists. Some had 300 sheep and maybe 100 heads of cattle. But many lost animals during the journey as the animals had to get used to new pastures. Some managed to reconstitute their herds after that. Others lost everything and had to come back and cultivate. Among those who failed in the first run some managed

---

this group travels more extensively than others, being away form their household for many months during the lean season. Also the success of certain herd-owners who have been able to build up a particularly large herd is attributed to special magical powers. Several times during visits to particularly rich herd owners, people have come to seek their mystic services. Such mystical powers play an important role in the self-knowledge regarding herding skills. According to the richest herder in the area, the reason why he managed to get his, indeed extremely, large herd across the Senegal River form Mauritania in the midst of the fierce hostilities between Mauritania and Senegal was that he was able to make them invisible. Invisibility was also used to explain the relative success of those herders who where able to cross the river to 'raid back' part of the Fulani herds during the hostilities.

[208] A survey carried out for the CSE (Juul, 1990) in 1988/89 showed that 17 % of a sample of 93 houscholds were involved in gum collection, 20% in commercialisation of livestock (but at a very variable scale) while 4% were involved in retail sale. In the course of the years retail trading has merely exploded and villages as Barkedji have at least 20 different shops. Often the shops function as a meeting place for different groups of a more or less clientelistic stamp and as a meeting point for trading smallstock etc.

to build-up a flock after some time. And among these, some have now left to go on transhumance in the south. Others, however, can't make it." (Ardo[209] Ururbe DjougonaBe, Madina Ndiatabe (Fuuta), 1995).

As illustrated in the quotation, the post-drought migration process is in itself an indicator of how rural dwellers may shift between preferred resources as a reaction to internal and external changes, adopting a more or less mobile lifestyle accordingly. And clearly, such patterns of resource use are likely to give way to more flexible resource management arrangements, than those adduced by the Common Property approach.

Indeed, the whole history of post-borehole settlement affirms the picture of African communities as porous and fluid social entities. They are comprised of individuals who have shown themselves apt to respond to new opportunities and constraints in a fluctuating physical and social environment, as discussed in chapter 3. This adaptability is reflected as the histories of the different agglomerations of the Ferlo, which are characterized by constant shifts in relation to changing population. Indeed they resemble the Zambian situation, recollected by Berry, according to which "*the village is not a permanent social entity, but rather an institution through which a large and varied company of people pass at different speed*" (Kay, 1967 quoted from Berry, 1993:162).

Accordingly, the distinction between the rightful user and the foreigners against whom the resources should be protected becomes less obvious than it would appear at first sight. Distinguished as it is by fluid ethnic boundaries, high levels of mobility and little permanent attachment to a particular geographical space, the Ferlo fits well into what Kopytoff characterised as a 'frontier region' (see above). In conformity with the 'frontier ideology', a continuing reorganisation of ethnic identities is taking place, making the distinctions between who is currently labelled 'foreigner' or 'newcomer' and who falls under the heading of 'first-comers', 'local' or 'indigenous' less clear-cut than originally anticipated. In the case of the Ferlo, a closer look into the 'age' of settlement of various groups around a borehole shows, that while many of the so-called 'foreigners' have stayed in the area for more than 25 years and have invested considerable sums in the maintenance of the boreholes and other crucial equipment in the area, many of those labelled 'first-comers' turn out to have settled in the area only a few

---

[209] *Ardo* is the title of the Fulani sub-clan leader. The *ardo* is similar in status to the village chief.

years before or maybe even after the arrival of the first FuutankoBes. This was for example the case of a group of FafaBe's in Velingara who were considered as first-comers, although they had only moved in by the late 1960's[210]. In those cases the labels of 'local' and 'foreigner' tended to be more related to differences in herd management, to productive strategy and to political affiliation than to the actual age of settlement. In the same vein the constitution of the FuutankoBe herders as a distinct group is a recent phenomenon, in vigour only as a product of post-drought migration situation.

The recent tendency among a number of those FuutankoBe herders who had stayed a long time in the Southern Ferlo of discretely backing attempts aiming at excluding their newly arrived kin may also reflect such 'identitary volatility'. With this in mind, it turns out to be largely impossible to distinguish a group through some common objective as was proposed by North, Ostrom and others. For as identities are changed new groups are composed, underscoring the need to explain change historically and not just from what can be seen here and now.

Finally, it is questionable whether post-drought migration can be perceived solely as a one-way process of newcomers invading a previously stable and static resource space. As is shown in the case of the Loumbi UrurBe sub-village (south of Barkedji), the influx of FuutankoBe settlers in some cases contributed to increase the productive potentials of a certain area, thereby making it more attractive to the so-called local population. In this case the labels of 'newcomers' and 'locals' are turned more or less up-side down.

"We all come from Namarel [in northern Ferlo]. We came in 1973. When we settled there was no one here, only jackals, hyenas and even lions. We camped in one single, but very large camp. This was to protect our herds against the wild animals. But after a while the predators left [formore undisturbed environments]. And then the SanraBe agro-pastoralists started moving in. They started cultivating and that's when the trouble of crop damages started. We spend fortunes paying compensations for crop damages now. Some have even chosen to move away into the gazetted forest where there is no cultivation. The SanraBe's who have moved in, are people with very little livestock. They are attracted by the improved conditions for cultivation, now the predators are gone. At present

---

[210] This was revealed during the mapping exercise in Velingara in 1991 (see chapter 4).

there are 5 camps of SanraBe cultivators. But we fear that more will come."
(FuutankoBe herder from the sub-village of Lombi UrurBe, Barkedji).

The case illustrates how difficult it is to speak of the borehole and the adjacent pastures as a distinct resource management space. Most resource users operate across several resource management spaces or make use of different resource spaces in the course of their productive 'career'. Consequently, also the distinction between the rightful 'owner' of the resources and the deleterious 'foreigner' or 'free-rider' (in the terminology of the Common Property framework) will turn out to be more politically than neutrally defined labels, aiming at justifying the rights of certain groups at the detriment of others.

When the Ferlanke population of Naoré suggest a strong dichotomy between themselves: 'the local, sedentarised population' and the others: the 'vagrant' foreigners (or even 'refugees'), it is yet an example of how identities are redefined and traditions reinvented. As shown above restriction of access of so-called foreigners to the pastures or to key resource institutions is not tied to some mutually recognized primordial or ancestral right legitimising a differentiation in status. Rather, it is a political manoeuvre, a way of establishing a 'discourse' linking up to the policy framework of decentralisation and self-governance. Framing the conflict as a problem of local vs. stranger groups may therefore be perceived as a tactical move by certain layers of the local population through which they have managed to legitimise the intervention of the *sous-préfet* aiming to defend their postulated rights of exclusivity. On their side the newcomers may, as is the case in Loumbi UrurBe, claim equal rights as first-comers by stressing their own role as 'domesticators' of an otherwise uninhabitable area.

Evidently such 'politisations' or struggles over meanings do not preclude that the arrival of the large and highly expansionist group of FuutakoBe households carried with it many problems in terms of increased competition and partial marginalisation of those occupying the area prior to the FuutankoBe invasion. But to get a proper understanding of the unfolding of conflicts, as the one in Naoré, it remains critical to recognize that the call for exclusivity was not shared by the entire (local) population. Other interests than the pure defence of the local resource base may be just as important elements on the local political agenda. Therefore the meanings attributed to notions such as 'strangers' and 'locals' and the definition of who is a legitimate user and who an outsider often turn out to be highly political issues crucial for present and future alignment of political powers. This political dimension is largely neglected in the Common Property approach. This omission of the political dimension is, as will be shown below, even more apparent in the analysis of the relations between local institutions and the state.

The local institutional landscape and the myth of the obtrusive state

The negative effects of excessive state interference and the unclear institutional arrangements hold considerable weight in the arguments for (re)instauration of common property resource management arrangements. According to conventional analysis of local institutional capacities it is the over-centralisation of institutional arrangements, which constitute the prime obstacle for local participation and self-government. Through stifling of local initiatives, excessive state tutelage is considered a major obstacle to development of viable institutions of local resource management (Guellar, 1990:130). Such arguments are, as will be shown below, pervasive, but nonetheless incomplete.

There can be no doubt of the overly centralized character of the Senegalese state apparatus. As noted by Rondinelli and Minis (1990:451) much of the authority system to take action, on both major issues and seemingly routine personnel actions, is centralized in the Presidency[211]. Government structures are highly compartmentalized, as they are composed by many ministries, agencies, commissions and institutions that operate with little co-ordination and co-operation. Finally a hierarchic system of controls, inherited from French tradition of public administration, hinders the ability of ministries and agencies to take action. All of this contributes to create a situation where it is difficult to carry out government functions and make decisions unless the highest executive officer takes a personal interest in expedient action. This could be observed very clearly in the case of Naoré.

---

[211] In fact, the President of the Republic is responsible not only for political guidance and direction but also for a myriad of administrative details such as the approval, appointment, promotions, retirement of all administrative personnel down to the level of the department director. The president can also amend and discard any regulation or procedure, reason for which many conflicts over or recommendations for change can be resolved only by actions in the Office of the Presidency (Rondinelli et al. 1990:451).

With the administrative reform of 1972, a process of decentralisation was launched. It comprised both deconcentration of power from central government to local administrative offices and handing over of specific responsibilities to locally elected bodies, namely the rural councils and the well-committees. Administratively the country is now divided into regions, *départments* and *arrondissements*, headed by governors, *préfets* and *sous-préfets* respectively. At the lower administrative levels, the rural communities, state administration is handed over to a locally elected body, the rural council, formally endowed with legal status and financial autonomy.

For the present work, the administrative levels of primary interest are those of the arrondissement and of the rural community *(communauté rurale)*. At arrondissement level, the state administration is physically represented by a *sous-préfect*, a secretary and a *brigade de gendarmerie*, all of whom act on the behalf of the Ministry of Interior (Vengroff and Johnston, 1987: 274). To this adds the CER (*Centres d'Expansion Rural*) a multi-disciplinary team of extension officers[212] in charge of providing technical expertise for the implementation of rural community development efforts (Vengroff and Johnston, 1985:4).

At the level of the *Communauté Rurale,* the representation of civil servants is often restricted to a single extension officer, eventually in company of a representative of the police forces. At village level, the state is represented by one or several village chiefs[213]. The village chief is in charge of resolving minor local conflicts, of collecting taxes and of assisting the government technical officers in their activities. Nonetheless he holds no formal authority and has no means to sanction trespassing of local or national rules or regulations.

---

[212] In the pastoral areas the CER is comprised of extension agents in charge of agriculture, livestock and forestry. The" chef de CER" has an administrative background and is tied to the Ministry of the Interior.

[213] Within a larger village, for example a borehole-village, there may be several village chiefs as each of them represent their own 'sector' (ethnic group or subclan).

Localisation of local authorities:

Chief town of the Arrondissement	Sous-préfet CER/Extension officers Police Force	Arrondissement Council/ councillors	Well-committee	Village Chiefs
Chief town of the Communauté Rurale	Police Officer (Extension officers)	President of Rural Council/ Councillors	Well-committee	Village Chiefs
Borehole village		(Councillors)	Well-committee	Village chiefs
Village/sector		(Councillor)		Village chief

(Persons in brackets may be, but are not necessarily, represented).

In spite of the considerable efforts to de-concentrate state agencies, implementation is far from complete. As stressed by Rondinelli and Minis (1990:455) decision-making responsibility remains highly centralized and field offices lack the resources to carry out their functions effectively. Strong vertical lines of authority prevail among the field-staff of technical ministries at the local level. This counteracts their official intention of providing technical support through the CER. Technical agents often prefer to follow the directives of their own ministries (in charge of salary and future career advancement) instead of respecting the priorities and directives of the local councils. This obviously limits the ability of the CER chiefs technically in charge of the horizontal coordination of activities, to exercise real authority over the agents. This situation is further hampered by a general condition of poor equipment, insufficient staffing and financial constraints, which effectively limits the frequency of trips to the field.

Close collaboration between the administrative and technical officers and the local government is also frustrated by the policy of the central government of keeping administrators responsive to central policies. In order to make it more difficult to develop schemes to abuse their powers, subordinate administrative officers are always posted outside their home districts and ethnic groups. This, together with the rapid circulation of administrative personnel, makes it liable that anytime the administrator gets to understand a corner of what is at stake in local politics; he is transferred to another jurisdiction. (Thomson, 1991:6).

The Rural Councils

Also the devolution of power from the state to the locally elected and participative structures, the rural councils, is hampered by the pervasiveness of state centralisation and control. According to the design of the Administrative Reform of 1972, the most important local institution in charge of management of local resources is the rural council. It was, however, not until 1984[214] that these locally elected bodies had been established in every municipality (*Communauté Rurale*[215]) of the Senegalese territory. Rural Councils are elected by universal suffrage[216] on a 5 year term. According to the original text (*Loi 64-46 du 17 juin 1962 relative au Domaine National*) all adults residing in the area and engaged in 'rural activities' are elegible to the council[217]. In reality members are almost exclusively selected among the local sedentarised elites and mobilized through the factions of the ruling Socialist Party.

---

[214] In those parts of the Ferlo region comprised within *département* of Diourbel (Louga) the councils were set up in the course of 1970's. In those parts of the Ferlo comprised by Region du Fleuve, the councils were established in 1980 and in 1982 in Senegal Oriental. The process was completed when Dakars first municipal council was elected in 1984 (Vengroff and Johnston, 1987:276).

[215] A *communauté rurale* consists of a number of villages within an "*arrondissement*" i.e. 20 to 80 villages and a total of 5000 to 10.000 inhabitants. (Le Roy, 1980:562)

[216] The number of elected members varies according to the population density of the rural community. In the Ferlo, 16 members are elected through direct voting. Originally 2/3 of the members were elected by universal suffrage while one-third are appointed by the local cooperatives. Since 1996, all members have been elected.

[217] Art. 10 :" [Le conseil rural] peut comprendre [..] des membres élus parmi et par des personnes domicilés dans le terroir , y résident effectivement s'y livrant à des activités rurales a titre principal et jouissant des droits electoraux"

The Rural Councils are intended to act as a sort of interface between the territorial administrative hierarchy and the rural users. In principle, they enjoy considerable authority over local resources being responsible, first and foremost, for the allocation of use rights to land and resources as well as for land use planning i.e. the ability to reserve certain areas of the municipal land for specific purposes. To this adds the powers to regulate local markets, cattle walks and residential zoning patterns and of financing local community projects through the rural councils budgets.

In spite of the broad powers attributed to the rural councils, a number of constraints exist which limit the effective control of the councils over local resource use. First of all, the state maintains considerable powers over the rural council. As an agent of the state, the president of the rural council comes directly under the authority of the *sous-préfet*[218]. Until the 1990 revision of the law, the *sous-préfect* could suspend any decision taken by the president if it was considered untimely, illegal or not in conformity to the spirit of the rural council debate to which it applies (Ministère de l'Interieur, 1984:14 here quoted from Vengroff et al., 1984:12). This also applied for the resolution of local conflicts, which formally lay in the hands of the rural council. Nonetheless, the autonomy of decision was hampered by a clause according to which solutions were to be presented to the *sous-préfet* before application (Le Roy ,1980: 563). Since 1990, a majority of the prerogatives regarding local resource management were transferrred to the rural council leaving the *sous-préfet* a clearer role as the controlling party (Blundo, 1995b:14).

Furthermore, vast tracts of land in the areas in question are gazetted (as pastoral, forest or game reserves) and therefore remain under the direct authority of the state through the Forestry Services[219]. And finally, the councils dispose of few financial and logistical means to control the

---

[218] The text concerning the degree of state supervision of the councils has been subject to frequent revisions. Initially land attribution was a prerogative of the president of the rural council upon consultation with the other councillors. This was modified in 1980, where the *sous-préfet* was given the authority of final approbation. In 1986 further centralization was made as a decree transferred this approbation to the *Préfet*. Finally in 1990, the autonomy of the rural council was reinforced, as the control over local budgets and tax collection was transferred from the *sous-préfet* to the President of the rural council.

[219] This is particularly relevant for the Eastern part of the field area which is located entirely within the Reserve de Faune du Ferlo Nord covering 332.000 ha and the Reserve de Faune du Ferlo Sud covering 663.700 ha. Source: Grenier, 1987 p. 156-157.

implementation of their decisions notwithstanding the implementation of local development projects as proposed by the law. According to the intentions of the Reform, the activities of the rural councils are to be financed primarily through a rural tax which is managed and budgeted by the rural communities themselves. The rural council, however, has no control over the rate of taxation, which is fixed by the state. According to planners this 'investment budget' was to be the motor of the community budget. Local leaders were intended to commit the greatest share of the budget to economic investments such as tube-wells and larger boreholes, livestock vaccination pens, markets, irrigation schemes etc. promoting the development of the rural community (Vengroff and Johnston, 1987:276). These intentions have, however, had little impact on reality. Budgets are very limited and in most cases no development projects are actually carried out[220]. In the pastoral area, the large of logistical and financial support is particularly problematic as each council is in charge of vast areas[221] over which the councillors are spread.

So although the rural councils are designated to play a central role in local resource management, few means are provided for regulating and securing pastoral land from agricultural encroachment. As will be shown below, the legal framework is both contradictory and ambiguous, making it very difficult for the councillors to carry out any efficient land use planning.

A main problem is the agricultural bias of the legal framework. According to the Land Law of 1964 (Loi 64-46 du 17 juin 1964 relative au Domaine National) land is inalienable. Plots may be allocated individually only in the form of leasehold to producers who will ensure its productive use either by physical or financial investment in the land (the principle of *mise en valeur* i.e. land development). As long as the peasant uses the land productively and hence respects the *mise en valeur* he will not be deprived of his means of production (Decret 86-445). For herders, however, the

---

[220] According to Vengroff and Johnston in 1983-84 total annual budgets ranged between 1 - 17 million CFA i.e. 2700-42.000 US$. The budget of the *communauté rurale* of Saldé amounted 22 million CFA in 1991 of which 1 million were given as subsidies to the running costs of boreholes in the area, 2 million were used to repair wells and boreholes, while 3,7 million were used for the drilling of a well.

[221] The *communauté rurale* of Barkedji comprises 2072 sq. kilometres; whereas the *Communauté Rurale* of Ogo, the country's largest is approximately 18.000 sq. kilometres.

situation is quite different. Due to the extensive character of the Sahelian grazing systems, grazing as such is not considered a productive investment in the land, and can therefore not serve as a justification for obtaining private leaseholds. So even if the right of access is left almost untouched by the law, herders have few means to protect their grazing lands once claims have been made by agriculturalists.

In the course of the years, attempts have been made to improve tenure security on grazing lands. According to a decree from the Ministry of Agriculture from 1980 it is prohibited to clear land for agricultural purposes within the boundaries of natural pastures. In the decree 72-1288, land which is designated as grazing lands may be used by any citizen (*ressortissant du terroir*). Here, one finds an attempt to bind the local resources to the local settled population. But as shown by Le Roy (1980:560) implementation of the regulation is seriously hampered by the fact that the concept of *terroir* remains undefined.

In the same way, the decree stipulates that it is the responsibility of the cultivator to fence and protect his fields from straying animals. But again, the legal value of these decrees is severely restricted, as none of the pastoral zones, except for the gazetted areas, can boast of clearly demarcated boundaries. The legality of a cleared field will therefore remain subject to negotiations and interpretations. One the whole, restriction on the room of manoeuvre of cultivators in search of new lands to clear is limited to singular regulations such as the prohibition to cultivate within a limit of 1 km from a pond and on cattle treks. But even such regulations may be difficult to put into effect due to the limited capacity of the institutions in charge of their control.

Finally, the central concept of *mise en valeur* is difficult for the councillors to handle: a fact, which is reflected in the minutes from council meetings by recurrent reference to almost all applicants as 'great workers'. Especially estimations of the capacities of modern farming units such as the Mouride *daaras* become pure guesswork. The lack of examples of '*desaffectation*" (fields taken away from leaseholders because of non-cultivation) and the enormous areas attributed to single families are telling for the difficulties (or lack of motivation) related to the evaluation of the productive capacities of the individual household[222]. The effect of such 'incapacities' is likely to be that priorities other than the plain productive capacities are decisive for how much and to whom land is attributed.

This is well illustrated by the sweeping practices of the Mourides of making claims of several hundred square kilometres of land often located within the limits of the gazetted forests, and the many cases where farmers, including the Mourides have started cultivating much larger tracts of land that originally attributed.[223] But it is also embodied in the new 'counter-strategy' put into effect by the big herd owners of Velingara in 1990 and 1991 that started soliciting large parcels of lands as private grazing grounds. This attribution of parcels covering 10, 15 or 20 km^2 of pastures (mainly to council members) aimed primarily at creating a buffer against the expansionist practices of the Mourides. As herders seldom possess agricultural tools or manpower to cultivate more than a single hectare or two, the practice was clearly not in conformity with the law. Nonetheless it was approved, at least passively, by the *sous-préfet* and the *préfet*[224], thereby providing yet an example of the partial non-application of the law.

In spite of these obvious deficiencies, it remains questionable whether the apparently meagre results of the decentralization process can be attributed solely to the insufficient devolution of real power from central government or to the deficiencies and contradictions of the legal framework, as assumed by Rondinelli and Minis, Guellar and Thomson. While it is true that decentralization remains imperfect and the fundamentally centralistic structure of the Senegalese state apparatus in many ways serves to undermine the authority and efficiency of the locally elected bodies, it remains doubtful whether clear structures of authority or the establishment of a lucid and unequivocal legal framework is likely in itself to improve local management significantly. Looking into the actual practices of the decentralized institutions in charge of local resource management a number of equally important issues are revealed, more related to the local practicing of politics.

---

[222] See also Le Roy 1980:565, Caverivière 1991:22 and Juul 1991c.

[223] Such 'overflowing' of field limits may even, is it said, entail movement of the boundary stones set up by the extension officers and councillors in charge of field delimitations.

[224] For a more thorough discussion of these practices see Juul, 1993.

Contrary to the somewhat amputated version of local resource management accorded to the rural councils, the well committees enjoy considerable autonomy both financially and legally. The measures taken by the state in 1984 to hand over the responsibilities for operation and maintenance of boreholes and pumps to locally elected well committees have in many ways therefore proven far more significant with regard to pastoral land use than the creation of the rural councils. Before passing on to the general discussion of decentralisation and the extents of state powers in the Senegalese countryside, these committees and their abilities in terms of efficient local management will therefore be presented and discussed.

The well committees

In contrast to the restricted powers of the rural council, the handing over of responsibility for the boreholes to locally elected committees is largely in line with the recommendations of the afore mentioned Common Property school. Although the state remains the formal owner of both water resources[225] and of the technical equipment, the well-committee enjoys extensive autonomy receiving almost no organisational support from the state.

The different degrees of autonomy result primarily from differences in the objectives of decentralisation. Obviously the driving force behind the establishment of the well-committees in 1984 was an attempt by the state to reduce public expenditure as part of the structural adjustment programme, an intent declared overtly in the legal framework of the transfer[226]. Although public parlance highlights the participatory elements of the transfer of responsibility, herders have tended to regard it mainly as a transfer of costs of operation and maintenance. Contrary to the implicit assumption that transfer of power is always welcomed by the local

---

[225] According to the Water Code Water resources are an integral part of the public domain. Such resources are a collective asset and their use of the national territory is subject to prior authorization and supervision. (Article 2 Law 81.13 of March 1981 Journal Officiel de la Republique du Senegal no. 4829 Here quoted from Allisoutin, 1997:3).

[226] Circulaire Interministerielle du 9 janvier 1984 visant a la création et a la généralisation de comites de gestion de forages en milieu rural, and Circulaire Interministerielle du 9 janvier 1984, Annexe 5 sur les Comites de Gestion des Forages.

population, herders feel that maintenance should remain the responsibility of the state, an opinion which helps to explain the widespread reluctance to pay for even minor repairs. This results in surprisingly frequent cases where the vital source of water is blocked for months despite considerable inconveniences for the users[227].

The (rudimentary) legal framework affecting the well committees is interesting on several counts. First of all, it is stated that the committee is a public non-profit making organization, established in accordance with the President of the Rural Council of the locality. Secondly, the recommended 12 members of the well-committee are elected by the local population for a period of 2 years. With regards to membership, this is open for any user paying correctly their watering fees. Thirdly, the objectives are restricted to ensure supplies of diesel and lubricants as well as proper maintenance of the pump and engine. Nothing in the law confirms that 'indigenous' occupants of a certain area, should have preferential rights with regards to representation in the boards of the well-committee, as it is often argued by 'local' residents and even by the personnel of the Ministry[228].

In spite, however, of the requirements of the text, none of the well-committees visited during my fieldtrips could boast of having held any elections, since the initial election of 1984. In many cases, single members had been replaced with others of the Presidents choice, as in Naoré. In other cases the boards had been dissolved numerous times by the *sous-préfet* or the President of the Rural Council, who had used the opportunity to appoint a new committee, in some cases made up by adolescents or people without much cattle[229] acting more or less as stooges for more influential people.

---

[227] According to the *Services de l'Hydraulique*'s regional office in Linguère, 4 of the boreholes of the *département* have been paralyzed for more than 2 years, due to breakdown of the motor.

[228] It is a firm belief among the technicians of the regional office of the Ministry of Waterworks (Service de l'Hydraulique) that only those paying their (poll) taxes in the area can be appointed members of the board. *(those who pay their taxes down there can be part of the board, those who are outside cannot. The transhumants are outside').* This view is also the one forwarded by the local 'first-comer' population.

[229] Members of the board are officially compensated by a 10% refund of the fees collected.

"The present well committee has been in office 4 months. I don't know what happened to the old one, but the President of the Rural Council called upon one of his relatives and asked him to become President of a new well committee. It's very difficult to find anyone who is ready to volunteer for the job. We have all been appointed by the President of the Rural Council. Except for two representatives of the Wolof population, we are all his relatives. We are all young people" (Member of the well-committeee, Barkedji Febr. 1993.)

Alternatively, the composition of the board is a matter of eternal strive between various rival sub-clans and factions present around the borehole as in the case of Gueye Kadar, where standstill of the well has been a repeating feature ever since the handing over of responsibility due to internal competition between *IrlaaBe*, *UrurBe* and *DialluBe* Fulani sub-clans. Often these conflicts go on for many years. Contrary to the situation of excessive state tutelage of the Rural Councils, the well-committees cannot rely on much institutional support or organisational backing from the state services[230]. The Ministry of Waterworks formally in charge of the wells restricts its services to technical maintenance. Organisational support is, as can be seen in the text, restricted to the surveillance of the President of the rural council[231]. The *sous-préfet* is often quite reluctant to intervene in the frequent and uncompromising strives between different factions of the population over the wells.

In several instances the situation has however become so chaotic that the *sous-préfet* has taken to dissolving the existing borehole committees replacing them with committees composed by the available extension officers. (This was also the proposition made by the *sous-préfet* in the case of Naoré). But in 1989 this praxis of 're-engagement' of the state was

---

[230] The Services de l'Hydraulique do not intervene in organisational matters *(questions de sensibilisation)*. In the original conception of the handing over a special unit for 'sensibilisation' or awareness- raising, was intented. Due to budgetary limits it was never implemented.

[231] Also the Chef de CER laments the lack of clear rules and control: *"There is nobody to make revisions of the budgets and accounts of the well-committee: There are lots of financial problems, but no one is in charge of taking care of that problem. It is up to the sous-préfet currently in office whether he will designate someone to supervise the accounts"*. (Chef de CER, Barkedji Febr. 1993).

explicitly condemned in a note from the government (Circulaire de Jean Collin 30 Juin 1989) enjoining the *sous-préfet*s to leave the management of the boreholes to the local population. The composition and functioning of the board is also a matter of serious divide between those with only few animals and those with many:

"To become a member of the well-committee you must live in the village and have a few heads of livestock. No, I don't know whether that written down anywhere. If the boreholes were handed over to those with many heads of livestock, there would be no more problems. At present it's the poor, who are in charge. They need the money they can earn and what surplus they might embezzle for the survival of their families. In Ranérou, they get 20 % of the turn-over [against normally 10%]" (Veterinary assistant, Ranérou).

On the other hand, the large herd owners, first-comers and newcomers alike, have until recently tended to give the well-committee little attention, claiming that they are herders and have other more important thing to do than to hang around at the well.

The high level of embezzlement is condemned vigorously by all parties. Nonetheless it remains characteristic for the vast majority of boreholes legitimated as it is by a general dislike among herders to count their animals, leaving taxes to be evaluated as a rough estimate of the size of the herd[232]. Lack of transparency in accounts further facilitates informal agreements in favour of influential indigenous herders who by way of clientelistic relations and informal negotiations have managed to keep their contributions to a minimum[233]. Many wells are now financed almost exclusively by taxes applied to FuutankoBe herds, a practice which seriously questions the non-profit character of the well-committees.

---

[232] Such estimations were not made easier by the fact that a considerable part of the herd was watered at the encampment with the tubes.

[233] According to Grenier (1987:138) the fees paid in 1987 had been unchanged for 10 years, hence corresponding to notoriously false herd size estimations.

In spite of the profits made, cases are frequent where the pump is shut down several days or weeks because of lack of fuel and lubricants, of spare-parts or of other repair. Such perpetual embezzlement of funds evidently generates a climate of general mistrust. As noted by the regional livestock officer in Linguère:

"There are many problems with the boreholes. Even if the transhumants weren't there, there would be problems. There are simply too many animals at the wells. At Warhock [a borehole with little or no FuutankoBe representation], *they have arrived to a situation where they pay for watering on a daily basis."*

With regards to the process of decentralization, it is important to stress that borehole committees were never intended to play any significant role. The boreholes remain under state ownership guaranteeing everyone who will pay the fees agreed a right to use the facilities. With regard to regulation of access to the watering facilities notwithstanding the adjacent grazing lands, they do not officially hold any authority. Nonetheless, the well-committees have found themselves to be holders of no less than the key institution to control management of local resources, the ability to limit access to pastures through regulation of the number of users of the well. The unintended consequence of state withdrawal becomes all the more paradoxical when one recalls that in contrast to the rural councils who are under tutelage of the Bureau in Charge of the Decentralization located in the Ministry of Internal Affairs, boreholes and well-committees remain separated from the decentralisation process, under the supervision of the Ministry of Waterworks.

The important role of the well committees became apparent particularly in relation to post-drought migration. Obviously the growing number of "foreign" herders on transhumance in the area, especially in years of rain deficit, increases competition on the pastoral resources, just as it wears the pump machinery which in most cases is old and fragile[234]. Hence, excessive use in order to satisfy the large number of animals contributes to frequent breakdowns which force otherwise sedentary agro-pastoralists to

---

[234] The level of suspicion is so that certain herders even suspect the wells committees of letting the pumps function 24 hours a day in the deliberate intention of making them break down, so that transhumants will leave.

move over to the neighbouring well for longer or shorter periods of time. In order to limit pressure on the borehole pump and not the least the pressure on the adjacent pastures, some first-comers holding office in the well-committees have used the tool, out of the reach of the Rural Council, of limiting the number of users of the well. This may be done either by direct exclusion (which is illegal according to the law) or through the exorbitant taxing of herds belonging to the migrant population.

But although emergence of more exclusive practices would appear to be a natural consequence of increased competition on resources, this trend is accompanied by its apparent opposition - a similarly strong inclination towards inclusive practices, generated primarily by economic concerns. For with the arrival of the FuutankoBe herders, the turnovers of the well-committees have increased dramatically, and have turned them into important means for extraction of economic revenue. The result of these contradictory interests has been that the policy of most well-committees has been a constant oscillation between exclusive and inclusive strategies with regard to foreigners' access to water; between the desire to limit competition on pastures through restrictions on the number of users and the temptation to increase revenues of the well-committee by expanding the number of "foreigners" to finance the bulk of running costs.

Contrary to the improved management anticipated by the Common Property framework, the handing-over of boreholes to locally elected bodies has resulted in generally poor management of the wells. Breakdowns of the equipment of the wells are frequent and local herders generally reluctant to pay for something which they regard essentially as a state responsibility.

It is, however, important to notice that in spite of the newly acquired ability of borehole members to regulate the number of herds grazing in the adjacent pastures, conflicts centre increasingly on problems related to the financial management of the borehole, rather than on management of the pastures. For apart from turning into a key institution in resource management, the deep-wells have also proven to be important means for extraction of economic resources in a region otherwise largely deprived of other objects or resource flows prone for misappropriation.

In the controversy between protection of local resources and the economic advantages related to increased mobility, many well-committees are incited to a constant oscillation between inclusive (and financially attractive) strategies and exclusive practices where the access to wells is used as a means to limit 'free-riding' by 'foreign' herds. Contrary to what was envisioned, the chosen policy turn out to be motivated more by short-term economic (and political) gain than by long-term ecological concerns.

Excessive state centralisation or politisation of institutions?

The process of decentralization in Senegal comprises both devolution of power from the central government to the local administration (deconcentration) and a handing over of specific responsibilities from the state to more or less autonomous and locally elected bodies; namely the rural councils and the well committees. Where the rural councils and the local administration are closely knit together in a web of obligations and control, the well committees enjoy, for better or for worse, a high degree of autonomy.

As illustrated by the case of Naoré, the direct effect of this handing over of control over local natural resources was not necessarily more efficient management. Rather the effect was in the first place that new arenas of struggle were being created with regards both to structures of authority and to the rights of access *per se*. Goheen explains this in the following way:"As access to land and authority over natural resources are being redefined by the state through the process of decentralization, contradictions, paradoxes and unintended consequences increase, and struggles over meaning and power intensifies". (Goheen 1992:403)

With regards to decentralisation, one could, as Sheldon Guellar, choose to perceive of the role of the state administrators as the prime obstacle for self governance and the rural councils as being deprived of their capacities for local initiative by flagrant state tutelage (Guellar, 1995:140). According to this interpretation, the well-committees would stand out as the example of genuine local associations characterized by institutional independence and financial autonomy.

Seen in the light of the Naoré conflict, it seems reasonable to question whether the unfolding of local initiative is in fact hindered by state interventions and whether the remedy likely to bring about the administrative efficiency advertised for is transfer of increased responsibilities to the local population. Is it at all possible to analyse the interrelation between the rural population and the state solely from the point of view of administrative efficiency, as a relation between simple order and an obedient rural dweller?

As discussed above, rules do not automatically determine people's behaviour. Many situations may force people to circumvent rules, just as they may chose to do so in order to fulfil some political or economic objective. Whether or not local initiatives are stifled remains an open question. Indeed, it seems more reasonable to analyse the 'management' of both well-committees and rural councils as a both creative and, and at least to some extent, functional adaptation of local institutions to the new management requirements. Such adaptation may take place in many unintended ways, as could be seen with the key role suddenly placed with the apparently insignificant well-committee. In the same vein, the considerable formal power attributed to the agents of the territorial administration as compared to that of the local institutions does not necessarily reflect the 'real' relations of power between these two parties. As could be observed in the checkmate situation of the *sous-préfet* in the Naoré case, formal authority does not necessarily go hand in hand with actual control. In many cases the area of state control turns out to be surprisingly limited.

Hence, a first problem when evaluating the extent of state control at local level relates to state representation. In areas as sparsely populated as the Ferlo region, each *communauté rurale* covers a vast area. Herders' relations to the state administration may therefore be very distant, a situation which is further aggravated by a permanent lack of vehicles, fuel etc. The rural council tends to be far better represented in the *chef lieu de l'arrondissement*, the central village, where also the *sous-préfet*s office and the *gendarmerie* are located, than in the small villages scattered over a vast territory.

Due to the extensive distances, the lack of information about the actual situation in the more remote areas and a generalized practice of informal arrangements, few of the conflicts played out in the field follow the official routines and formalised structures of decision making. In fact, many of the decisions concerning land attribution which formally are under the authority of the rural council, are taken locally without consent or approval of those formally elected. Accounts collected in the Ferlo as well as literature on tenure problems in Senegal abounds with examples of how land is attributed by the president of the rural council and 'officialised through his stamp on a typed petition' without any control or measurement by the CER or *sous-préfet* or even consent from the other members of the *Conseil Rural*[235] (see Blundo, 1995b:13; Le Roy, 1980; Mathieu, 1996 and Juul, 1991c). In other cases land is distributed by the village chief or simply taken by the user without any form of formal approval.

In short, the situation surrounding land attributions in large parts of Senegal may at best be characterized as imperfect. Attributing the responsibility for this chaotic situation solely on the excessive state interventions therefore seems unjustified.

In reality the control and influence of the state is severely restricted by the ambiguous position of the *sous-préfet* and the CER vis-à-vis the local population. For contrary to the vision of the state administration giving orders to an obedient population, it turns out that the local population to a wide extent evades, obstructs or transforms the orders of the authorities as part of a defensive strategy. As shown by Spittler, such defensive strategies may take many forms ranging from hiding or direct movement of villages into the bush to escape tax collection, labour demands or other forms of bureaucratic pressure, to ignoring or deformation of the commands and prohibitions of the state. Also simulation of agreement is a means by which herders or farmers hope to bargain with the minimum of annoyance and bring the subject to an end as quickly as possible (Spittler, 1979:30-32).

---

[235] The prospectings (missions de prospection) prescribed by the law before any attribution of land is carried out, are highly infrequent (communication of the President de Conseil Rural of Barkedji 1993, see also Blundo, 1995b:13). Only a small part of the plots attributed are registered in the books (*cahiers de délibération*) of the rural council (see Juul, 1991c). And in those cases where registration is carried out the actual size of the plot only in few cases corresponds to the extent registered, while its geographical location in most cases is omitted.

The effect of such strategies of defensive communication is obviously a low level of information on the part of the administration at local as well as at the central level. According to Spittler (ibid: 35) this lack of knowledge may be partly compensated for by force. For contrary to other forms of influence which implies some consideration of the situation as a whole, this is less a requirement with threat of force. This makes it easier to handle for the administrative authority. Alternatively, the administration may chose to give up the areas in which it is hardest to achieve success. The reaction of the state therefore becomes a paradoxical mixture of laissez-faire and force, a situation which also characterised the role of the state administrators in the Naoré case.

While the analysis proposed by Spittler of the interrelation between peasants and the state fit well with the situation of the Ferlo, his focus on the defensive aspects of the peasants' reactions tends to overlook the political power struggles going on between different groups of herders and peasants and the role of the administration herein. For where according to Spittler peasants attempt as much as possible to avoid situations which could bring them into contact with the holders of office in the government, herders in for example Naoré played a very active part in influencing or discrediting the agents of the administration as part of the struggle for political power[236].

The Naoré case also showed, how the *sous-préfet* acts within a highly politicised local environment where the administration is under strict control by the (ruling) Socialist Party[237]. Any *faux pas*, stemming from insufficient understanding of the intricacies of local politics, is likely to cost the local administrative officer his career or at least put a halt on any aspiration of moving closer to civilization and away from the dust storms and the heat of the Ferlo by way of a promotion. This situation was well recognized by the representatives of the local administration and was obviously a source of great frustration to the *sous-préfet* of Ogo. As a result,

---

[236] Where Spittler here seemingly approaches Hydens 'uncaptured peasant' in his focusing on peasant's autonomy from the state I prefer the view expressed by Berry (1993: 62) according to which people in general seek to activate ties to the state when gains can be made from it, and escape when state resources dwindle or political opponents gain the upper hand.

[237] The state administration is to a considerable degree interwoven with the structures of the ruling Socialist Parties. The large majority of administrative cadres are party members, just as all councillors, at least until the latest elections were members of the ruling party.

the *sous-prefét* and his officers, who are paralysed by the joint pressure from the Ministry, the political party structure and not the least the local politicians, tend as long as possible to adopt a *laissez-faire* attitude and to limit interventions and hence active responsibility to a minimum.

According to Spittler (1979:35), such circumstances forces the *sous-préfet*, who is under the obligation of reporting regularly and extensively to his hierarchic superiors to resort to the creation of a fictive reality in his monthly reports. This tendency by the local administrators of trying to keep out local disorder is labelled *institutional autism* by Geshiere (1984:22, see also Spittler, 1984:36[238] and Blundo, 1995b) and stems from a mixture of deficient knowledge of the realities of the vast area under his command, and out of fear of presenting local conflicts to the higher levels of an administrative hierarchy who will conceive of such local disorders primarily as disturbances, issue of the insufficient capabilities of the administrative officer.

Institutional autism and attempts to avoid getting to know about local conflicts may be traced in the many cases of local dispute where the pragmatic intervention of the local *sous-prèfet* or *chef de CER* has been to urge the local population of *"trouver un arrangement"*[239]. In this way, the administrator signals that even diversions of the law will be tolerated if only the administration is not concerned and peace reinstalled. The frequent cases of 'minimalistic' or overtly deficient minutes from council meetings engaged in conflict resolution also reflect such generalized reluctance towards 'officialising decisions' by writing them down and hence run the risk of giving cause for precedence[240]. Finally, it can be traced in the often

---

[238] Spittler (1984:37) refers to the disastrous situation of 1930-31 created by the colonial administrators in Niger when the district commissioners in spite of severe famine continuously reported of high input pr. hectare and an adequate provision for the population. Hence the blame for a bad harvest was attributed to the natives and their laziness. As the famine was finally recognized in 1932, the bureaucratic machinery was able "with its usual seeming precision to evaluate the victims to 26,167 dead and 29,311 emigrated to Nigeria".

[239] "Find a mutual arrangement" An example of such state 'disengagement' is given by Niasse (in Mathieu, 1996:67-68). But also the example of the administrations passive accept of pastoralist councillors attribution of large tracts of grazing lands to themselves (Velingara in 1990) is an example of such deliberate overlooking of trespassing of the law.

[240] It was interesting to note, that in the case of Naoré the decision of making a large meeting with representation from all the parties involved, including the extension officers,

surprisingly low level of information on the part of the administration for example regarding the amplitude and implications of post-drought migration. Obviously such lack of interest goes hand in hand with a tendency among administrators and extension officers of disregarding the mobile population. Having been educated in a system which regards nomadic herders as a residual category and an obstacle for any 'real' development of the rural areas, these administrators tend to favour the local, and settled population with which it is easier to establish stable relations and who fit better into the general picture of an *"administré"*.

A highly fluid situation prevails with regards to the arbitration of local conflicts, a situation in which decisions are frequently contested and renegotiated. As in the example of Naoré, local decisions are often overruled while decisions taken by the state very often are open ended. This leaves open space for renegotiations while the local administration is left in a sort of power vacuum. For the individual administrator this is often a source of frustrations leading to attempts to 'professionalize' the tasks assigned to the locally elected bodies:

"We ought to make a committee in charge of installing the newcomers. It should be formed by the extension officers in charge of agriculture and livestock production. The well committee is not able to evaluate the carrying capacity of the pastures. They would install people in a completely arbitrary manner. It should be a task for the local administration. (..) It's not the Rural Council which is in charge of pastures. They can make cattle tracks, but that's it. In each arrondissement the sous-préfet is the representative of all the Ministries, so he is in charge of coordinating the activities at local level". (Chef de CER, Barkedji, Febr. 1993).

But such attempts to defend the 'administrative territory' do not receive backing from above[241]. Decisions taken by the government tend to

---

the UNHCR representative etc. was criticised by some of the attendants for being an *un-african* form of problem-solving. The idea was that with so many witnesses present possibilities for individual negotiations were hampered just as the solution which was written down in the minutes could make room for precedence.

[241] See also the fate of the attempted re-engagement of the local state administrators into the well-committees above, which was dismissed by the government.

be vague and characterized by partial application of laws and decree, as in the example of Naoré.

The situation is further aggravated by the ambiguities and overlaps of the different legal texts juxtaposing the free and open access determined in the Law on the National Domain and the decentralization process according to which some authority of exclusivity is granted to the local resource management institutions. According to Mathieu and Hesseling (1986:309-325), this partial non-application of rules is neither accidental nor an example of the impotence of the state apparatus. Rather the gap between on the one side rules and principles and, on the other side, its effects in reality, must be seen as a sort of 'functional ambiguity', a situation of fluidity in which and through which arrangements can be made on the margin of legality in its strict sense. In this way a non-expressed consensus can be obtained between state and the different parties at local level, which is crucial for the process of transformation.

Inherent in this process is of course a constant strive for adjustment and accommodation where the different social actors seek to manoeuvre themselves into those positions which are most beneficial to his or her objectives and take most advantage of the opportunities offered by the moment. Here the dispute related to who is to be considered a 'regular' user eligible to the board of the committee is of course central.

Hence, penetration of state structures into the countryside is obviously far more restricted than anticipated by the critics of the obtrusive state. Farmers and herders often choose to ignore or circumvent state policies which do not fit into their particular interests, while bureaucrats to a wide extent limit their sphere of intervention into those areas where they do not get into conflicts with the ruling elites. The relation between state bureaucrats and the representatives of the local population can therefore not be described just as a one-way power relation between the 'administrator' and the *'administré'*. Rather it is characterized by a constant struggle for power and authority between different parties each disposing of different political means. Although critics are right when they claim that the decentralisation process in Senegal, particularly until 1990, was stifled by the excessive controlling powers attributed to the *sous-préfet* and the ministries of tutelage, the critique tends to underestimate both the political abilities of the local rural elites and the complexity of the task assigned to the administrative authority. Squeezed as they are between claims and diverging interests of the *marabouts*, the rural councils and the political party, the sphere of influence of the *sous-préfet* and his officers will often turn out to be extremely restricted.

As a result cases are many where strategies of peacekeeping and accommodation has dominated state intervention rather than attempts of keeping strictly to the letter of the law. Blundo even speaks of the process of '*socialisation de l'administration de tutelle*', referring to the ways in which any newly appointed *sous-préfet* will tend to cling to the political faction or tendency in majority and otherwise keep a minimum level of governmentality, in order to avoid administrative trouble (Blundo, 1995b:14). Contrary to what is anticipated, there is not necessarily any conflict between the locally elected representatives and the administrative personnel. Excessive state intervention is therefore seldom a proper diagnosis to understand the limited efficiency of local resource management institutions and transfer of power to local institutions no panacea to improve local management practices. As highlighted by the quotation below, rules do not necessarily determine people's behaviour, just as many different institutions may compete for the control over the same resources.

"It's difficult to talk of rules in relation to the Rural Council, for among Fulani people, one does not follow what is written down. Formally it's the rural council who should decide everything in relation to the management of the territory here. But that's not possible because of Pulaaku [Fulani solidarity]. People should make a request before settling in the area. But people just settle where they feel like. The Rural Council isn't informed of anything. People only negotiate with the Borehole Committee". (Agro-pastoralist, former president of the Rural Council, Thiargny, February 1993.)

6. POLITICAL AND SOCIAL REALIGNMENT IN A POST-DROUGHT CONTEXT

In the introduction, the importance of getting politics back into the study of natural resource management' was emphasized together with the need for uncovering the often unexpected and innovative ways in which drought victims have adapted to and eventually taken advantage of the post-drought situation. In fact 'getting politics back in' turns out to be an essential requirement if one is to explain the successful and dynamic adaptation of the FuutankoBe herders. But the success of the FuutankoBe herders also has to do with their ability to manoeuvre adeptly within the existing power relations and to take advantage of the current political opportunities. The present chapter contains the disentanglement of the political processes of adjusting the political and social institutions to a new emerging order - the political inception of the FuutankoBe herders and the impact on the post-drought migration movement on the institutions controlling water and pastures.

Not the least in areas as the Ferlo, where resources to a great extent are state-owned and governed as open access, normative codes play a crucial role in the regulation of access to resources. As socio-economic conditions change, in this case as a result of improved herd management, contradictions in the existing order, between for example individualized and communal property claims may be become more apparent. As a result new attempts to safeguard local resources and enforce exclusive rights are likely to emerge. In such situations, where the open pursuit of material gain and political power is acquiring new legitimacy, specific events such as droughts may, as mentioned above, play a vital role in providing a moral pretext for rendering legitimate claims and social practices that have been considered socially unacceptable. Under the guise of caring for the well-being of the local community, a process of transformation of the normative codes regulating access to crucial resources such as water and pastures is set in motion.

As mentioned earlier, opportunities for such social and political adjustment have been provided through the smaller and more localised droughts which have occurred on several occasions during the 1990s, notably the drought of 1990-1993. For the old sedentarised elites these events provided the opportunity for re-enforcing their position in relation to local power relations and for positioning themselves more favourably in the competition over local resources. For the emerging elites of rich newcomer pastoralists it respresented an opening for driving a wedge into the existing institutions involved in local resource management in getting part the control over key institutions in local resource management.

Increased mobility and exclusive management practices

The attempts to restrict access to local resources and enforce exclusive rights became particularly pronounced between 1991 and 1993 when failing rains in the Northern Ferlo during two successive years propelled a new wave of migration from the Senegal River Valley southward to the less affected areas south of the Linguère-Matam axis. Already in the beginning of the rainy season of 1991 when it became clear that rains would be deficient, the most livestock-rich herders from the Senegal River Valley started moving southward to join their kin in the southern Ferlo. The movement of these animals took place at a steady pace, giving the animals the opportunity to graze and recover at the various boreholes or wells traversed.

At certain wells these movements resulted in a tripling of the number of animals presumed to share the meagre pastures available. Obviously, this created anxiety among the local population who foresaw that they would be forced to migrate themselves, once the large foreign herds had stripped the area of fodder. Transhumance for these, in some cases relatively poor agro-pastoralists, implies numerous constraints, as it is demanding in terms of labour and logistics just as it is likely to hamper carrying out of other supplementary income-generating activities. In an attempt to reserve the meagre resources for themselves, new and hitherto untried methods were therefore put into service to limit access to the pastures. As can be read out of the statements below, this resulted in a rising level of conflict throughout the Ferlo:

"In the entire Ferlo people are doing things to limit the access of foreigners. As far north as Tessekre, the well committees have closed the borehole a few days to avoid that herders from the waalo settle. It's mainly to avoid illnesses. But in some areas people have even taken to burning their own pastures to avoid the arrival of foreigners". (FuutankoBe herder on transhumance near Loumbi Aly Thedy febr. 1993)

"The local population will do anything to get rid of the foreign herds. Either they do not fill up the reservoirs properly, so that animals cannot drink adequately. In other cases they force you to continue your voyage after having paid a fortune for a single watering. At the boreholes of

Linde and Thiel they closed off the pump for a whole week, and told people that it was broken, just to get the foreigners to move away. Many herders from the north are beginning to be afraid of moving south after these latest experiences." (Transhumant herder, Thiargny febr. 1993)

"The transhumant herds have completely finished the pastures here, and we'll all be forced to leave. I have stayed put around the borehole of Djagueli for the last many years, moving only between my dry season and my wet season camp. But with all the newcomers, my animals cannot any longer find pastures on the day where they go for watering. Herders here wanted the well committee to limit the number of newcomers, but they want to earn money. Personally I don't want to prohibit installation of newcomers, but it would be good to limit the numbers coming at each well. In that way the motor-pump could be spared without increasing the taxes". (FuutankoBe herder, resident of the southern Ferlo since 1973, Djagueli, Febr. 1993).

"Last year we were forced to limit the number of transhumants. They say that all Senegalese have the same rights. All the village chiefs around Djagueli got together and held a meeting. It was decided that transhumants could come and let the animals drink, and then continue elsewhere. We're saturated here. We contacted the souspréfet and the rural council. After that people have respected the decision." (Chef de village Djagueli, Oct. 1994).

"There is much more jealousy now than was the case in 1983/84. It's now, where they have started copying on the newcomers and have large herds themselves, that the problems of rivalry arise"..(Herder from Mbiddi, on transhumance near Loumbi Aly Thedy, Febr. 1993).

Comparing the level of conflicts and competition (or as phrased by the Fulani 'the degree of jealousy') over resources from the great drought periods of the 1970's and 1980's till now is of course a hazardous endeavour. For obvious reasons, it is problematic, in retrospect, to assess the degree of conflict which resulted from the insertion of the first contingent of "drought refugees" in the beginning of the seventies and eighties. Sufficiently reliable sources concerning the acceptance and tolerance of the local population vis-à-vis refugees of the droughts in the seventies and eighties are not available. In addition, reference to a traditionally high degree of solidarity in an undefined past would be tantamount to undermining the previous arguments where it was stressed how pastoral production strategies tend to be based mainly on individualistic decisions.

The impression is, nonetheless, that although conflicts and contradictions are recurrent phenomena in both intra-herder and nomad/sedentary relations (Hussein 1998), the general porosity and latent mobility inherent in these communities ensured a relatively peaceful reception of foreigners in what might be characterised as the first wave of drought related migration.

This peaceful insertion was also assured by the FuutankoBe herders, who kept a relatively low profile vis-à-vis the settled population. They camped mainly in remote areas and endured, to a wide extent, the malice inflicted upon them by the 'first-comer' population. The general impression is that herders in accordance with the passive co-ordination strategy described by Niamir (1900:32) in general sought to avoid conflicts and confrontations and accepted their status as 'strangers' with all it's connotations of marginal representation in the local resource management institutions.

In the course of the late 1980s and early 1990s the large majority of foreign' herders had managed successfully to rebuild their herds and could no longer be considered as drought ridden and destitute kin, victims of climatic hazards and calamities. On the contrary, concurrently with the economic consolidation of the foreign herders, it became clear that what distinguishes the settled first-comer population from the so-called strangers was not so much the date of installation but rather the very mobile lifestyle and the new herd management strategies which they had adopted. It was these differences in strategies, which have contributed to what by some first-comers has been considered as a situation of unequal competition.

When a new wave of southward movement began to take shape in connection with the drought period of 1991/93 the indigenous population began to fear that these herders too would settle in the area on a more permanent basis, thus increasing the ratio of foreigners to locals. Claims for exclusive rights, which had been addressed ever more fiercely during this period, erupted into genuine struggles to secure control over key institutions of resource management such as the well committees. Without stretching the argument too far, it seems liable that this pressure was stronger than was the case during the drought years of the seventies and eighties. In this sense the drought of 1991/92 which affected only the northern half of the Ferlo[242], fits well into the label of revelatory crises or event of articulation, characterised as shorter and evanescent events used as a pretext for rendering formerly illegitimate claims acceptable. As will be shown below,

---

[242] Mainly north of Tessekre.

the drought contributed not only to an upsurge of distinctions between (more) settled first-comers and mobile newcomers but also opened up for a process of privatisation of former common property resources and of commoditisation of formerly reciprocal arrangements.

Limiting access to water: the technical' solutions

As described above the migration wave prompted by the failing rains involved considerable inconvenience for the local population. As a means of self-defence a variety of new measures were taken by the local well committees to limit the access of strangers to the wells. Although methods varied, they aimed above all at making watering of large (foreign) herds as difficult as possible.

"Many of the small boreholes [puits-forages] do not function at present. They aren't even broken. People just don't want to make them function. They want to avoid having the transhumants to come. Therefore people have been getting together and have decided not to start the pump. They will turn it on once all the transhumants have passed. It's the first time that we hear of such measures being brought to use".(Agropastoralist Loumbi Sanrabe jan.1992)

"The pumps of Lour and Lombi Balaï have been closed to avoid that transhumants settle there. It's the first time that this method is employed. If you are ready to haul water by hand they let you stay, but those who have many animals are forced to continue. I think that it's evil. The wells were drilled by the state, they are meant for watering of animals. Its not because there are too many animals that they do this. It's because they want to stick to themselves". (Mauritanian refugee, Loumbi Sanrabe, Jan 1992).

Discouraging large herd-owners by forcing them to haul water manually is however only possible at the *puits-forages*. This well type, where water may be drawn either by hand or by pump can be installed only in those areas where ground water tables are relatively high-lying, as in certain parts of the eastern Ferlo. At the deep artesian boreholes found over the rest of the Ferlo, hand drawing is impossible. Therefore certain well committees obstructed the connection between the reservoir and the drinking troughs of the animals so that the individual herders had to draw water by means of a hose sunk into the reservoir. Animals were then watered at an oil drum. In this way the time and effort spent on watering increased significantly.

The event depicted in the box, describes some of the controversies which arose as the flow of water from the reservoir to the troughs was constrained as part of the politics of keeping away foreign herders.

> **"We are now paying to water the soil, not to water the animals"**
>
> During the dry season of 1992/93 the well-committee of Ranérou did not open the connection between the water reservoir and the troughs. Herders were forced to water their animals by means of a hose whereby only 10-15 animals could be watered at a time. For the well-committee the aim was that to make the deep-well less attractive, particularly for those herders possessing large herds, and to make it easier to survey if any (foreigner) was watering without paying. According to the well-committee, it was also a way to force 'foreigners' to install themselves at the same distance from the borehole as themselves. This was justified, among other things, by a wish to protect the gum producing *acacia senegal* stands from marauding 'foreign' goats. As a result of the new practice large amounts of water was wasted and a huge mud puddle was created around the borehole, increasing the liability of cholera infestations to occur and seriously damaging the foundation of the reservoir. As expressed by the herders: "We are now paying to water the soil, not the animals".
>
> A first attempt by the FuutankoBe herders to protest against the actions of the well-committee did not give any positive result. Rather the foreigners were told to submit to the regulations made by the
> indigenous population. Later on, however, the case was brought to the local representative of the Ministry of Waterworks who showed up to object to the on-going destruction of state property. Nonetheless, the practice was continued.
>
> .../

> .../
> In the opinion of the local veterinary assistant, it is primarily the FafaBe herders who are pressuring for closing off the connection. This group of cattle-rich herders is the ones competing most directly with the newcomers over the pastures. They are, according to the veterinary: "against the FuutankoBe herders". According to rumours it was these FafaBes who managed to bribe the well-committee president into keeping the connection closed in spite of the recommendations of the Ministry of Waterworks.
>
> As in many similar cases, the incidence ended by getting to a violent outcome. In mid-November when Bathil Ba returned from transhumance the troughs of the deep-well of Ranerou were still blocked. While watering his animals by means of the hose, another herder wanted him to move away, claiming that it was his turn. Bathil refused, fearing that if he stopped watering before his animals were satisfied the man's cattle would trample down his sheep. As he didn't obey the other herder hit him twice in the head with a machete causing Bathil to go to hospital. They were taken to court and the herder had to make his excuses and pay him a compensation of 50.000 CFA. The day after, the troughs were opened.

Obviously, considerable ambiguity reigns regarding both the legality of these actions and what state institutions are responsible for stopping such actions. On the one hand everyone seems well aware that both wells and boreholes are public and access therefore is open. On the other hand the intervention of the Ministry of Waterworks was strictly limited to the eventual damage to public infrastructure (the undermining of the foundation of the reservoir) and did not go further into the question of restriction of use rights. On the contrary, they refrained from reacting when the malpractice persevered. And as access to water is not denied (which would be against the law) but hauling only made more difficult, the motivation for the *sous-préfet* or the police-forces to intervene was likely to be low. For as discussed above, local administrators in charge of securing law and order are generally favourable to local solutions aiming at restricting uncontrolled migration and free-riding on the local resource base. Besides they tend in general to be unwilling to mingle in local disputes, not the least if spheres of competence are as unclear as is the case here. It was therefore only when the hostilities developed into open violence that an intervention on behalf of the state administration was carried out.

Finally, the case is interesting in the sense that it shows how certain individual herders or well committees have taken advantage of the migration wave to try and discourage some of the 'old' FuutankoBe households, such as Bathil's, from resettling in the area, when returning from their periodic transhumance.

Scarcity and other justifications

Justifications for keeping out the migrants are various but often centre on the prospects of a situation of scarcity and on the fear of infestation from diseases presumably carried around by transhumant herds:

"The transhumants have destroyed the pastures. They come from the waalo or they are refugees from Mauritania. If they hadn't come, pastures would have been sufficient for us and there wouldn't have been any problems with the sheep. But they have brought with them diseases that affect both sheep and cattle." (Rural Councillor, Jaen Fuuta Jan. 1992).

Also concern over the state of the mechanical equipment of the borehole or, in the Eastern Ferlo, the question of protection of the gum producing *acacia senegal* stands are prominent causes for worry. As herders are spread around in the bush it becomes difficult to protect this important source of income from the hungry goats of transhumant herders[243].

"We have received many more animals than usually this year. The pump works from 7 in the morning to midnight with a 2 hour break in the afternoon. There are at least 700 foreign heads of cattle and a much larger amount of smallstock for each transhumant bring with them 50, 400 or 200 smallstock[244] *They eat up all the pastures and bring with them*

---

[243] While goats devouring of the gum arabic bubbles exuded from the trees are frequent also among indigenous herds, the transhumants themselves are also cause for worry among the gum-tappers who frequently accuse them of having and sold the gum exuded from trees tapped by others.

[244] The importance number of transhumant herds arriving at certain deep-wells during the 1991-93 drought can be read out of the data collected by the local veterinary assistant of

diseases. The well committee cannot do anything to control the situation. There is no way we can regulate it. We started out trying to force the foreigners to camp away from the acacia groves, but it isn't possible. The only place where you find some pastures is in between the acacia trees. It isn't possible to prohibit people from coming. The problems is the lack of rain, not the arrival of the transhumants. But there are too many animals now[245]. *If more arrive we won't be able to provide sufficient water"*. (President of the well-committee, Jaen Fuuta. jan 1992.)

Herders generally express considerable ambiguity towards attempts at excluding transhumant herds. In the present case this is expressed through the competing explanations between the neutral notion of failing rains and the more subjective reference to excess of animals. Justification for limiting the numbers is therefore often expressed in other terms. Very often common 'environmental flaws' such as bushfires or illegal cutting of trees, are attributed to the uncivilised behaviour of foreign herders, just as the growing problems of theft of animals is assigned to the foreigners, either as deliberate robbery or in terms of local animals joining foreign herds.

Finally the authorities have pointed to the fact that the early arrival of the transhumants contributed to increasing the cases of crop damage. This is true not the least for the number of officially recognised cases. For just as the increased number of animals present in the cultivation season increases the chances of trespass and crop damage, the more distant relations between foreign herders' and local farmers also put a strain on tolerance and friendly relationships[246]. As more cases are brought for settlement by the administrative authorities, the number of cases known to a wider public automatically increases. An obvious cause for worry is the

---

Velingara in January 1992. According to him 18.000 heads of cattle were watered at the well, of which 5.000 were 'foreign'. To this was added at least 10.000 foreign heads of small-stock.

[245] According to the accounts of the well committee, the borehole of Jaen Fuuta hosted 23 'foreign' households during the month of January. This relates to a local population which according to the national census of 1988 (Repertoire des Villages, Region de St. Louis) is of approximately 95 households or 500 persons.

[246] The intervention of the CER and the extension officers had, according to the agricultural extension officer in Barkedji, been requested in no less than 20 cases of crop damage during 1990. In a normal year this is restricted to only a few particularly serious cases.

limited or at least contradictory authority and restricted means held by the local institutions in charge of managing access to resources. Views expressed by different interviewees clearly verbalise this confusion:

"The councillors and the village chiefs have discussed what to do. They have proposed to get the President of the Rural Council to mobilise the Police Forces, but they haven't yet made use of this means. It's much easier to convince the well committee to deny access to water to those foreigners who do not accept to camp where it is proposed by the councillors. In one case a herder refused to move to the allocated spot. He was denied access to water and within a week he had moved out". (Rural councillors, Jaen Fuuta. Jan 1992).

Nonetheless, it is clear that few legal means for restricting the access of foreigners are available. Considering both the absence of restrictions in the letter of the law and the distance (over 50 km's) to the police forces, the call upon the police to expel Senegalese citizens from a public well, seems a hollow threat. As expressed below, the use of "technical" and hence not directly illegal dispositions seems a more adequate manner to deal with the increased number of transhumants:

"With the law on the National Domain it is very difficult to prohibit people using the well and the pastures. There are no rules to apply. The wells are private property. Nonetheless, it's very difficult to limit access. The only way to limit the number of newcomers is to block access to water. If the well contains little water, the foreign herders are likely to abandon the area within a short time, but if the well has plenty of water, it is almost impossible to persuade people to go elsewhere." (Rural Councillor, notorious for having chased many foreign herders away, BemBem. Febr. 1993).

The various attempts at making the borehole unattractive for foreign herds listed above indicate the increased resource competition experienced in the Ferlo in years of partial or total rain deficit. Evidently the arrival of large numbers of transhumant herders often possessing very large herds constitutes a considerable constraint for local agro-pastoralists. The migratory movements from the North tends to trigger a "domino effect", whereby herders in the less affected areas are forced to follow the migrants once the scarce local fodder resources have been devoured. Such movements are likely to further social differentiation as small herd-owners tend not to have the same capacities for moving to more abundant pastures as have the more livestock-rich. Indeed it seems that the attempts directed toward discouraging large foreign herd-owners from settling were more widespread in the eastern Ferlo, where the indigenous population primarily consists of relatively fixed agro-pastoralists possessing herds and flocks of more moderate sizes. As shown below, attempts to take economic advantage of the increased mobility have been adopted more frequently in central Ferlo.

Taking advantage of the drought situation: the economic solution

The most frequent strategy set forth was the enforcement of exorbitant watering fees on foreign herds. This practice has, as mentioned above, been frequent throughout the Ferlo since the 1980s. Nonetheless, the increased mobility of the early 1990's encouraged the development of still more excessive taxation policies. During the dry seasons of 1991/92 and 1992/93 migrating herders in the *arrondissements* of Ogo and Barkedji could unanimously recount how excessive taxes or direct denial of access had forced them to zigzag through the area in order to find a well where, as a minimum, the livestock could be watered before the voyage towards more friendly localities could be resumed.

Many herders claimed to have used significant sums to bribe the various well committees and/or pay sums equivalent to a full month of watering at their usual well just to use the watering facilities of certain wells for a few days[247]. The considerable variation in taxing practices is well illustrated by the record made by Bathil of his transhumance trip in 1992/93:

"At our first stop in Fourdou I didn't pay anything. People there are all our relatives. In Naoré where we stayed 2 weeks, prices were reasonable. I paid 2.500 CFA for 14 days. The well of BemBem was the most expensive. There we had to pay 6000 CFA just for one week. After that we stayed in Loumbi, where the price was 14.000 CFA per month. At the well of Diamel, we paid 15.000 per month in salary to those who were hauling water. We had to provide bucket and tackle ourselves. Then I paid 10.850 at the borehole of Loumbi Aly Tedy for one month of watering.

---

[247] Due to the lack of transparency it is difficult to get an accurate picture of the prices paid. Arrangements are variable as are the services involved. One herder for example complained that the price of 3000 CFA Francs for donkey-carts in some boreholes covered several carts, while at other one had to pay separately for each cart.

Finally in Malem Ba where we stayed 1 month and 19 days, I had to spend 36.000 CFA corrupting people and 20.000 in total on watering fees at the borehole. This is to compare to the fees I pay back home in Ranerou of 7.250 CFA per month".

As mentioned, extraction of higher taxes for foreign herds normally means lower taxes for what is considered to be the 'indigenous' population. Whether that is the case is obviously difficult to assess as the number of animals in the herd seldom are counted and taxation of 'local' herds to a wide extent is based on estimates which are not written down. Nonetheless it seems obvious that the alleviation of watering taxes contributes to make the arrival of large contingents of transhumants more acceptable to the local population. Securing such external 'funding' has, as mentioned, at some boreholes become a more a less deliberate strategy (where taxes are deliberately set a little lower than at the neighbouring well, in order to attract the maximum number of transhumants). In fact, a three layer taxation system may be discerned whereby FuutankoBe herders who have been residing in the area for several years are overtaxed according to 'usual' rates, while new transhumants are more excessively taxed.

This graduation of taxing could be read out of the common practice of using a *diategui*, a host, in whose name you can water your animals or who can negotiate the taxation rates which are to be applied. This practice of using a host, also points to some of the many ways in which the presumed 'victims' of these policies of exclusivity manage to evade attempts at discrimination. Such services are of course reciprocal in the sense that they often release granting of certain favours to the host, just as they contribute to increase the host's personal status:

"I arrived to Loumbi in 1973 as part of a larger group of FuutankoBe herders. But I was the only one to stay. I'm a hunter and there was a lot of deer in this area. When the drought of 1983/84 pushed a new wave of FuutankoBe herders to the area, I helped them to get installed, The local population wasn't too friendly, so I undertook the negotiations concerning access to the well. There are always some of the locals who want to chase away the newcomers, but I'm there to help settle the matters. Now there is a better understanding between the two parties". (FuutankoBe, Loumbi Aly Thedy, Koumpentoum 1993).

Not only legal means have been used in the attempt to make the best of the situation. The installation of foreigners also provided certain political notabilities a new possibility for extraction of material gain. At a public meeting with the Governor of Louga in Barkedji in 1993, a new practice was revealed where certain rural councillors abused their authority to make transhumant herders pay for the right to install themselves in the pastures. This clearly illegal practice was vigorously condemned at the meeting. Whether the practice was widespread or not remained unclear as no one would stand up and admit to have received or have been given anything as part of a negotiation regarding provisional settlement. Nonetheless no one seemed to doubt the existence of such practices:

"People negotiate their provisional settlement with the village chiefs[248]. It's not in conformity with the law, they are all Senegalese. Nobody will admit to have received or given anything to anyone as payment for their installation. As rains have failed again this year the illegal commercialisation of rights of settlement will probably resume again". (Sousprefet, Barkedji, Oct. 1994).

According to other sources, such illicit commoditisation of the right of settlement may be carried out under different guises. Frequently, the councillor will claim that the transhumant has settled on what is a recognised cattle path (an issue under the authority of the rural council).'Payment' then takes the form of a "fine" paid to the councillor. In this way it represents yet another example of how such commoditisation of former reciprocal arrangements (the free movements on the range) is given a 'legal guise', thereby making it socially more acceptable.

Exclusivity and the heterogeneity of interests

Nonetheless, this transgression of Fulani norms of hospitality is not necessarily acceptable for the population as such. In line with the ambiguities running through many of the statements cited above, many local herders have expressed their concerns over the ill-treatment of foreigners:

"Closing off the wells is not correct behaviour. The calamities which have forced these people to move could affect us next time - and besides where there are many people there is also more happiness."

---

[248] It's interesting that the sous-préfet blames village chiefs for this illicit practice, as all other sources pointed to the councilors. Apart from the possibility of it being a slip of the tongue, one explanation could be that the position of the sous-prefet is under far more pressure from the politically elected councilors than from the village chiefs.

(President of the well-committee, Loumbi Sanrabe 1992).

Neither the denial of access to the watering facilities, the differential and excessive taxing of the migrating herds nor (few) the attempts at trading the rights of camping on the open range are in accordance with the customary norms and regulations related to local resource management. Nor do they conform with the legal framework covering watering and grazing facilities, which stresses the equal and open access rights of all Senegalese. Putting forward claims of exclusivity to resources that have previously been free for all has therefore required considerable efforts in terms of constructing a moral pretext for transgression of Fulani solidarity.

Notwithstanding, the reaction of the local population is full of contradictions and ambiguities. Especially at the smaller *puits-forages* in the eastern Ferlo, which are normally not used by more cattle-rich agro-pastoralists due to the labour constraints attached, the gestures of closing the pumps must be interpreted as clear acts of panic from a population with few alternative means of survival.

At the larger boreholes the situation is less clear. Here the cry for exclusive rights is promoted primarily by the politically strongest groups of herders and agriculturalists. It is mainly among these groups that the situation of scarcity is put forward as justification for restricting the use of commonly owned resources such as water and pastures. In this way they seek to adjust the system in their favour. For while high degrees of permeability and free access to water and pastures are preconditions for a mobile and extensive livestock system, the indigenous system of production has been in a process towards increasing sedentarisation ever since the installation of boreholes in the 1950's. Such a system evidently works in favour of development of more exclusive rights. For these groups mobility no longer contains the same predominance as a risk management strategy whereas exclusive rights may enhance possibilities for more pragmatic herding strategies where pastures are preserved for a limited group of users. It is also among these groups that scarcity most frequently has been used as a means to legitimate the tendency towards a commoditisation of social relations, as could be traced in the attempts to generate revenues on their drought ridden kin, both through watering fees and by trading the rights of camping on the range.

The call for exclusivity is nonetheless not without its contradictions. First of all, the arrival of the economically potent foreign herders increases prosperity not only though the deep wells, but also in the general economic life of the villages. Local trade in livestock, often an important supplementary activity of the local agro-pastoralists is boosted, as are the weekly markets. The same goes for sale of grain from the peasants and the turn-over of the local shops, owned to a large extent by the settled agro-pastoralists. Furthermore, the foreigners may contract local youth as salaried herders just as a wealth of services and gifts are exchanged to improve the relations between the two parties:

"I get along very well with the transhumants. I do not wish them to leave. We help each other hauling and transporting water. When they go looking for hay, they always provide us with a cart-load, and they lend us their oil drums and their hose so that we can draw water from the reservoir. If they go to the market in Galoya [in the Fuuta] you can always get a lift on their cart. At present the transhumants don't get any milk, but otherwise they would be sure to offer you some". (Sedentarised herder with few animals, Loumbi SanraBe, 1992).

"The only one who has shown some hospitality to us is the shopkeeper. He also defended us at the meeting". (Transhumant herder, Thiargny, 1993).

And even at borehole level one finds examples of well committees which have intervened more directly to ensure more peaceful relations.

"Last year rains were good and many transhumants herds stayed in the area. All went well. The well committee had engaged a griot [traditional praise singer] to travel around in the settlements to tell people that the transhumants have the same rights as the rest of the population". (Agro-pastoralist, Thiargny 1993).

In reality the opposition between 'foreigners' and 'locals' is less antagonistic, than what could be anticipated from the conflicts described above. Many alliances and social relations are created and upheld between the two groups, alliances which may be brought into effect for example in the struggle against the encroachment of peanut farmer upon grazing lands. Part of the explanation for the significant decrease in requests and attributions of land to Mouride *marabouts* and peanut growers in the course of the 1990s could be attributed to the numerical and economic reinforcement of herders vis-à-vis the cultivators, provided by the FuutankoBe 'invasion' in the area. This situation enforced herders' possibilities of presenting their protest at higher state-administrative levels.

Furthermore, it is important to note that, although mobility for these relatively sedentarised herders has decreased in some ways, it has not disappeared altogether. In a highly risk-prone area as the Ferlo, local or generalised drought, bush fires, ticks, disease, or failure of crops still requires the possibility of seeking refuge in less affected areas[249].

Also the frequent breakdown of borehole equipment favours a less hostile relationship with neighbouring communities. In fact the tendency for increased sedentarisation is paralleled by a tendency towards increased mobility. As described in chapter 4, the technological innovation provided by the tubes has largely been taken up by local agro-pastoralists who now attach more importance to raising small stock. Together with this strategy goes the adoption of more mobile lifestyles, although seldom as mobile as those followed by the FuutankoBe herders.

This brings about a paradoxical situation where herders stress mobility and the need to move across the range when describing their herd management, but their fixed location when discussing rights to water and pastures[250]. Consequently motivation for co-ordinating resource use has seldom been sufficient to support development of an extended set of rules and of institutions capable of the implementation and sanctioning of such regulations. Struggles to limit the number of users should therefore not be confused with a desire to improve local resource management or an urge for more sustainable methods of resource extraction. For as conflicts tend to be related more to struggles to gain control over key institutions than to competition over presumably scarce pastoral resources, it becomes the political power likely to be generated through securing of control over the productive resources rather than ecological concerns which are at stake.

Before passing to a general discussion of the struggles over resource control in post-drought Ferlo, it is interesting to have a closer look

---

[249] Among the more sedentarised herders who have been most eager to exclude foreign herds are the herders from Widou Thiengoly and Tessekre. Nonetheless, these herders have, at several occasions, been forced to move southward because of large bush-fires (1988) and droughts (1991 and 1993) and have been forced to capitalize on a solidarity to which they did not contribute in their area of origin.

[250] A similar situation is described by Peters from Botswana (1994:108)

at the reactions of the FuutankoBe herders to these attempts to strengthen local control with the resources crucial for pastoral production: water and pastures.

The reaction of the FuutankoBe herders

As noted above, nomadic societies are generally characterised by a lack of central institutions and systems of political representation. Reactions to harassment therefore tend to be individual and passive (as the 'passive choreography' described by Niamir above) in order to avoid conflicts. In those cases where the herder disposes of sufficient means he will try to settle conflicts through individual arrangements This will in many cases involve bribing neighbours, local politicians or eventually local administrative authorities. Ultimately herders under pressure may chose to make use of their mobile lifestyle and move away from areas of conflict. As a result Fuutanke herders in the first period of settlement in the southern Ferlo have involved themselves very little in local affairs.

Confronted with the general mismanagement of the wells and with an increasing number of attempts by certain 'local' groups to use the well committees as a means of exclusion or extraction of revenues, the FuutankoBe herders have embarked on a set of new strategies.

Improving the bargaining position

Increasingly, well committees have come under pressure from Fuutanke herders who demand representation on the board in order to ensure proper functioning and to control the considerable financial resources collected by the well committee.

"Those who are in the well committees hardly possess any animals themselves. It has been almost impossible to react against all the abnormalities. Now, after the dry years, we are more egge-egges, and we are better able to react against the malpractice. We are getting organised to get more control over the well-committee and more information about the money, the turnovers etc. We have the means to go to the authorities. For us it is an advantage if many FuutankoBe herders come to settle here. That could make things change, but the inconvenience is that it would increase competition on pastures". (FuutankoBe herder, Ranerou Febr.1993).

"We have tried to make a well committee comprised of only herders with many animals. We ensure that the reservoir is always full of water, and that transhumants are received on the same conditions as those settled around the well. Often those who come will have a relative who is member of the well-committee, and this relative will explain the modalities to the newcomer. We receive a lot of transhumants every year. That's because we are friendlier. After the FuutankoBe herders are represented in the well committee, they function much better. Now it's recognised that the well is for everybody and everybody pays. The local population recognises the rights of the newcomers, although in the beginning we had to keep quiet." (Accountant, well-committee, Fourdou)

The first-comers have in general exhibited fierce resistance to any division of power, an attitude which in most cases has been backed by the local administration. Such resistance is most frequently legitimised by suggesting a dichotomy between 'strangers' and 'locals'. In this way the 'local' population seeks to establish a discourse linking up with a central assumption in the decentralisation framework, the existence of a homogeneous and fixed group of local users, which should be given more firm property right including the rights to exclude 'foreigners' from use and decision making[251]. But as mentioned, the existence of such clearly defined groups of users is certainly a matter of (re)definition in areas such as the Ferlo which, due to variability in climate and resource use, are characterised by high degrees of mobility and therefore a very fluctuating population.

The perpetual embezzlement of funds which characterises the large majority of well committees in the area has, nonetheless, lead to an almost chronic financial deficit. This has opened up for a new situation where wealthy FuutankoBe herders are able to trade representation in the committee in exchange for financial help in emergency situations. If the pump breaks down, herders are forced to move their herds to a neighbouring borehole, located approximately 25 km away. This involves considerable risk for herd-owners (notably those used to a more sedentary lifestyle). Purchase of expensive spare-parts has therefore proved to be a comfortable platform for negotiating a partition of power within the committee[252].

---

[251] See for example Bromley and Cernea, 1989:15.

[252] This strategy had been used successfully in at least 3 cases (in Djagueli, in Yonofere and in Fourdou).

"Later there was a problem with the borehole pump. The rural council told us to decide among the village chiefs whether we would pay and have it repaired or wait until the brigade of waterworks could find the means to repair it. The local herders had no possibilities of paying. We decided to take it in charge and collected 700.000 CFA for the repair". (Village chief of Fidjiti, Djagueli).

In return for this favour, the *UrurBe* population, who have been present around Djagueli in large numbers since the beginning of the 1970's were granted two key positions within the well committee (that of president as well as that of accountant).

Such decisions are nonetheless always open for renegotiation. In spite of the feeling of superiority expressed in the underscoring of the limited economic resources of the local users, the new (and evidently more adequate) representation proved short-lived. Within a period of less than a year, the first-comers managed, in spite of their numerical inferiority and restricted economic assets, to overthrow this new board and re-conquer the central key-position of president. Needless to say all these transactions have been taking place without any preceding elections.

The attribution of seats in the well-committee is not solely a matter of making the well function properly. Along with the growing recognition of the key status of the well committee, the committees have also become the scene of local power struggles between representatives from different factions (see the *souspréfets* condemnation of the battles between tendency A and tendency B in Naoré, for example). Being vital institutions in local economic and political life, the well-committees are used by the local political elite to gain support for their own political career within the ruling and (until recently) all embracing Socialist Party. This is particularly true for those smaller villages where other state connected institutions (such as the Rural Council or the *sous-préfet* and CER) are not present.

In such cases, FuutankoBe herders have managed to play very skilfully on the internal rivalry between opposing political candidates of the local community. Local purchase of party cards plays a crucial role in the internal alignment of candidates as they are used to measure the support that opposing tendencies within the ruling Socialist Party can mobilise on the local level (see Cruise O'Brien 1975:174). In times of approaching elections, FuutankoBe herders who constitute an important economic backing for some of the local candidates, have refused to purchase any party cards before the posts of treasurer or president were granted to a representative of the FuutankoBe population.

> **Bargaining party cards for representation**
>
> *"In 1987 when many FuutankoBe herders were present in Yonofere we held a meeting. It was decided that as it was the FuutankoBe population who paid the bulk (80%) of the running costs of the borehole we wanted to be represented in the board with at least 2 members. It was in connection with the presidential elections. FuutankoBe herders therefore conditioned their purchase of party cards by the granting of board membership.*
>
> *Last year the indigenous population wanted to over throw the board. This is why we called upon the sous-préfet. The indigenous population did not want to have transparency in the running of the borehole, although it worked very well. There were more than 750.000 CFA set aside for repairs and maintenance.*
>
> *Then the local rural councillor died. He had always received the FuutankoBe population very well. After he died the indigenous population took up their hostile behaviour again. At present the local population is hoping that the FuutankoBe herders want us to foot the bill and pay to repair the motor. But we won't do it unless we get posts in the board in return.*
>
> *Lately, they [the indigenous, primarily SanraBe board members] have confined a number of donkeys. To set them free, they demand 2000 Francs. They claim that it's to cover their watering fees."* (FuutankoBe accountant of the well-committee, Yonofere).

Also in other cases (as in Naoré), it seems that political support for certain members of the well committee, was a term of trade for the 'foreign' herders to gain access to the board of the committee.

Both cases point not only to the fluidity of political representation but also to the importance of personal political relations. As can be seen, decisions regarding board representation in the key institutions are always open for renegotiation. Rather than determined by the existing rules and regulations (concerning transparency of accounts or democratic representation), the outcome is to a wide extent determined by the ability of the various actors to manoeuvre skilfully in the power structures reigning at the moment, taking advantage of the various opportunities (such as the national elections or the mechanical breakdowns) offered.

Investment in clientelistic networks

Evidently many of these victories are temporary and may be modified once the power relations at the local level turn in favour of the 'locals'. In the words of the deputy of the *Préfet* of Matam:

"Every time there is trouble in the management of the wells, some FuutankoBes are integrated into the well-committee in order to get hold of some money; afterwards they get rid of them again".

In order to strengthen their positions, FuutankoBe herders therefore increasingly participate in political power struggles and seek to position themselves to gain control over resources. In this process investment of their newly acquired economic wealth into social capital is also used.

Until recently many FuutankoBe herders, conscious of their weak political position as foreigners, sought to settle conflicts through individual negotiations. *Arrangements a l'amiable* (arrangements on friendly terms) have been the most common way of settling for example cases of crop damages. This ranges from "tolerating" (i.e. making no demand for compensation) to open negotiation between the two parties, eventually in the presence of witnesses or of the village chief) over the size of the compensation. The frequency of the latter type to be employed tends to increase as harvesting approaches.

From the beginning of the 1990s the number of complaints presented before the local officials seems to have increased dramatically partly in response to the many conflicts which occurred in 1991-1992[253]. As a new tendency many herders have tried to gain support further up the political-administrative system in those cases where no satisfactory solution

---

[253] This is also reflected in the increasing number of conflicts over crop damages which are not settled locally between the two parties but negotiated by the extension officers.

was found locally. This has however, presupposed a higher degree of consensus among the often very dispersed and individualized FuutankoBe herders than had been prevailing until then. One way of generating such consensus has been through the increasing number of religious festivals, such as the *Maouloud* (the prophet's anniversary) celebrated for members of particular sub-clans by *marabouts* in the area of origin[254].

> *"Maouloud is an occasion for all SowonaBe to meet at Mbiddi, where they have their marabout. We come to pray and to celebrate the anniversary of the Prophet. Everybody brings something, even those who cannot come themselves. Women give some butter, the men sent an oxen or a sheep. It is a festival of religious songs. It's not for making politics, but of course there is a lot of debate going on. At the boreholes the SowonaBe talk with each other. They find someone to whom they can present their grievances. Either they go to the Souspréfet, but if that doesn't satisfy them, they continue to someone higher up in the system. They may even demand to be received in audience by Djibo Ka [the Minister of Interior]. This can be organised through his servant at a cost of approximately 25.000 CFA. Also Amadou Talla [Director of the Dakar cattle market, see below] can help. Anybody may help us."* (Interview with Yerim Sow and his brother in Ganina,1994)

Whereas herders vigorously deny that these religious meetings have political functions, the possibility of discussing common problems with people of one's own lineage, have materialised in several co-ordinated actions on behalf of the migrants. The ethnic gathering of the SowonaBe undoubtedly had an impact on the formation of a delegation of SowonaBe herders who were sent off to Dakar during the dry season of 1992/93 to obtain interviews with the Minister of Interior, a post which at that time was held by Djibo Ka, a Fulani closely related to the settled first-comer herders. The protests concerned the sweeping practice of discriminatory watering taxes and direct exclusion of transhumant herders at the wells. Also other delegations were sent off during 1993. These protests conveyed much of the same message, but also included denouncements of the new practice among counsellors and village chiefs of 'selling' rights of installation to

---

[254] This is of course a very bleak parallel to the very active associative life sustained by periodic ritual in terms of pilgrimage and songs, characteristic of the Mouride Muslim community. According to Cruise O'Brien (1996:459) associative life among the Mourides constitutes what amounts to a religiously based civil society, more or less the social foundation of the Senegalese state.

transhumant herders described above.

The 'protest initiative' of the FuutankoBe herders, turned out quite successfully. Shortly after the delegations had passed, the Minister sent the Governor of Louga out on a tour in the *arrondissement* of Barkedji to mediate. The Governor vigorously stressed how all users were supposed to contribute on equal footing in the functioning of the deep well. He further condemned the way that transhumant herders were badly received in the area and that they were over-taxed at the boreholes and eventually even denied access after only a few days of watering. He also denounced that foreign herders in some cases were forced to move their camps from the bush to stay at the same distance from the deep well as the sedentary, and that cases had occurred where they had been forced to pay for their settlement. "*Transhumants,* he said, *have the right to settle and do not have to pay more than others*". Instead the Governor invited the audience to strive for peaceful cohabitation, among other things by avoiding straying of animals into areas of cultivation, by resisting the purchase of animals of unknown origin which might be stolen and by refraining from admitting foreign animals into their herd (common accusation of egge-egge implying 'unconscious' theft). Finally the audience was asked to abstain from using the term "egge-egge"[255] considered by some as pejorative. "*We are all Senegalese!*" he proclaimed.

In doing so, the Minister of Interior and his representative, the Governor, fully acknowledged the rights of the migrants to move freely over the range and confirmed the equal rights of access to water and pastures, whereas the dissent of the first-comer population was overheard.

Evidently the channels of political influence seem to have been accessed though a variety of (clientelist) channels and intermediaries, revolving around the two main properties of Fulani life, Islam and livestock. The first is represented through the *marabouts*, notably the Tall family, who occupy central positions in the Tijanya brotherhood and are extremely influential among the herders from the Senegal River Valley; the latter through the influential Director of the Dakar cattle market who according to my informants "is much listened to in government circles". In contrast to the *marabouts*, the latter provides the advantage of being easily accessible either through personal interviews in his noisy and untidy office in the heart

---

[255] In FulBe egge-egge means:"those who are always on the move".

of the cattle market or through the two continuously busy telephones through which he keeps in permanent contact with both the herders in the interior of the country and his relations in the highest government circles.

> **Amadou Talla, Foirail de Dakar. Nov 1994.**
>
> *"I'm the boss here. I even represent the head of state. I take care of people's problems and try to reconcile them and settle disputes. I try to help people to find out who is right and who is wrong. If that doesn't work out, we have no other means than to call the police.*
>
> *Normally the problems brought to me from herders in the interior are about thefts of animals or the problems of herders being refused at the boreholes. I also take care of cases where people have problems with the police or the custom officers.*
>
> *A lot of people call me on the telephone; they call even from Mali or Mauritania. Everybody, all over the territory who is concerned with livestock, seller or buyer, know that I'm ready to help them. I do what I can with for example the Governor or the state administration. I can get in touch with the Minister of Interior or the Director of the Department of Livestock.*
>
> *With regards to the problem of watering taxes, it's obvious that all should pay on equal footing. Now that it has rained well there aren't as many problems. Now people have become closer to one another.*
>
> *The problems are mainly created by the indigenous population. They use the borehole to do politics, giving favours to some, at the detriment of others. When the village chiefs complain, I tell them that all Senegalese have equal rights. But if the problems do not stop, I'll get the name of the person creating problems and I will go and present the problems to the Minister of Interior".*

Although the above quotation primarily reflects the influence held by Amadou Talla in his own self-knowledge, his doings in connection with the FuutankoBe delegations of protest clearly show how the distance from the presumably marginal herder from the remote bush to the centre of decision often turn out to be far shorter than anticipated. Not the least the extremely personalised[256] and clientelistic features of Senegalese politics (the so-called clan politics mentioned in the first part of this chapter) contribute to the establishment of connections between the bureaucratic centres and the largely illiterate rural population which by and large have proven both viable and efficient[257]. The relative facility with which one can get access to the centres for decision-making is further illustrated by the recent introduction of public telephones in some of the larger villages of the Ferlo[258]. Very quickly these telephones booths, which constantly attract a large group of 'listeners', eager to pick-up the latest gossip, have turned out to be important instruments for disseminating rural protests. Indeed, the local politicians do not hesitate to call the politically most influential persons, such as the Minister of Interior, if decisions are taken at local level of which they do not approve[259].

In Senegal, the use of intermediaries between the different levels of society is no recent feature. The relations between state and local communities have always been ensured through brokers and networks of political patronage where favours are exchanged for political allegiance. The most well-known example is that of the Mouride saint, the *marabouts* (see Cruise O'Brien 1971 and 1975). The use of intermediaries is not unique to Senegal. Also Sara Berry describes how the outcome of rural disputes in those cases where disputes are regulated outside formal judicial proceedings

---

[256] In spite of Talla's claimed impartiality it is nonetheless precisely his position as a *ressortissant* (citizen) of the Senegal River Valley which provides him with the qualities required for ethnic identification.

[257] Apparently they are accessible even for people with relatively limited means, as in the case of Djibo Ka, whom one apparently could reach by bribing the servant (*planton*) of Djibo Ka with the fairly accessible amount of 25.000 CFA i.e. 250 French Francs

[258] The public telephone booth in Barkedji was installed in 1991.

[259] This was for example the case when the Mouride farmers of Samali (near Barkedji) illicitly had started cultivating some fields which apparently were the property of some local non-Mouride farmers. A local politician telephoned the Minister of Interior and shortly after he visited the place in question.

hinge on relations among neighbours and kin and how situations of increased competition over land and labour encourage investment in social relationships (Berry 1993:162).

In the case of the settled Fulani of the Barkedji *arrondissement,* complaints have tended to pass through Daouda Sow, former president of the *Assemblée Nationale* and after his dethronement in 1989, through his nephew Djibo Ka. In many cases this takes place even before they have been presented to the local administrative officers. In relation with the 1994 case of a Mouride *marabout* transgressing and cultivating someone elses fields, a villager explained how the upset villagers instead of warning the sous-préfet, had sent a politician from the locality to the new telephone booth of Barkedji to complain directly to Djibo Ka. "*No*, he explained, *we did not have the souspréfet to intervene. He is not part of the family. Here we are SanraBe; we are the kin of Djibo Ka*" (Barkedji 1994).

But while such political interventions until recently were the terrain of the (highly politicised) settled kin of the Dakar politicians, the increasingly difficult conditions for gaining access to water and grazing lands and growing economic potentials, has incited the transhumant herders to present their claims further up in the Senegalese political hierarchy to protests against local practices of exclusion.

Therefore, the perhaps most interesting aspect of the protest delegation incidence was how the Minister of Interior (although only by means of an emissary) chose to stress state ownership to pastures and wells (thereby overruling his own kin). Obviously his interpretation was in conformity with the letter of the Land Law. It seems, however, that the ambiguities of the legal framework and the general trend towards granting more rights to local population framework could have provided for a more subtle expounding of the texts. This would obviously also have facilitated the position of the decentralised state administrators who have long traditions of favouring the local settled elite and who have been socialised under the incessant urge of settling nomadic pastoralists. On the other hand, it seems that the message delivered should be interpreted more as the continuation of *status quo*, than as a firm victory to the mobile population. For as long as crucial issues such as the discrimination of FuutankoBes in the composition of well committees is left unacknowledged, the local power relations have largely been left untouched. Hence the incidence is yet an example of the functional ambiguity, described in the beginning of this chapter whereby the state, by maintaining a situation of fluidity, manages to obtain a situation of non-expressed consensus between the different stakeholders at local and at national level.

Straddling between different identities:

In general, the legal framework concerning local resource management is contradictory and vague and the limit between what is state ownership, free access and local control rather unintelligible. With regard to the wells no clear definitions exist which could specify, for example, who is to be considered a 'regular' user eligible to the board of the committee. The distinction between insider and outsider being contested terrain, this situation obviously lends itself to considerable manipulations and redefinitions of rights and status.

As mentioned briefly above, one of the means employed by FuutankoBe herders to position themselves most favourably in the struggle over access and control over resources has therefore been to straddle between different identities. In the cases described above, transhumant herders have chosen to launch their protest in their capacity of strangers claiming their free rights to make use of publicly owned resources. Djibo Ka, who has close family ties to the majority of the "local" politicians of the area, was therefore forced to intervene against the interest of his own relatives and in favour of their adversaries, the FuutankoBe herders. In the other cases of conflict, namely those relating to the functioning of the well committee, the battle stands more between those claiming to be the genuine 'locals' (and therefore the sole legitimate caretakers of the wells) and the FuutankoBe herders who claim to be legitimate users while refering to their protracted presence in the area and, not the least, to their significant contributions in terms of watering fees.

Consequently, it is important to bear in mind that, although the position of 'foreigner' may offer substantial advantages in certain cases, herders also strive to acquire the status of 'local' with all the rights and privileges pertaining to that role. Depending on the nature of the dispute, the same individuals will select the most appropriate social identity and appeal to both customary tenure rules and national land ordinances, singly and sometimes in combination and will invoke whatever ideology and cultural symbol are appropriate to substantiate the claim. (Goheen 992:403). In the main themes of conflicts played out at present, the free access to pastures and the control over the deep wells, herders are likely the choose opposing identities in the two cases although the roles may change in the course of the conflict where this proves more convenient.

Transgressing from stranger to local: officialising strategies
a). The role of taxes:

"Here the population is not very friendly. But we pay our taxes and have our vaccination documents in order, so that we can prove that our animals are not ill. Then they can't chase us away even though they have tried. Back home in the Fuuta, we used to receive many foreign herds, when the pastures were abundant there. Even during the drought of 1983/84, people were more hospitable. Now everyone want's to fill up his pockets. The change is related to the state of poverty. The transhumants are richer than the first-comer population". (Transhumant herder, Thiargny, 1993)

The need to have documents in order and to be in conformity with the law is generally recognised as important preconditions for moving freely on the range. Lately also tax paying has acquired prominence as a theme played through at the local level when determining how and when the FuutankoBe herders can transmute from the status of "foreigner" to that of "local". The taxes referred to are those collected by the rural council of which a certain percentage is returned to the local community for development purposes. Although taxes are moderate even for small producers a very small minority of the FuutankoBe herders pay them[260].

Many of them, however, claim to pay their taxes in their area of origin in the Fuuta. This has evidently been the case of those migrants who have wished to retain rights over land in the Senegal River Valley but were afraid of loosing these rights in case the land was subject to development of irrigation.

Once people have left for the South they don't have time to come back here and pay their taxes, and I don't have time to go down there to collect them. Some village chiefs do go there to collect taxes. People want to pay here. This is their territory and they want to keep their rights over the waalo land. (Ardo Ururbe DjougonaBe, Madina Ndiatabe (waalo))

---

[260] Rural taxes are head taxes of a fixed amount, generally 1000 CFA. The taxes are collected by the village chief who transfers the funds to the tax collector of the Rural Community. In principle they are given a receipt for the total amount of payment, and by way of remuneration for the services rendered, an indemnity of normally 10% of the tax collected is provided (Blundo 1998:6).

Obviously, the large majority do not pay anywhere, a situation which they share with a large part of the local population[261].Nevertheless the payment of taxes has all of a sudden become the symbol of division between locals and strangers. Although tax payment is a requirement for those wishing to present themselves as candidates to the rural councils, payment of taxes is no exigency for obtaining more secure rights over pastures and water. It seems, however, to have acquired some sort of symbolic meaning as it is often referred to by both FuutankoBes present in the area on a more permanent basis and by the local leaders as a sign of political allegiance, a sort of tribute paid to the local notabilities. In this way tax payment seems to have become one of several ways of signalling integration, an act which is expected to materialise in some sort of protection of use rights.

Bourdieu terms such activities "officialising strategies" as they aim at transmuting "egoistic" private and particular interest into disinterested, collective, publicly avowable, legitimate interests" (Bourdieu 1977:40). Within this line of thought, payment of taxes represents a way of officialising one's presence in the area of reception. Another interlinked strategy is that of being recognised as village chief.

Precisely because of these officialising attributes, the payment of taxes and the appointment of village chiefs (in charge of collecting these taxes) have become a matter of fierce opposition among parts of the first-comer population. For just as local herders use the lack of tax-payment as justification for limiting the rights of newcomers, very strong political pressure and creativity is invested in constraining development of tax-collection among foreigners. The various political agendas involved in the simple act of tax paying is expressed very pertinently by the FuutakoBe accountant of Yonofere:

"It's true that conflicts are increasing. There are more people and more animals now. More and more transhumants arrive from the North. The indigenous population fear that these people also decide to settle

---

[261] It is interesting to note that while tax payment is gaining some prominence among newcomers, the latest administrative reform of 1991 which transfers the responsibility of tax collection from the sous-préfet to the rural council has resulted in a dramatic decline in the amounts collected. One reason is that the rural councilors, in contrast to the sous-préfet, do not collect taxes accompanied by the police forces. According to the Minutes of the Rural Council of Barkedji only 900.000 CFA out of a possible 5,9 million CFA had been collected by the newly elected councilors in 1991.

here for good. They fear that as the FuutankoBe population increases they will start claiming to be represented in the Rural Council. But this goes only for those who pay their taxes here. That is why it is sometimes very difficult to get to pay your taxes. This has caused many transhumants to give up paying taxes".

b). The long road to recognition; the appointment of 'foreign' village chiefs

It is symptomatic that although officially appointed by the Ministry of Interior, the status of village chief is a fairly hollow title endowed with little actual powers. The rights to distribute land and control local resources were lost already with the passing of the 1966 Land Law (Loi sur le Domaine National). Today village chiefs are first of all in charge of overseeing that national laws and regulations and decisions of the rural council are observed within his village. He is furthermore in charge of keeping the civil register and, more important, of collecting rural taxes in his village[262].

The interest of the FuutankoBe herders in the office of village chiefs lies primarily in its official attributes[263]. By acquiring the symbols and roles of traditional chiefs, these herders validate the legitimacy of their claims. In assuming the role of traditional head of lineage (a sort of local representative of the *ardo*, the traditional clan leader) they reproduce a social, not an individualised identity for these are social not individualised roles, with obligations as well as rights attached (Goheen 1992:402).

This symbolic value is clearly recognised by the local population and is manifested in the fierce opposition to any official appointment of FuutankoBes as village chiefs:

---

[262] Decret 72-363, Ministère de l'Interieur.

[263] Yerim Sow expresses his priorities in this way: *"I'm not very often asked to participate in any meetings. It isn't very important for me. There is a guy at the borehole who informs me of what's going on. Sometimes he is my stand-in at the meetings. I can't go by cart all the time to Barkedji, I risk getting ill".*

> "When our relatives started arriving in large numbers the local herders did all they could to try and chase us away, but they didn't succeed. The FuutankoBe people are very earnest and responsible people. We don't steal cattle or anything else. It's 13 years ago that the village was officially recognised. People didn't approve of it. But we have contributed a lot to the functioning of the borehole, so now people leave us alone. There are 11 different FuutankoBe sub-villages around Djagueli but only 3 villages managed to be officially recognised. To be officially recognised, you have to pass by the Rural Council and the sous-préfet. Barkedji is very well represented in the higher spheres of the state. Djibo Ka, Daouda Sow and Bira Sy Sow all come from that area[264]. When they are displeased they can make a lot of noise. But they couldn't do anything against our 3 villages because we had paid our taxes and everything was according to regulations. But they did manage to get the Sous-préfet mutated".
(FuutankoBeVillage chief of Fidjiti, borehole of Djagueli).

Although many FuutankoBes have applied for recognition, only a few hold office. The rest have been rejected, officially on the basis of their villages being too small or located illegally within the borders of a gazetted forest (as above), but in reality as a result of pressure from the local population who fear that official recognition will give the village more permanent rights and eventually enhance recognition of territorial claims also. Only in 3 cases have 'foreign' village chiefs gained official recognition and in those cases they still lack the final official approval from the Minister of Interior. This does not, however, prevent them from being involved in local decision- making on equal terms with the other village chiefs.

---

[264] All three are influential FuutankoBe politicians with close family ties to the Arrondissement of Barkédji and the Département of Linguère. Djibo Ka (from Thiargny in the Barkédji arrondisement) has occupied several Ministries, lastly the central post of Minister of Interior from 1991. In 1993 he was removed from this post as a result of the internal power struggles of the Socialist Party (PS). Daouda Sow, his uncle, was for numerous years President of the National Assembly. He was removed in 1989. Biram Sy Sow also occupied several central post within the state and party apparatus. The fall of Djibo Ka was highly lamented by the Fulani population of the Ferlo, who felt they no longer had someone to represent their interest in the highest political spheres.

THE IMPORTANCE OF BEING RECOGNIZED:

Sous-préfet of Barkedji, 1994:
"Normally it's the 'big' families that occupy the post of village chief. Normally there is no conflict or election. Villages are almost always made on basis of ethnicity. If they are mixed, it's because the foreigners make up a very small minority. It isn't common that a newcomer is appointed village chief, but if they make a well or a vaccination pen, or make a donation of some kind it's not unusual that they are appointed village chief. If people are not organised in a village, the administration will not be aware of their existence, if there are food aid packages or seeds to distribute. They have an interest in being recognised.

If a village is to be recognised, the rural council will make a deliberation to accept the name given to the village and send it to the Prefet for approval. There are two village that are recognized here, Yiera Lopé [Yerims village] and Belel Thiabouli. But they are located within the gazetted forest. The problem with the FuutankoBe and their villages is not that they are FuutankoBe but that the villages are installed in the forest. That's not legal. Hence, the villages in the forest should not have been approved. But it's 15 years ago, so there isn't much to do about it."

Deputy of the Prefet of Matam 1995:

"Villages are created on government decree (arreté), whilst seasonal camps may be authorised by the sous-prefét, but the latter is only in case of conflict, to help them get installed'. Those villages that aren't characterised by fixed attachment are not recognised as villages: If an agglomeration is made up of rainy season camps it cannot be recognised and no village chief can be appointed.

..../

> *To officialise a new village, one criterion is the size: it has to contain a minimum number of households. Then you have to contact the sous-prefet and the President of the Rural Council. The request must be handed over to the sous-prefet, and after having passed by the Prefet it is transmitted to the Governor. He will then send a note to the Ministry of Interior. Then a small survey will be made to check the information given. If all elements are present, the village may be recognised. At present all existing villages in the arrondissement of Ogo are officially recognised. There are people in the forest reserve who have found a location and a name, but they are not recognised by the administration. The FuutankoBe of Yonoféré for example have written a petition to get them recognised as villages, but we responded that they were not officially recognised.*
>
> *People aren't always aware. We have had some cases where identity cards turned out to be invalid because the village indicated didn't exist. It's to the village chief that you have to pay your taxes. The newcomers are supposed to pay to the closest village chief. If they don't pay their taxes here they are not in acquiescence with the norms and regulations. If they don't pay, they have fewer rights".*

The explanations above give several hints to the room of manoeuvre available to participants in local struggles over access to resources. As stressed by the Deputy of the Prefet of Matam, foreign herders who do not pay their taxes in the area of settlement have less right. This is obviously the justification for both the actions of the foreigners and for those of the locals. But what these rights include is less clear and hence open for interpretations.

For the *sous-préfet* of Barkedji it is the location of the new villages within the gazetted forests which provides the justification for questioning their legality, while the Deputy Préfet of Matam stresses the provisional character of their settlements. Other arguments invoked during interviews with rural councillors are the size of the agglomerations, that they don't pay their taxes, and that they are too mobile to constitute a village.

"To create a village you must have a large family. If the village isn't large enough, it will not be recognised. For recognition you go the Rural Council. They will decide if your petition is accepted. Those who were rejected were not stable here. They went on transhumance to the Saluum all the time in search of pastures and they didn't even pay their taxes here". (Former president of the Rural Council, Barkedji)

The reference by the *sousprefet* to the legal framework concerning the gazetted forests is problematic, as this legislation from 1965 [265] was primarily aimed at limiting the uncontrolled expansion of peanut cultivation characterising this period by prohibiting cash crop production in certain areas. The law clearly stipulates the rights of local occupants to make use of pastures, tree products etc. as well as the right to cultivate annual crops if the choice of site is approved by the forestry services. Rights of settlement are not explicitly stipulated.

The size of the settlements is another open question as no official prescription exists[266]. With regards to the requirements of a candidate, the decree 72-636 of the Ministry of the Interior states that everybody over 21 years, who has principal residence in the village who has been listed regularly on the list of electorates is eligible. It is of course this paragraph that the deputy is referring to. Nonetheless, what is meant by principal residence in this area characterised by high levels of mobility among both first-comers and newcomers remains open to interpretation. And concerning the registration on the list of electorates, this goes back to the availability of a village chief to whom one can confide one's taxes. In the actual climate of distrust, this can, as shown below, not be taken for granted [267].

"When I first arrived, the people of the neighbouring village of Belkagne, were very much against us, but they didn't really dare to do anything against us. Two years after we had settled, I started paying taxes in Barkédji. Several of my relatives had settled in the vicinities and we

---

[265] Decret no. 65-078 du 10 février, 1965 portant code forestière.

[266] Interview with the préfet of Linguere 1994. His own proposition is a minimum limit of 50 persons.

[267] In a recent article Blundo gives numerous examples of how tax embezzlement is occurring not only at the level of the village chief but also among councillors and administrators (Blundo 1998).

decided to form a village. This was authorised by the sous-préfet. But the local population complained and at the end, the sous-prefet was mutated. Several other FuutankoBe groups had also tried to become recognised, but it only worked out for me and for the village chief of the UrurBe Daka of Djagueli[268]. The reason why we were recognised was that we could show the receipts for having paid our taxes. It was very fortunate that I had kept my receipts for the councillors had hidden away the book into which payments were registered". (Yerim Sow, FuutankoBe village chief of Yera Lopé in the gazetted forest of Barkedji-Dodji).

The limited security of tax registration to a foreign village chief creates a paradoxical situation whereby newcomers are condemned for not paying taxes while taxpaying of newcomers, with all its officialising attributes, is indirectly constrained. But as observed by the *sous-préfet* of Ogo, the reverse is also true:

"If the FuutankoBe want to pay their taxes here they should go the nearest village chief. But they do not want to. They want to make their own villages in the best pastures. They want to establish property rights." (Sous-prefet of Ogo 1994.)

The intricacies surrounding the official establishment of new villages and village chiefs furthermore illustrate the difficult situations of the administrative authorities. On the one hand, the incorporation of at least some of the 'foreigner' village chiefs enhances the legitimacy of local decision-making. For this reason the existing three village chiefs are incorporated in local decision-making despite of the lack of consent from the Ministry of Interior. On the other side, it seems that by omitting to proceed to a final approval, the local administration is keeping the decision open for later renegotiation. In this way the possibility is kept open for keeping them excluded or at least marginalised, as in Naoré where 70% of the population was represented by only two persons out of seven. Finally, proceeding towards full official recognition of these semi-officialised chiefs is, not the least in the highly politicised Barkedji arrondissement, a hazardous endeavour, unlikely to tempt the *sous-préfet* who keeps the mutation of his predecessor (see above) fresh in his memory. On the contrary, the present situation of partial recognition enables the authorities

---

[268] The interviewee has forgotten the third officialized FuutankoBe village of Loumbi UruBe

to blame the actions of their predecessors, should the legality of the village chief be brought into question.

Securing control through private ownership

Common for the FuutankoBe strategies mentioned above has been that they aim at protecting resources that have previously been open to all from attempts at reserving use rights to a more limited group. As will be shown below, this does not imply any stronger propensity among FuutankoBe herders towards collectivity than among the first-comer population. Indeed some of the most successful attempts to secure individual access to the range have come from the newcomers who have invested in digging a private well. Such operations evidently involve considerable investment and are therefore only within the reach of a small minority of (exclusively) FuutankoBe herders[269].

For natural reasons, the development of private wells is only taking place in the eastern part of the Ferlo where groundwater table is within more accessible reach. In this area distance between the existing boreholes tends to be higher than in the rest of the area, making private investment in wells more attractive than would be the case elsewhere. In 3 cases wells have been localised by the author, but according to the *sous-préfet* of Ogo, the number of FuutankoBe herders who have obtained permission to dig private wells is far larger.

"The borehole is where everybody meets. It's also where the animals contract diseases. That's why people want to dig a well. They want to be able to water their animals in peace. In the 20 years where I have roamed around in the Southern Ferlo and in the Saluum, I have tried many times to get permission to sink a well. This is the first time that I have had a positive response. I sent a demand to the Rural Council and to the Sousprefet of Ourosogui and to the officers from the Ministry of Waterworks there. The Rural Council gave the authorisation. It was the people from the Forestry Services who located the place to sink the well. I spent a lot of money on getting the authorisation. Gallo Gato [an extremely rich FuutankoBe herder, who has been long time in the area] helped. Once you have an authorisation to sink a well you also have the authority over the

---

[269] According to the examples given, prices for a well in this area ranges from 600.000 to 1 million CFA.

pastures in a radius of 5 km. Then you are in peace. You will not be chased away, and no one will hamper your watering. You will be the one to decide who is permitted to use the well. If people are thieves or in other ways doing wrong, you can tell them not to use the well. But you can't tell them to move out of the area. I think the well will be used mainly by my own family". (FuutankoBe well-'owner', Yonofere)

The digging of private wells is interesting for several counts. First of all, granting a permit for digging of private wells is officially subject to extensive bureaucratic procedures. They can be granted by the *Préfet,* after a technical approval by the Forestry Services, but are legal only after ratification by the Ministry of Interior.

In the present cases, the wealthy FuutankoBes had, however, literally "purchased" the permission directly from the local director of the Forestry Services. These purchases were all the more spectacular as they involved land which was part of a national game reserve. In order to protect the habitat of the (indeed very sparse) wild animals and fowl, settlement is authorised only near already existing infrastructure i.e. the areas already covered by the existing boreholes. Nonetheless, the former Director of the Park acting in collusion with the President of the Rural Council has illicitly granted permission for digging of more than 30 wells, a situation which was now under scrutiny by the state administration[270]. Despite the correct procedure depicted by the FuutankoBe well-owner above, it is therefore not likely that his permission was obtained legally.

Secondly, it is interesting to note how the FuutankoBe herders, otherwise fierce defenders of free grazing rights, apparently adhere to restrictions where their own wells are concerned. According to herders, the advantages of such private wells are mainly that they enable herders to settle in previously unused pastures, thereby limiting situations where transhumance might be necessary. Such advantages would easily be undermined if access to the well, as stipulated in the law, was held open for all herders. Asked whether such a well would not attract other users, one of the "fresh" owners responded that he had been granted not only rights of exclusivity to his private well, but also to pastures around. As mentioned

---

[270] The President of the Rural Council was obviously not aware of the illicit character of his doings as he proudly boasted of having approved the creation of more than 20 wells in the course of his presidency', just as he stressed that no demand had ever been turned down.

above this may be interpreted as a clear trespassing of both Islamic and customary law, as well as of national jurisprudence:

"We have had to intervene at several wells to tell the village chiefs that it's illegal to prohibit access to water. This the case even if people have paid all the expenses related to the sinking themselves". (Sousprefet Ogo 1994).

Herders' claims of property rights not only to the well itself but also to the adjacent pastures are therefore a revealing re-interpretation. The allegation (and the preciseness with which the extension of the rights was described) might well stem from a (very optimistic) reconstruction of an existing regulation prohibiting installation of fields within a distance of 1 kilometre around the wet season ponds[271]. Hence it is yet an example of the changes in mentality or transgressions of moral codifications which, according, to Solway often take place in a period of readjustment after a drought. For the appeal of such wells is not merely the need for more secure watering facilities. The attraction lies just as much in its attribution of being a **man-made** well, a feature which lends more readily to its being claimed as exclusive property. Indeed, the fact of being man-made is interpreted as providing the otherwise communal water sources with more extended rights in direction of private property.

Heterogeneity of interests and politisation of resource management institutions

As can be seen, the emerging claims of rights of exclusion towards strangers, are no longer only forwarded by the settled indigenous population, but are increasingly shared by 'older' FuutankoBe herders. Among these well-established newcomers, moral rules and old solidarities are transforming as part of their adaptation to changing conditions and new opportunities. Increasingly they desire to restrict access of 'new' transhumants i.e. those of their relatives from the Fuuta who at present have rebuilt their herd sufficiently to take up a more pastoral way of living and

---

[271] The idea that control over a source of water also confers control over land within a certain radius of the well may also stem from the many mapping exercises and delimitation of resource-regimes and "pastoral units" (*unités pastorales*) in vogue among development projects (such as PAPEL and PRODAM) working along the same logic in the area.

who are ready to start copying on the production strategies of their prosperous kin. Much seems to indicate that these herders are developing into just as fierce defenders of the rights to exclude 'newcomers' from the local resource base, as were another group of relative newcomers, the FafaBe of Ranerou.

The incidences described above are thus illustrative of the ways in which groups and solidarities tend to emerge or dissolve according to the opportunities available and of how ethnic' identities are under constant recreation. For while the labels 'FuutankoBe', 'egge-egge' or 'foreigner' contributed to give the drought-refugees of the Senegal River Valley a group identity they had not hitherto possessed, the economic and political consolidation of part of these herders creates a new situation where old solidarities seems to evanesce and be replaced with other types of alliances with for example part of the settled local elite.

Nonetheless this movement is not uni-directionnal. For it was by stressing their situation as foreigners being deprived of their rights to move freely over the range that the basis of their present success were established. Once more firm' rights have been yielded through official establishment of villages and village chiefs or through enforcement of 'private-property-like' rights over land adjacent to private wells, other preoccupations than the free and open grazing and watering rights have tended to take over. Nonetheless, it is still by referring to their group identity as "those who contribute most to the running costs of the well" or as "those who will ensure the well-being of the animals by making the well function properly" that claims for representation in the well committee and other similar institutions are made. (This explains the ambivalence towards their present numerical reinforcement expressed in many of statements made by 'old' FuutankoBes cited above). Furthermore the tendency for increased sedentarisation is paralleled by a tendency towards increased mobility, a situation which goes for first-comers and newcomers alike. Hence, claims towards more exclusive rights are likely to continue to coexist with claims protecting the free and open access to pastoral resources.

So where Solway states that drought hastens and renders visible what has previously been latent processes, and (in a somewhat unilineal interpretation of the revelatory process) stresses how vitality of reciprocal use entitlements is being undermined as a result of long-term structural changes towards commoditisation, privatisation and class-formation (1994:492), the case of Senegal seems to point towards a far more ambiguous and fluid situation, where several trends are at work at the same time.

Whereas it is true that acquisition of land by individuals and commoditisation of formerly reciprocal arrangements are becoming more recurrent features, this does not confirm a general trend towards individualisation or privatisation of hitherto communal resources. Apart maybe from the cases of 'spontaneous privatisation' of the range surrounding the private wells[272], few of the cases point towards individual acquisition. Rather these trends are inter-twined with more 'reciprocal arrangements'. For as noted by Shipton and Goheen (see chapter 3) people use resources such as water and land not only for survival and enrichment but also to gain control over others and define personal and social identities.

The attempts by certain villagers to appropriate the funds of the well committee are for example not so much a matter of personal enrichment. For apart from constituting a source of profit they are first of all important sources of social and political legitimacy for those who control them. In this way they have become vital institutions in local political life and are used as such by the local elites.

As argued in chapter 3, a person's status and influence hinges on his ability to mobilise a following. Well committees, especially those where incomes swell from transhumants' contributions obviously constitute a very important source of capital for clientelistic redistribution. For this reason they have not developed into closed corporations acting to exclude others, but have remained arenas for individual accumulation and mobility - acting to expand the number of supporters. This is not to say that maintenance of a clientele is financed overtly through the taxing of foreign herders (although this might be the case). Rather, as proposed by Blundo, control over such remunerative institutions puts the local bosses represented in the well committee in a situation where they cannot refuse their village clientele favours (such as tax exemption) as they are the basis of clientelistic exchange. In the same vein cases of financial borrowings are therefore also part of the explanation for the frequently empty accounts of the well-committees[273].

---

[272] But even here the owner acknowledged his inability to exclude others.

[273] This is not only the case at local level. Also the national banks of Senegal have in several cases been close to bankrupt as enormous sums of money had been lent to political and religious notabilities with limited motivation for paying off their mortgages. (See also Boone, 1990:440).

It is however important to recognise that this monopolising of (scarce) resources for political power is not only a matter of a divide between first-comers trying to retain control over their local resources against the economically more powerful immigrants. First-comers do not speak with one voice, but are engaged in their own internal struggles over the available resources. The attempts to maintain monopoly over the well committees are, therefore also part of another logic related to the internal strives between political factions at local level. As revealed maybe most clearly in the case of Naoré, disputes over the composition of the board of the well-committee are just as much struggles to gain control over the means to compensate the clients who have supported the winning faction,- and with the equally important addition made by Blundo (1998:2) of depriving the opponents of the benefits which they in turn could have derived from these resources. In this struggle, the rich new-comers are not only being used by the various local political factions. They also manage to play adeptly on the internal oppositions in order to get their share of the political power and resources which are redistributed. In this way it is an example of the processes described by Kopytoff of how immigrants attempt to take over local political systems and remould them to their own purposes by skilful political manoeuvring.

With regards to the role of the administration, what characterised the situation was how deviation of funds, as in the case with the overtaxing or exclusion of foreigners or in the attempts of technically constraining watering, was left strangely without any sanctions. In general the administrative centres appear uninterested in the misappropriation of funds taking place at the local level and only intervene if protests become too overwhelming - or if violence is involved. This is the result partly of the submission of the administrative authorities to pressures stemming from the game of factions and from the political and religious notabilities which may be mobilised in the course of struggles. But it is also because many of these actions not necessarily imply collective reprobation as they to a wide degree are accepted as legitimate, although not uncontested, means in the general bid for political power. Involvement of the administrative authorities is therefore no neutral act, but is immediately used in the political battle, as shown in Naoré.

Transfer of competence and delegation of the responsibility for local resource management to local community has, as can be seen, not generated a political culture based on well-defined rule-making authorities anticipated by the Natural Resource Management Framework. Rather local institutions whether 'new' or 'traditional' have remained contingent and indeterminate in character, as a result of their embeddedness in specific political and economic structures. As shown above management of local resources cannot be regarded as an activity in isolation irrespective of time and space. For precisely as proposed by the negotiated development approach (see chapter 3), the perception of both first-comers and newcomers of the object of negotiation changed in the course of the process from being a matter of competition over access to water and pastures to a strive centred primarily on control over the key resources for accumulation of political power (as expressed in the curiously pertinent quotation below). And in consequence of this also the social relationships between the negotiating parties were altered.

"People don't want us here. If they could they would chase us away. We haven't even made any attempt to integrate the well-committee, or the Rural Council. We haven't even participated in the meetings among the FuutankoBe village chiefs, and we haven't contributed to the delegation of protest". (Village Chief, Loumbi UrurBe, Barkedji April 1995).

Ensuing this cognition, the need, expressed in chapter 3, of studying tactics and strategies, not merely the rules of the game cannot be sufficiently underscored.

7. CONCLUSION

The principal objective of this research was to analyse the changes in access to water and pastures triggered by post-drought population movements and to study the changing configurations of power and obligations which have resulted. This was part of a more general exploration of the institutions and processes through which individual and groups gain access to, exploit and exercise control over resources and how these processes interact with other social and political processes over time. A number of questions were raised concerning the ways in which migrant herders had adjusted their production systems to the opportunities offered in their new environment and how access to resources was negotiated with the first-comer population. Issues concerning the impact of migration on local institutional mechanisms and the role of the decentralisation process herein were also advanced in order to open a more general discussion on how these processes have shaped the arenas of resource competition.

Preliminary conditions for answering these questions were that the crisis scenario and the conception of herders as passive victims of the on-going deterioration of their fragile environment were abandoned. To capture the ingenuity and adaptive capacities of rural producers of the Ferlo a more open- ended framework was developed. Using this as a backdrop, it became clear that the situation of post-drought Ferlo was neither an absolute nor a structural decline in the number of animals in the pastoral areas. Rather than a de-pastoralisation of household economies, development seems to have favoured the adoption of more specialised, mobile and labour intensive systems of production. The 'drought refugees' have, together with the indigenous population, been able to adjust to the new situation through conscious adaptation of a large number of different innovations. This has enhanced the ability of both groups to cope with constraints and to take advantage of new opportunities.

One important explanation of this ability to adapt and persist is that eco-systems such as the Ferlo are unstable, i.e. they do not have as a prominent characteristic the ability to return to equilibrium after a temporary disturbance or crisis. Instead, frequent occurrence of random perturbations such as drought, bush fires, etc. produce instability in the sense of large fluctuations (turbulence). Such production systems encourage resilience and exhibit considerable capacity to absorb changes and disturbances. This in turn fosters flexible and opportunistic management systems where local producers seek to take maximum advantage of the resources available at any given moment. When analysing the fluid and porous social relations within such unpredictable and highly variable production systems, constancy of behaviour therefore becomes less important than persistence of relationships.

Persistence, in the sense of flexibility and ability to manoeuvre economically as well as politically have been pertinent elements in the success story of the Fuutankobe herders and of their (more or less involuntary) hosts, the sedentarised agro-pastoral Fulani. It is the ability to absorb changes and disturbances, which explains the smooth incorporation of the large contingent of drought 'refugees'. The relatively trouble-free integration of foreign herds and herders may partly be explained as a result of a generally flexible environment where both herders and animals are in a position to respond to externally driven change such as drought and other climatic hazards. In consequence of their restricted possibilities to influence or control localised fluctuation in range land productivity (as fodder is scarce due to deficient rains, not because of too many animals), herders in such non-equilibrium environments are seldom motivated to co-ordinate or restrict access to available resources. Rather, pastoral strategies tend to be individualistic and opportunistic, geared towards seizure of opportunities and avoidance of hazards. Such opportunistic systems tend in general to favour open and unrestricted movement over the range. This openness is reproduced in local interpretations of 'Fulaniness' as hospitality towards foreigners and in the belief that it is shameful to deny other herders access to water and pastures.

Also the human capacities to persist, absorb and adapt to new conditions contribute to explain the success story. As shown above, individual economic and social strategies are far more flexible than is usually assumed. As exposed throughout the case study, people are often very alert when it comes to directing their investments and labour efforts towards the most profitable activity at any given time. This goes not only for the changes and disturbances brought about by the drought and the proliferation of irrigated agriculture in the Senegal River Valley. Indeed, breaking with the crisis scenario and the idea of drought as an epochal change also implies recognition of a turbulent past in the course of which herders have been forced to adjust their productive capacities by making the best of the opportunities given. Watershed events, such as the boosting of the groundnut economy in the beginning of this century or the borehole 'revolution' in the 1950s, provided for substantial changes in the production systems as well as in the social relations. In both cases it provided for constraints as well as for new possibilities. The rapid proliferation of the groundnut economy brought along an unprecedented encroachment on former grazing lands, but it also brought about a substantial boosting of cattle markets and hence of herders prosperity. It even triggered the venture of some Fulani herders into groundnut cultivation. Hence, no uni-lineal trend of deterioration can be extracted.

Likewise, the introduction of government owned boreholes could be interpreted as as a first step towards overgrazing, as proposed by certain preservationists focusing on the presumed undermining of previously well-functioning management systems. But if focus is set on resilience instead of on degradation the picture revealed is rather one of adaptation, of herders taking advantage of the opportunities by abandoning the large energy-consuming transhumance movements and creating a more 'pure' pastoral space, freed from the perpetual confrontations between farmers and herders. This did not, however, involve total sedentarisation or intensification as was expected by the planners. Instead a system of micro-nomadisation was adopted, whereby mobility was preserved as a crucial means to limit the risks related to climatic variation. In short, the drought-related migration acted not only to increase population and animal pressure in the area of reception. On the contrary, the influx of drought refugees acted as the prime catalyst for technological innovation of pastoral production, a process which triggered off a whole series of other technological and institutional innovations.

For herders the crisis was perceived just as much as persistence of relationships as a rupture or an epochal change. Adjustment of the production systems to the new conditions was a less insurmountable constraint for migrants than anticipated. Persistence of relationships in the post-drought context included for example the ability to move and exploit various resource regimes as well as the ability to shift between various productive strategies according to what proved most profitable for the moment. The adaptation or unwrapping of the different technological and institutional innovations available can also be understood as an expression of the creativeness of local entrepreneurs in ensuring the perseverance of relations. Through this capacity to innovate, pastoral producers were been able to 'enlarge', so to speak, the commons from 'within'. But such interrelations between individuals turned out to be governed more by individual interests and needs than by consideration for the weaker or by collective ecological concerns.

With this interpretation it would be easy to fall into the trap of the rational herder as the lone hunter for benefit, where all needs are reducible to rational economic calculations. The bargaining, manipulations and counterattacks played out in connection with the well committees and the ongoing negotiations over access to pasture and water witness are nonetheless examples of actions and operations that fall short of any resemblance to economic rationality. The frequent and often prolonged inactivity of the boreholes due to simple fuel shortages or delayed repairs are provoked mainly by the unwillingness of herders to pay the taxes due or by the perpetual deviation of funds. Together with the many cases of standstill prompted by struggles between different political factions or clan groups, they constitute considerable economic constraints for both first-comers and new-comers. Their frequent occurrence cannot be explained through rationales related to pure economic gain. The key to understand this apparent mess must instead be found in the multiple and competing claims to legitimate use governing resource allocation in the Ferlo and elsewhere. These conflicting claims indicate that resource management institutions serve many purposes at the same time. The well committees are concerned not only with the operation and maintenance of the borehole and its equipment but also with regulation of access to adjacent pastures and, not least, with the generation of support for local political elites by nurturing a village clientele through favourable taxing arrangements. These priorities may at certain moments overshadow the simple question of securing accessibility of water. Getting to grips with the functioning and malfunctioning of these local institutions therefore become impractical if the political dimension is omitted.

Comprehending how rights of access and control over resources change over time requires an understanding of how rules are made and remade through peoples' practices. This in turn requires an appreciation of power relations. The Ferlo case certainly shows that peoples' use of rules, norms and moral obligations far from being constant are re-interpreted continually as a function of the prevailing power relations, of the position of the individual actor and of the resource priorities entailed. The dissimilar attitudes towards transhumant herds experienced during the dry years of 1991 and 1993 highlight such differences in resource priorities. In the eastern Ferlo, (at the *puits-forages*) where producers are predominantly settled agro-pastoralists, priority was given to the fabrication of technical constraints to watering so that large herd-owners were discouraged from settling. In contrast to this, the well committees of Western Ferlo, where the indigenous herders are more prone towards mobility, displayed a more ambivalent stategy towards the FuutankoBe. Here the newcomers were seen both as competitors, as sources of economic and political prosperity and as a numerical and political reinforcement of the pastoral population vis-à-vis the perpetual pressure from the *Mouride* agricultural expansion.

Over the years, resource priorities and power relations between FuutankoBe and indigenous herders changed considerably as newcomers and certain layers of the indigenous population increased their wealth and influence. This had obvious repercussions both on the claims raised by the newcomers and on the rights granted them by the first-comer population. For as prosperity increased and power relations altered, the objects of struggle tended to shift from pure safe-guarding of productive resources towards other types of assets more closely related to the generation of political power. As shown in the Naoré case, struggles around the well-committees moved away from being solely a question of ensuring proper watering to becoming just as much a struggle over political power and influence as a means to gain control over others and define personal and social identities.

Within this fluid situation, the FuutankoBe herders managed very adeptly to position themselves favourably in the struggle over access and control with the natural resources in the pastoral area. Although they were 'used' by the local political elite as part of a strategy to reinforce political positions, the FuutankoBe played very skilfully on the internal oppositions within the firstcomer group in order to get their share of the political power and resources, which were being redistributed. Until now they have exhibited considerable intelligence and 'clairvoyance' in analysing the content of ongoing transformations. In spite of their relatively weak institutional organisation and not least the geographic and political distance between the centres of power and their own remote encampments, they have managed to a wide extent to influence the rules of the game. The result can, among other things, be read out of the changing attitudes towards transhumant herders exhibited by government officials, notably those in central positions.

Hence, the apparently simple story of increased competition leading to greater claims for exclusivity does not lend itself to equally simple conclusions. Although some first-comers were united in a clear interest in limiting competition on resources, there was no general interest in a total exclusion of foreign herders. The 'foreigners' who generally displayed a considerable interest in maintaining free and open access to water and pastures have, on several occasions, shown a strong propensity towards limiting further influx of members of their kin groups who are moving southwards to settle near their prosperous kin.

In the ongoing transformation of social and cultural systems strife for adjustment and accommodation is ever present. Different social actors seek to manoeuvre themselves into those positions which are most advantageous to his or her objectives and seek to maximise the opportunities offered by the moment. Indeed, a closer look at so-called communities and interest groups shows that multiple interests are at stake in the process of securing access to and control over the key resources of the area. In this struggle, defining who is and who is not a member of a community becomes the subject of considerable manipulation and reinterpretation just as redefinition of custom and invention of tradition are submitted to considerable political manoeuvring. Myths, ritual and symbolic systems are therefore interesting not because of their regulatory role in ensuring the balance of economic and social systems, but because the struggles over the meaning of key concepts such as who is and who is not a legitimate user, a legitimate well-owner or a legitimate taxpayer or tax collector have turned out to be essential parts of peoples' social manoeuvring. The struggles over meaning as well as other forms of invented traditions and symbolic rituals have turned out to be crucial factors in the transformation of local systems of resource access and control. It is these struggles and contradictions that run through the many political and social alliances from which local politics is fabricated.

But in many cases, such adjustments and manoeuvrings tend to transgress existing moral standards and codes of proper conduct. In the Ferlo case, the most prominent examples were where indigenous herders denied access to water to herders victims of drought, where rural councillors charged foreign herders for settling on the range or when parts of the range became subject to private appropriation by individual herders through the establishment of private wells. Obviously processes towards increasing degrees of exclusivity, commodification and even privatisation were in motion before the droughts. But, like in Solway's cases, it was events such as droughts, overgrazing, desertification and deficient precipitation that provided the necessary licence for actors to extend these codes of conduct to previously unacceptable levels. The post-drought rehabilitation period can therefore be perceived as a series of events through which people actively contested and revised key notions and representations. In this way, they are part of a practical political struggle through which people defend their interests and advance claims. A vast range of direct and indirect strategies are employed, involving action as well as inaction, compliance as well as resistance, all of which demonstrates the considerable skills and adeptness of both elites and subordinate groups to identify sources of power and leverage.

The opportunities actors take are, however, not entirely random, nor are they entirely predictable. They consist first of all in the maintenance of flexibility, in the diversification of options and in keeping opportunities open. As a result one sees no clear-cut trend towards increasing privatisation and consolidation of economic resources. Instead, such attempts coexist alongside with efforts to consolidate the free and open access to resources because mobility, diversification of income sources and maintenance of diversified networks linger on as fundamental attributes of pastoral production strategies.

Returning to the question concerning the impact of migration on the local institutional mechanisms regulating access to natural resources and the effects of decentralisation, it seems obvious that the direct effect of post-drought migration on resource management in the area was considerable. This is less the case with the decentralisation process. The establishment of rural councils and the handing over of responsibility over the boreholes to the local populations provided relatively little change in local resource management practices. Instead, it was the swelling accounts of the well committees derived from the new and exorbitant taxing policies, which conferred a new and central role in local resource management to these hitherto fairly insignificant well committees. It was, however, through reference to the decentralisation policy that the indigenous population legitimated their rights to restrict access of 'foreign' herds to the boreholes and to the adjacent pastures. Such emerging claims of exclusivity have been nurtured not only in the rhetoric surrounding the rural councils and other decentralised management institutions, but also by various projects aiming at controlling overgrazing through the establishment of locally regulated pastoral units or fenced paddocks. As such it has entered into the discourses used by the various parties to legitimate and support claims of exclusive rights over particular resources or tracts of land

Finally, attributing responsibility for deficient local resource management on excessive state tutelage may not be the most fruitful entry for understanding the intricacies of local resource management. Neither state control nor local authorities have been capable of ensuring efficient management of the wells. Nor have they been able to secure that attribution of land is carried out according to the requirements of the law. In reality many decisions regarding attribution of land or provisional restriction of access to watering troughs or wells are taken locally without consent or approval of those locally elected. Often the decisions are in direct contradiction with the norms and regulations governing the legal framework. Due to a combination of logistical deficiencies, widespread politicisation of resource management and the active role played by local politicians in the rise and fall of local administrative officers, administrators are severely restricted in their room of manoeuvre when trying to impose a new order. Furthermore, independent initiatives seldom receive any backing from the central state administration and may even, as was the case with the ban on administrative involvement in the functions of the well-committee[274], be directly obstructed. Confronted with the overwhelming tasks assigned them, many administrators instead resort to what has been termed *institutional autism*. By avoiding any upward reporting of local trouble, they hope to avoid the fate of the *sousprefet* of Ogo who in the moment of interviewing was contemplating demotion or at least postponement of any prospect of transfer to a more 'civilised' posting.

The process of decentralisation has not given way to the anticipated development of a political culture based on accountability. Instead it has contributed to reinforce a system based on clientelistic redistribution. As demonstrated above, such a system hardly conveys efficient management or transparency in accounts. Nonetheless, it does provide a sort of functional adaptation to the rapidly changing management priorities and power relations of the local communities through the creation of working compromises and alliances such as those emerging around the control over key resources and institutions. Such alliances, based as they are on the expectations of reciprocal benefits among people of unequal status, obviously facilitate privileges and have therefore contributed to increase the strength of certain layers of the political and economic elite. Nonetheless, they also contribute to create space for the more disadvantaged as power in such systems can always be contested and as the redistributive features of these clientelistic arrangements to a certain extent inhibits identification of clear winners and losers.

As conflicts shifted to be directed towards the control over assets as part of a larger bid for political power and private gain, the simple and mutually exclusive categories of group identities and group interests between first-comers and newcomers, which guided the initial hypothesis of this work, tended to evaporate. The objects of struggle and even the meaning of certain strategies shifted in the process of adaptation.

---

[274] The letter (circulaire) from Jean Collin, discussed in chapter 5.

Understanding the changing arenas of resource competition increasingly resembled the act of hitting a moving target. Mutually exclusive categories such as before /after, crisis/recovery, turmoil/order, degradation/rehabilitation, private/common, insider/outsider, newcomer/first-comer and even rich and poor, which had structured the initial hypotheses proved increasingly invaluable. Presumably fixed analytical dichotomies (between the politically well-consolidated sedentary agro-pastoralists and the marginalised and individualistic foreigners, between those settled in comfortable distance of the wells and the newcomers avoiding conflicts by settling far away in the bush, and even between rich and poor) tended to dwindle away as the process of post-drought rehabilitation proceeded.

Likewise the meaning and value attributed to certain objects or strategies transformed in the course of time. The strategy of settling in the bush which, for example originally had character of a largely defensive strategy, shifted within a relatively short time span into a 'winners' strategy through which it was the foreign herd owners who had positioned themselves most favourably in the on-going competition over fodder resources. Hence far from the first impressions of marginalisation, settling in the bush transmuted into one of the prime markers of the successful strategy carried out by the drought refugees.

Similarly, the opportunities provided by the new watering techniques, implied that the value and importance attributed to pastures located farther away from the boreholes changed, prompting also previously settled herders to move out into the bush. In some cases, this even entailed a 'domestication' of previously 'under-utilised' land as grazing within bushy areas contributed to improve the palatability of species composition and to keep away wild animals, making the area more attractive to the 'indigenous' population. Where it initially was access to the presumably scarce fodder resources that was at play, the objects of struggle shifted. Once the herds had recovered from the most immediate effects of the drought, conflicts became more related to control over key institutions and eventually, it became the political and financial gains that were generated through these institutions that were at the heart of the struggles.

Finally, the successful rehabilitation in itself provided an opportunity for the drought 'victims' to transgress their previous status as politically marginalised. Through skilful manipulation and negotiation with political contacts (in the broadest sense) they have managed simultaneously to reinvigorate or recreate hitherto unacknowledged institutions in the area of departure (such as the *Maouloud*, the local *marabouts* and their religious networks, the *ardo's* and the association of pastoralists to mention but a few) and to establish new alliances and platforms for bargaining in the area of reception. In this process new interest groups and alliances have been moulded across previous divides just as certain former communities have lost importance. Hence, at the end of the analysis both the arenas on which the struggles were played out, the claims expressed as well as the social actors staging the scene, had transformed and have merged into new and unexpected combinations.

It is likely that the succes story of post drought migration described here is particular for Senegal, and therefore does not lend itself readily to generalisations. Nonetheless, the case does stress the need, expressed by Salzman (1995:163), of adopting a pluralist perspective which stresses multi-causality and which focuses upon the interaction of many different factors as the processes generating the patterns of human custom and action that we wish to understand. Although human adaptation to an area takes account of the environmental conditions, it is important to stress that there are many different kinds of adaptation and many liable outcomes.

It also seems clear that it is impossible to understand local management of water and pastures independent of the political and economic context within which it was set. Due to the economic, human and political resources that were generated from the process of post-drought adjustment, the struggles ensuing over access to and control over resources inevitably became part of a wider struggle to get new objects and new rules under local control. And therefore even small conflicts over local resources tended to become politicised as they mixed with struggles over larger political goals. Such fluid, contradictory and politicised environments are not ideal for fostering either equitable or sustainable development. Nevertheless, omitting to address the political environment as such, and directing intervention towards imagined homogeneous communities driven by mutual agreement about long term sustainable production goals is likely to fuel further social differentiation and increase social conflicts.

8. BIBLIOGRAPHY

Abrams, Philip, 1982: *"Historical Sociology"* Ithaca, New York.

Adam, J.,1915:" Le Djoloff et le Ferlo". *Annales de Geographie* 132.

Adams, Martin, 1982: The Baggara Problem, Attempts at Modern Change in Southern Darfur and Southern Kordofan (Sudan) *Development and Change* vol. 13.

Allisoutin, Rosnert Ludovic, 1997: "Pond Management in the Podor department, Senegal" *Issue Paper* no. 72. International Institute for Environment and Development (IIED), London,

Amanor, K.S., 1995: "Dynamics of Herd Structure and Herding Strategies in West Africa: A study of Market Integration and Ecological Adaptation." *Africa* vol. 65 no. 3.

Ammitzbøl, K., 1997: "Decentralisering af Naturressourceforvaltning - en arena for institutionel synergi". Speciale Internationale Udviklingsstudier, Roskilde Universitetscenter.

Anderson, David M., 1993: "Cow Power: Livestock and the Pastoralist in Africa". *Africa Affairs* nr. 1 1993.

Aubreville, A., 1949:*"Climats, forêts et desertification de l'Afrique Tropicale"*, Sociéteé d'Edition Géograpiques, Maritimes et Coloniales, Paris

Audiger, Jeanne 1961: "Les Oulof du Bas-Ferlo" *Les Cahiers d'Outre-Mer,* No. 54.

Ba, Oumar, 1975: "Les Peul du Diolof au XIXe siècle", *Bulletin IFAN* T.37, série B no. 1.

Ba, Cheick, 1986: *"Les Peul du Senegal, Etude Géographique"*, Dakar.

Barral, Henri, 1982:*"Le Ferlo des Forages; Gestion ancienne et actuelle de l'espace pastoral"* ORSTOM, Dakar.

Barrows R. and Roth M., 1989: *"Land Tenure and Investment in African Agriculture: Theory and Evidence",* Land Tenure Center, University of

Wisconsin-Madison.

Barth, Fredrik, 1973: "A General Perspective on Nomad-Sedentary Relations in the Middle East", in Nelson, C.: *The Desert and the Sown, Nomads in a wider Society.* Institute of International Studies, University of California, Berkeley.

Barth, Fredrik, 1969:" Introduction" in Barth (ed): *Ethnic Groups and Boundaries, The Social Organization of Cultural Difference.* Oslo, London.

Baxter,P.T.W., 1991: Introduction in Baxter,P.T.W*: When the Grass is Gone; Development Intervention in African Arid Lands".* Seminar Proceedings no. 25: Scandinavian Institute of African Studies, Uppsala.

Baxter,P.T.W and R. Hogg., 1990: *Property, Poverty and People: Changing Rights in Property and Problems of Pastoral Development,* Manchester. University of Manchester Press.

Behnke, R.H., 1985: "Open Range Management and Property Rights in Pastoral Africa: A case of Spontaneous Range Enclosure in South Darfur, Sudan". ODI Pastoral Development Network Paper 20, London.

Behnke, R.H., 1992 "New Directions in African Range Management Policy", *ODI Pastoral Development Network Paper* 32c, March 1992.

Behnke, R.H. and I. Scoones, 1993: "Rethinking Range Ecology; Implications for Range Land Management in Africa" in Scoones et al.: *"Range Ecology at Disequilibrium; New Models of Natural Variability and Pastoral Adaptation in African Savannas"* ODI, IIED Commonwealth Secretariat, London.

Benoit, M., 1988: La Lisière du Kooya; Espaces pastoral et paysages dans le Nord du Sénégal (Ferlo), *L'Espace Geographique* no.2.

Berkes and Farvar, 1989: "Introduction and Overview" in: Berkes (ed)1989: *"Common Property Resources: Ecology and Community Based Sustainable Development"* London.

Bernard, Claire, 1993: "Les débuts de la politique de reboisement dans la Vallée du Fleuve Sénégal (1920-1945)" *Revue francaise d'histoire d'outre-mer.* T. LXXX no.298.

Berod-Inard, Thierry and Di-Meo, Guy, 1985: " Crise du nomadisme pastoral et modernisation des transport dans le Sahel sènegalais du Ferlo".Travaux de l'Institut de Geographie de Reims 63-64.

Berry, Sara, 1994: "Resouce Access and Management as Historical Processes" in Markussen and Lund (ed) "Access, Control and Management of Natural Resources in Sub-Saharan Africa - Methodological Considerations" *Occasional Paper* no. 13 IDS.,Roskilde.

Berry, Sara, 1993: *No condition is permanent; The social dynamics of Agrarian Change in Sub-Saharan Africa*, University of Wisconsin Press, Madison, USA.

Berry, S., 1988: "Concentration without Privatization? Some Consequences of Changing Patterns of Rural Land Control in Africa" in Downs and Reyna (eds.), *Land and Society in Contemporary Africa*, University Press of New England.

Berry, Sara, 1989: "Social Institutions and Access to Resources" *Africa* no. 59 no. 1.

Bierschenk, Thomas, 1995: "Structures spatiales et pratiques socials chez les Peuls du nord du Bénin". Working Paper 9, Centre for Agriculture in the Tropics and Subtropics, Universität Hohenheim.

Bierschenk, Thomas, 1995: "Rituels politiques et construction de l'Identité etnique des Peuls au Bénin". Cahiers des Sciences Humaines 31 (2) 1995 : 457-485.

Biot,Y. P.M. Blaikie, C. Jackson and R. Palmer-Jones, 1995: "Rethinking Research on Land Degradation in Developing Countries" *World Bank Discusion Paper* 298, World Bank Washington DC.

Bloch, P.1986: *Land Issues in River Bassin Development in Sub-Saharan Africa*, Land Tenure Center, Madison, Wisconsin.

Bloch, P., 1989: "Land Issues in the Senegal River Valley: Report on a Reconnaissance trip", mimeo. December 1988." Land Tenure Center, University of Wisconsin-Madison.

Bloch, P., 1990: *An Egalitarian Development Project in a Stratified Society: Who ends up with the Land?*, Land Tenure Center, University of Wisconsin-Madison.

Blundo, Giorgio, 1995a: "Les courtiers de développement en milieu rural sénégalais". *Cahiers d'Etudes africaines* 137,XXXV-1.

Blundo, Giorgio, 1995b: "Gerer les conflits fonciers au Sénégal: Le rôle de l'administration locale dans le sud-est du Bassin Arachidier". Unpublished Draft, Institut d'Etudes de Développement, Université Catolique de Louvain.

Blundo, Giorgio, 1998: "Decentralisation, Participation and Corruption in Senegal". Paper presented at the 14th International Congress of Anthropology and Ethnological Science, Williamsburg, Virginia.

Blundo, Giorgio and Jean Pierre Jacob et al., 1997: "Socioanthropologie de la décentralisation en milieu rural africain; bibliographie sélective et commentée", *Itineraires, Notes et Travaux* no. 49, IUED, Genève.

Bonfiglioli, A.M. and Yiero Doro Diallo, 1988: "Kisal, production et survie au Ferlo (Sénégal) Dakar": Rapport préliminaire préparé pour OXFAM.

Bonte, Pierre, 1993: "Terres collectives , droits coutumiers et conflits fonciers", in Moorehead and Lane (eds): Rapport de l'Atelier Sous-Regional sur Le Foncier Pastoral et le Developpement au Sahel, Nouakchott 1993. Annex II. London, International Institute for Environment and Development (IIED).

Boone, Catherine, 1990: "The Making of a Rentier Class; Wealth and Accumulation and Political Control in Senegal", *The Journal of Development Studies*, vol. 26, no. 3, April 1990.

Boserup, Ester, 1983:"The Impact of Scarcity and Plenty on Development" in: Rothberg, R.I. and Rabb, T.K., *Hunger and History*.

Boserup, Ester, 1965: *The Conditions for Agricultural Growth*, London.

Bourdieu,P., 1977: *Outline of a theory of practice*, Cambridge University Press.

Boutillier, J.L., 1982: "L'Aménagement de fleuve Sénégal et ses implications foncières", in: Le Bris E, Le Roy et Leimdorfer (eds.): *Enjeux fonciers en Afrique Noire*.Paris.

Bovill, E.W., 1921 "The Encroachment of the Sahara on the Sudan" *African Affairs, Journal of the African Society*, vol LXXX Juli 1921.

Breman, H. and C.T. de Wit : Rangeland Productivity and Exploitation in the Sahel", *Science* nr. 221 p. 1341-1347.

Breman et al.,1985: "Analyse des conditions de l'élevage et propositions de politiques et de programmes, Burkina Faso". Etude preparée pour le Club du Sahel et le CILSS.

Brink, Roger van der, D.W Bromley and J-P. Chavas, 1995: "The Economics of Cain and Abel: Agropastoral Property Rights in the Sahel". *Journal of Development Studies* vol 31, no 3.

Bromley, D.W and M. Cernea, 1989: "The Management of Common Property, Some Conceptual and Operational Falacies". *World Bank Discussion Paper* 57.

Bromley, D.W., 1972: The Commons, Property and the Common Property Regimes", in Bromley (ed): *Making the Commons Work, Theory, Practice and Policy*. San Fransisco.

Brown, Lester and E.P. Eckholm, 1974: *By Bread alone*, New York.

Brox, Ottar, 1990: "The Common Property Theory: Epistemological Status and Analytical Utility". *Human Organization* vol. 49, no. 3. pp. 227-235.

Bruce, J., 1990: *Community Forestry, Rapid Rural Apraisal of Tree and Land Tenure*. FAO, Rome.

Bruce, J. 1988b: "Do Indigenous Tenure Systems Constrain Agricultural Development?" mimeo, Land Tenure Center, University of Wisconsin-Madison.

Bruce, J. 1988a: "A Perspective on Indigenous Land Tenure Systems and Land Concentration", in Downs and Reyna (eds.): *Land and society in contemporary Africa*, University Press of New England.

de Bruijn, Mirjam de and Rijk van Dijk and Dick Focken (eds.) 2001: *Mobile Africa; Changing Patterns of Movement in Africa and beyond.* Leiden, Bostion, Köln, Brill. .

de Bruijn, Mirjam and Hans van Dijk, 1994: 'Drought and Coping Strategies in FulBe society in the Hayre (Central Mali) : A Historical Perspective'. *Cahiers d'Etudes Africaines* 133-135 XXXIV- 1-3.

de Bruijn, Mirjam and Hans van Dijk 1995: *Arid Ways: Cultural Understandings of Insecurity in FulBe Society, Central Mali,* Thela Publishers, Amsterdam, 1-32.

de Bruijn, Mirjam and Hans van Dijk, 1992: 'Changing Fulani Society and Fulani Security'in F. Von Benda-Beckmann and M. Van der Velde (eds): *Law as aRresource in Agrarian Struggles.* Wageningse Sociologische Studies no.33. Wageningen Agricultural University.

Carl Bro International, 1988: A Livestock Development Study in the Sahel to Assess the Potential Role of Livestock in Integrated Farming Systems, Country Report, Senegal.

Carney, J, And M. Watts, 1990: "Manufacturing Dissent: Work, Gender and the Politics of Meaning in a Peasant Society", *Africa* Vol. 60, no. 2

Caverivière, M. and Debene M., 1988: *"Le droit foncier sénégalais",* Mondes en devenir, Berger-Levrault, Paris.

Caverivière, M. 1991: "Problematique foncière et amenagement de l'espace rural; le cas du Sénégal", Atelier sur les nouvelles approches de la planification regionale, Nations Unies, Dakar 4-8 mars 1991.

Centre de Suivi Ecologique (CSE) 1992: "Estimation des effectifs du bétail par vol systématique de reconnaissance dans la moitié nord du Sénégal. Rapport de campagne". Document NT 92.

Centre de Suivi Ecologique (CSE), 1991: "Etude de la distribution spatiale et des mouvements de bétail par enquêtes aériennes; 1989-90". Document NT 91-02.

Cohen, A.P.,1985 *The Symbolic Construction of Society*. London. 125 p.

Colvin, L.G., 1982: "Land Tenure and Irrigated Agriculture in the Senegal River Basin", USAID and OMVS Design Team, Dakar.

Comaroff, J. and Comaroff, J., 1992: "Goodly Beasts, Beastly Goods" in Comaroff, J. and Comaroff, J.: *Ethnography and the Historical Imagination*. Westview Press, Boulder, Colorado.

Coppock, D.L., 1993:"Vegetation and Pastoral Dynamics in the Southern Ethiopian Rangelands: Implications for Theory and Management. in Behnke et al.: *Range Range Ecology at Disequilibrium*, London, Overseas Development Institute.

Croll, Elizabeth and David Parkin, 1992: "Anthropology, the Environment and Development" in Elizabeth Croll and David Parkin: *Bush base: Forest Farm*, Routledge London.

Cruise O'Brien, Donal, 1996: "The Senegalese Exception" Review article, *Africa* 66 (3).

Cruise O'Brien, Donal, 1975: *Saints and Politicians: Essay in the Organization of Senegalese Peasant Society*, Cambridge, Cambridge University Press.

Cruise O'Brien, Donal, 1992: "Le contrat social sénégalais à l'epreuve". *Politique Africaine* no. 45.

Cyriathy-Wanthrup S. and R.C. Bishop, 1975 :"Common Property' as a Concept in Natural Resources Policy" *Natural Resources Journal* 1975.

Dahl, Gudrun, 1979: *Suffering Grass, Subsistence and Society of Waso Borana*. Stockholm Studies in Social Anthropology.

Dahl, G and A. Hjort, 1979: *Having Herds; Pastoral Herd Growth and Household Economy*. Stockholm Studies in Social Anthropology vol 2.

Davis, Lucy, 1995: 'Opening Political Space in Cameroun: the Ambiguous Response of the Mbororo'. *Review of African Political Economy* no. 64.

Degnbol, T. 1996: "The Terroir Approach to Natural Resource

Management: Panacea or Phantom: the Malian Experience" Unpublished Paper, IDS Roskilde.

Diop, Amadou Tamsir, 1987: "Les ressources de l'aire pastorale de Tatki: Inventaire et étude du mode d'exploitation, proposition de plan d'aménagement et de gestion rationelle". Dakar-Hann, ISRA/LNERV

Diop, Momar Coumba et Mamadou Diouf, 1990: *Le Sénégal sous Abdou Diouf.* Editions Karthala, Paris.

Diop, Mamadou Coumba(ed), 1992: *Sénégal, Trajectoire d'un Etat.* Dakar.

Diop, A-B., 1968: "La tenure foncière en milieu rural wolof (Sénégal): Historique et Actualité. *Notes Africaines* n°118, avril 1968.

Diouf, Makhtar, 1994: *Sénégal, Les ethnies et la Nation.* UNRISD/ Forum du Tier Monde, Paris.

Dupire, Marguerite, 1957: " Les forages dans l'economie peuhle" in: Gouvernement du Sénégal, Services des Eaux et Forëts, Inspection Forestière du Fleuve: *Elements d'une Politique Sylvo-Pastorale au Sahel Senegalais.* Dakar, Sénégal. Fascicules 1-7.

Dupire, Marguerite, 1970: *Organisation Sociale des Peul*, Paris.

Dyson-Hudson N.& JT McCabe, 1983: "Water resources and livestock movements in South Turkana,Kenya" *Nomadic Peoples* 14:41-46.

Dyson-Hudson N. 1985: "Pastoral Production Systems and Livestock Development Projects: An East African Perspective" in M.M. Cernea (ed), *Putting People First.* Oxford: Oxford University Press.

Ellis, J. 1995: "Climate Variability and Complex Ecosystem Dynamics: Implications for Pastoral Development" in Scoones (ed): *Living with Uncertainty:New Directions in Pastoral Development in Africa.* London.

Ellis, J. Coughenour, M.B. and Swift D.M.1993: "Climate Variability, Ecosystem Stability and the Implications for Range and Livestock Development" in Behnke et al. *Range Ecology at Disequilibrium; New Models of Natural Variability and Pastoral Adaptation in African Savannas*, London

Ellis, J. Coughenour, M.B. and Swift D.M.1991: "Climate Variability, Ecosystem Stability and the Implications for Range and Livestock Development" in: New Concepts in International Rangelands Development; Theories and Applications", Proceedings from the 1991 International Rangeland Development Symposium, Society For Range Management. Logan, Utah.

Engelhard, Ph.et al., 1986: *Les enjeux de l'après-barrage*, ENDA, Dakar.

Fairhead, J. and M. Leach, 1996.: *Misreading the Arican Landscape. Society and Ecology in a Forest-Savanna Mosaic*", Cambridge University Press.

Fatton, R.Jr., 1986: "Clientelism and Politics in Senegal" in *African Studies Review* 29 no. 1, December 1986.

Faye, A. and Marks M., 1990: "Rapport de la cinquième campagne d'enqêtes aériennes: décompte du bétail", Document du CSE, Dakar.

Faye, A. et Malcolm Marks, 1992: "Aerial Monitoring of Sahelian Livestock and Determination of Rangeland Pressure. Dakar, Centre de Suivi Ecologique (CSE).

Faye, Malick, 1995: "Gestion des ressources pastorales au Ferlo. Quelles orientations".Communication du Seminaire-Atelier sur la production de Viande en Afrique Sub-Saharienne, 13-17 Mars 1995 a Saly Portudal, Sénégal, multigr.

Feder and Feeny, 1991: "Land Tenure and Property Rights: Theory and Implications for Development Policy". *The World Bank Economic Review*, vol. 5 no. 1.

Feeny, David, 1992: "Where do we go from here; Implications for a research agenda" in: Bromley (ed): *Making the Commons Work, Theory, Practice and Policy*, San Fransisco.

Feeny, David, Fikret Berkes, Bonnie Mc Cay and James Acheson, 1990: "The Tragedy of the Commons Twenty Two Years later". *Human Ecology*, vol. 18, no. 1. 1990.

Ferguson, James, 1990: *The anti-politics machine; Development, depolitization and bureaucratic power in Lesotho*, University of Minnesota Press.

Fjellman S.M. and Miriam Goheen, 1984: "A prince by any other Name? Identity and Politics in Highland Cameroon", American Ethnologist, *The American Anthropological Association* Vol 11. No.3.

Fortmann, Louise, 1995: "Talking claims: Discursive Strategies in Contesting Property". *World Development* vol.23 no.6.

Fratkin, E., 1997:"Pastoralism: Governance and Development Issues". *Annual Review of Anthropology* 26.

Freudenberger, Karen Schoonmaker 1991: "The Incongeneous Destruction of a Forest Reserve: The case of Mbege, Senegal." *IIED Issues Paper.*

Freudenberger, M.S. 1991: "Losing, Protecting and Regenerating the Gum Arabic Tree: Constraints to the Emergence of Local Level Resopurce Management in Northern Senegal" Draft, Land Tenure Center, University of Wisconsin, Madison.

Freudenberger, M.S., 1992 "The great Gum Gamble: A Planning Perspective on Environmental Change in Northern Senegal". Unpublished Ph.D. Dissertation, University of California, Los Angeles.

Freudenberger, Mark Schoonmaker, 1992: "Le règlement des conflits en matière de gestion des terres" in "La gestion des ressources naturelles par les collectivites locales" Actes du séminaire organisé a l'Université de Saint Louis du 3 au 5 novembre 1992.

Freudenberger, M.S. and P.Mathieu, 1993: "The Question of the Commons in the Sahel" Preeliminary Version Land Tenure Center, University of Wisconsin-Madison.
Gallais, Jean, 1972a: "Les sociétés pastorales ouest-africaines face au développement", *Cahiers d'Etudes Africaines* 12,3. Paris.

Gallais, Jean, 1972b: "Essai sur la situation actuelle des relations entre pasteurs et paysans dans le Sahel ouest-africain", *Etude de Géographie Tropicale offerte a Pierre Gourou*, Paris.

Gellar, Sheldon, 1995:" State Tutelage vs. Self-Governance: The Rhethoric and Reality of Decentralization in Senegal" in Wunsch J.S. and D. Olowu: *The Failure of the Centralized State; Institutions and Self- Governance in Africa.*

Gérard, Jerome, 1994: Un parti vert au Sénégal: Une participation militante. *Politique Africaine* no.53.

Geschiere, Peter, 1984: 'Segmentary Societies and the Authority of the State - Problems in Implementing Rural Development in the Maka Villages of Southeastern Cameroun' *Sociologia Ruralis* vol. XXIV (1).

Gibbs, C.J.N. and D.W. Bromley, 1989: "Institutional Arrangements for Management of Rural Resources: Common Property Regimes." in Berkes (ed) *Common Property Resources; Ecology and Community Based Sustainable Development.* Belhaven Publishers, London.

Gilles, J.L. and Jamtgaard, 1981: "Overgrazing in pastoral areas: the commons reconsidered" *Sociologia Ruralis* 21(2).

Glantz, Michael H., 1977: "The U.N. and Desertification: Dealing with a Global Problem" in Glantz (ed.): *Desertification; Environmental Degradation in and around Arid Lands*, Boulder, Colorado.

Godwin, R.K.and Shepard W.B., 1979 :"Forcing Squares, trianmgles and ellipses into a circular Paradigm: The use of the commons dilemma in examining the allocation of common resoources" *The Western Political Quarterly*, Salt Lake City, Utah, 1979, Vol.32 No. 3.

Goheen, Mitzi and Parker Shipton, 1992: "Introduction. Understanding African Landholding: Power, Wealth and Meaning". *Africa* Vol 62, no.3.

Goheen, Mitzi, 1992: "Chiefs, Subchiefs and Local Control: Negotiations over Land, Struggles over Meaning" *Africa* Vol 62,no.3.

Goody, Jack, 1971: *Technology, Transition and the State in Africa*, London.

Gore, C., 1993: "Entitlement Relations and 'Unruly' Social Practices: A Comment on the Work of Amartya Sen". The Journal of Development Studies, Vol. 29, No.3.

Graham, Olivia, 1988: "Enclosure of the East African Rangelands; Recent Trends and their Impact" *ODI pastoral Development Network Paper* 25a, London, March 1988

Grandin, B., 1983: "The importance of wealth effects on pastoral production" in: *Pastoral Systems Research in Sub-Saharan Africa*, ILCA, Addis Abeba.

Grannovetter, M., 1992:"Economic Action and Social Structure: The Problem of Embeddedness" in Grannovetter, M. and R. Swedberg: *The Sociology of Economic Life*. Boulder.

Grenier, Ph., 1960: "Les Peuls du Ferlo", *Les Cahiers d'Outre-Mer* no. 49, t. 13.

Grenier, Ph., 1987: " Les Problèmes énergétiques du Ferlo (Sahel sénégalais) in "Energie et espace au Sénégal", *Travaux et documents de géographie tropicale* no. 60.

Gromaire, 1957: "Elements de Politique sylvo-pastorale au Sahel du Sénégal", Fascicule 1-17.

Groot, W.T.de, J.C.J. van Wetten and C.A. Drijver, 1995: "Drawing the Boundary: An Explorative Model of the Defense of the Coomons" in: Van der Breemer et al.(eds.): *Local Resource Management in Africa*, John Wiley and Sons, Chichester.

Gueye, Babacar, 1994: "Historique de la Décentralisation au Sénégal: les deux premières phases" in: La décentralisation au Sénégal : l'Etape de la Regionalisation, Actes du Séminaire de 2 au 4Mai 1994: Mise en place de la régionalisation au Sénégal". Dakar.

Gueye, Mamadou Bara, 1994:"Conflicts and Alliances between Farmers and Herders: A Case Study of the "Goll" of Fandène Village, Senegal" *IIED Issues Paper* no.49. International Institute for Environment and Development, Dryland Networks Programme. London

Guyon, G., 1989: "Faut-il se préoccuper des questions foncières? Jusqu'ou et comment?; Les enseignements du developpement rural en Afrique de l'Ouest". Note de reflection, Caisse Centrale de Coopération Economique, Paris.

Hanan, N.P. Prevost, Y, Diouf, A and Diallo O, 1991: "Assessment of Desertification around Deep Wells in the Sahel using Satellite Imagery" in *Journal of Applied Ecology* 28.

Hansen, Tina og Kurt Skårup Kristensen, 1991:"Pastoralister, Bistand og Bæredygtig Udvikling. Speciale, Institut for Geografi og Internationale Udviklingsstudier, RUC.

Hardin, Garett, 1968: "The Tragedy of the Commons", *Science* 162:1243-1248.

Hardin, Garett, 1977: "Living in a Lifeboat", *BioScience* vol. 24 no. 10.

Hardy Golan, Elise, 1990: "Land Tenure Reform in Senegal: An Economic study of the Peanut Basin", Land Tenure Center, University of Wisconsin-Madison.

Helland, J., 1982: Social organization and water control among the Borana". *Development and Change,.* 13(2).

Hellden, Ulf, 1984: "Drought Impact monitoring. A Study of Desertification in North Kordofan, The Sudan, *Rapporter och notitser,* nr. 61, Department of Physical Geography, University of Lund, Sweden.

Hellden, Ulf, 1988: "Desertification Monitoring: Is the Desert Encroaching?", *Desertification Control Bulletin* no. 17.

Henriksen, G., 1974: *Problems of Development in Turkana*. Skriftserie no. 11, Occasional Paper, Socialantropologisk Institut, Bergen.

Herskovits, Melville J., 1926: "The Cattle Complex in East Africa". *American Anthropologist* 28.

Hesseling G.,and Matthieu, P., 1986: "Stratégies de l'Etat et des populations par rapport à l'espace." in: Crousse,B. Le Bris et Le Roy (eds): *Espaces diputes en Afrique Noire*. Paris.

Hesseling, G., 1985: "La reforme foncière au Sénégal : Consensus entre paysans et pouvoirs publics?" in van Bingsbergen, W. Reyntjens, F, and Hesseling, G. (eds.) *State and Local Community in Africa*. Bruxelles.

Hill. Polly, 1986: *Development Economics on Trial; The Antropological Case for Prosecution.* Cambridge University Press.

Hjort A. and Mohamed Salih, M.A.(eds), 1989: *Ecology and Politics: Environmental Stress and Security in Africa.* Scandinavian Institute of African Studies, Uppsala, Sweden.

Hjort af Örnäs, G.Dahl, 1991: *Responsible Man; the Atmaan Beja of Northeastern Sudan.* Uppsala.

Hobsbawm E. and T. Ranger, 1983: *The Invention of Tradition*, Cambridge University Press.

Hogg, Richard, 1986: "The New Pastoralism: Poverty and Dependency in Northern Kenya" *Africa* 56 (3).

Holling, C.S., 1973: "Resilience and Stability of Ecological Systems". *Annual Review of Ecology and Systematics*, Vol. 4:1-23.

Homewood, Katherine, 1995: "Development, Demarcation and Ecological Outcomes in Masailand", *Africa* vol. 65. no.3.

Hussein, Karim, 1998: Conflicts between Farmers Na Herders in the semi-aid Sahel and East Africa: A Review. *Pastoral Land Tenure Series* no.10, Overseas Development Group, School of Development Studies, University of East Anglia, IIED, London.

Haan, Cees de, 1990: "Changing Trends in the World Bank's Lending Program for Rangeland Development" in: "Low Input Sustainable Yield Systems: Implications for the Worlds Rangelands" Proceedings from the 1990 International Rangeland Development Symposium, Nevada, USA.

Haan, Cees de, 1994, "An Overview of the World Banks Involvement in Pastoral Development". Mimeo, Draft.

Ingold Tim, 1986: *The Appropriation of Nature; Essays on Human Ecology and Social Relations*, Manchester University Press.

International Fund for Agricultural Development (IFAD) 1995: *Common Property Resources and the Rual Poor in Sub Saharan Africa.* Special

Programme for Sub-Saharan Countries affected by Drought and Desertification. NewYork/Amsterdam.

ISRA 1992: Groupe de Travail sur l'autosuffisance en moutons de Tabaski au Senegal, Mars 1992, Dakar.

Jacobs, Allan H., 1980: "Pastoral Masai and Tropical Rural Development" in Bates, R.H. and M.F. Lofchies: *Agricultural Development in Africa: Issues of Public Policy*. New York, Praeger.

Jamin, P.Y. et J.F. Tourrand, 1986: "Evolution de l'agriculture et de l'elevage dans une zone de grands amenagements: le delta du fleuve Sénégal", *Les Cahiers de Recherche Developpement*, no. 12

Jamin, P.Y., 1986: "La double culture du riz dans la vallée du fleuve Sénégal: Mythe ou réalité?", *Les Cahiers de Recherche Developpement*, no. 12

Juul, K., 1996: "Post-drought Migration and Technological Innovation among Fulani Herders in Senegal: the Triumph of the Tube!". *IIED Issues Paper* no. 64, juli 1996.

Juul, K., 1994:"Opportunistiske Græsningsstrategier i det Nordlige Senegal". *Den Ny Verden* no.2. Vol.27:38-49. Copenhagen, Denmark. Center for Development Research.

Juul, K. 1994: "Arealanvendelse og forvaltning af naturressourcr blandt hyrder og bønder i det nordlige Senegal" *Kulturgeografiske Hæfter* no 45, 14 årg.

Juul, K 1993a: "Pastoral Tenure Problems and Local Resource Management, The Case of Northern Senegal", *Nomadic Peoples*, no. 32:81-91.

Juul, Kristine, 1993b: "Spontaneous Privatization of Rangelands as a Means of Pastoral Self-Defense; The case of Northern Senegal" in Markussen: "Institutional Issues in Natural Resource Management" *Occasional Paper* no. 9 Institute for Development Studies, Roskilde University.

Juul, K.1991a: "Animal Counting in the Northern Senegal (Ferlo) -a comment in the reliability of quantitative livestock data." in Poulsen and

Laweson: *Dryland Degradation; Causes and Consequences;* Proceedings from Danish Sahel Workshop 1990.

Juul, K. 1991b: "Commentaires a la cartographie du forage de Velingara, Mai 1990". Unpublished paper, Centre de Suivi Ecologique, Dakar.

Juul, K., 1991c: "Problèmes Fonciers et aménagement territorial en zone agro-pastorale: Le cas de l'arrondissement de Barkedji. Mimeo. Centre de Suivi Ecologique, Dakar.

Juul, K. 1990a: "Notes sur la Pre-enquête sur les stratégies des producteurs" Unpublished, CSE, Dakar, Senegal.

Juul, K. 1990b: "Pastoral Tenure Systems in Senegal - A Discussion of Pastoral Management and Exclusion Rights", Documents du CSE, Dakar.

Juul, K., D. N'Decky et O. Touré, 1989: " Comptage de bétail dans 14 forages du Nord Ferlo. Avril 1989". Publication du Centre de Suivi Ecologique, Dakar.

Kabeer, Naila and Subrahmania, Ramya, 1996:" Institutions, Relations and Outcomes: Frameworks and Tools for Gender-Aware Planning". *IDS Discussion Paper* 357, Sussex.

Kasberger-Sanftl, G.,Richter, M. et Tluczykont, S., 1991: Le pâturage controlé: Un système d'exploitation sylvo-pastorale comme modèle pour la sauvegarde des ressources naturelles". Mission Forestière Allemande, Saint Louis, Senegal.

Khazanov, 1984: *Nomads and the Outside World.* Cambridge, Cambridge University Press.

Klute, Georg, 1996:"Introduction" in Nomads and the State, *Nomadic Peoples* no.38.

Kopytoff, Igor, 1987: "The Internal African Frontier", in Kopytoff (ed) *The African Frontier; The reproduction of Traditional African Societies.* Bloomington.

Lamprey, H.F. 1988: "Report on the Desert Encroachment Reconnaissance in Northern Sudan 21 October to 10 November 1975", *Desertification*

Control Bulletin no. 17.

Lamprey, H.F: 1983: " Pastoralism Yesterday and Today: The Overgrazing Problem" in Bourliere F.(ed) *Tropical Savannas. Ecosystems of the World* vol 13. Amsterdam

Landais, E. and Philippe L'Hoste: "Association agriculture-élevage en Afrique intertropicale: un mythe confronté aux realités du terrain" *Cahiers de Sciences Humaines* 26 (1-2).

Lane C., 1994: "Introduction" in "Pastoral Tenure Overviews" Draft Manuscript submitted to UNRISD.

Lane, C., 1993: "Past Practices, Present Problems, Future Possibilities: Indigenous Natural Resource Management in Pastoral Areas of Tanzania" in Markussen: "Institutional Issues in Natural Resource Management " *Occasional Paper* no. 9 Institute for Development Studies, Roskilde University.

Lane, C.,1990: "Barabaig Natural Resource Management: Sustainable Land Use under Threat of Destruction" Geneva: *UNRISD Paper* no.12

Lawry, S. 1989: *"Tenure Policy Towards Common Property Resource Management in Sub-Saharan Africa"*, Land Tenure Center, University of Wisconsin-Madison.

Lawry, Steven W., 1990: *Tenure towards Common Property Natural Resources in Sub-Saharan Africa.* Land Tenure Center, Univeristy of Wisconsin.

Le Roy, Etienne, 1980: Le sous-préfet, le President de la Communauté Rurale et les paysans; Limitations de la compétences judiciaires et adaptations du contentieux adminsistratif dans le règlement des conflits fonciers au Sénégal" in: *Fonction de Juger et Pouvoir Judiciaire, Tranformations et Déplacements.* Publication des Facultés Universitaires, Saint Louis et Bruxelles.

Le Houérou, H.N. 1977: The Nature and Causes of Desertization" in: Glantz, Michael H. (ed). *Desertification; Environmental Degradation in and around Arid Lands.* Boulder, Colorado.

Le Roy, E. Karsenty and Bertrand, 1996: *La Sécurisation foncière en Afrique*, Editions Kartahala, Paris.

Leach, M., 1991: "Engendered Environments: Understanding Natural Resource Management in the West African Forest Zone". *IDS Bulletin* vol 22 no. 4..

Leach, M. Mearns, R and Scoones, I., 1997: "Environmental Entitlements; a Framework for Understanding the Institutional Dynamics of Environmental Change" *IDS Discussion Paper* 359, Sussex..

Leach, M and Mearns, R. 1996: " Environmental Change and policy; Challenging recieved Wisdom in Africa" in Leach, M. and Mearns, R.: *The Lie of the Land; Challenging received wisdoms on the African Environment*, Oxford.

Lericollais, André, 1989: "Risques anciens, risques nouveaux en agriculture paysanne dans la Vallée du Sénégal", in Eldin, M. et P. Milleville: *Le risque en l'agriculture*. Editions ORSTOM, Paris.419-437.

Lhoste, P., 1984: *Enquêtes en milieu pastoral au Sine-Saloum au Sénégal*, GERDAT, Montpellier.

Lhoste, Ph. et P. Milleville, 1986: "La conduite des animaux; techniques et pratiques". in Landais (ed.): Actes de l'Atelier Méthodes pour la recherche sur les systèmes d'élevage en Afrique Intertropicale. ISRA/IEMVT. Mbour, Senegal

Li, Tania Murray, 1996: "Images of Community: Discourse and Strategy in Property Relations" *Development and Change* vol 27.

Little, Peter D. 1985: "Social Differentiation and Pastoralist Sedentarisation in Northern Kenya", *Africa* 55 (3).

Little, Peter D., 1987: "Land Use Conflicts in the Agricultural/Pastoral Borderlands: The Case of Kenya" in: Little, P.D., M.M. Horowitz and A.E. Nyerges (eds): *Lands at Risk in the Third World*. Westview, Boulder.

Livingstone, Ian, 1977: "Economic Irrationality among Pastoral Peoples: Myth or Reality? *Development and Change* no.8 (1977).

Long, N. and van der Ploeg, J.D., 1989: "Demythologizing Planned Intervention: An Actors Perspective" *Sociologia Ruralis*, vol XXIX, 3-4.

Lund, Christian, 1995: *"Land, Power and Politics in Niger; Land Struggles and Rural Code"*. PH.D.dissertation, International Development Studies Roskilde..

Lund, Christian, 1994a: "Law Power and Politics and the Rural Code in Niger". *Project Paper* 12, International Development Studies Roskilde.

Lund, Christian 1994b: "The rural code in Niger: A social process of formation and transformation. Preliminary fragments of an analytical framework". Unpublished draft, Institute for Development Research; University of Roskilde.

Lund, Christian, 1994c: "Tinkering Methodology" in Lund (ed): Access, Control and Management of Natural Resources in Sub-Saharan Africa-methodological considerations." *Occasional Paper* 13, International Development Studies Roskilde.

Mac Manus, Patrick, 1995:'Dagen og vejen - om nogle livsstrategier i fattige samfund' *Den Ny Verden* no.2.

Markakis, J., 1993: "Introduction" in: Markakis, J (ed.) *Conflict and the Decline of Pastoralism in the Horn of Africa*. Macmillan Press, London.

Mc Cay and Acheson (eds.), 1987: *The Question of the Commons, the Culture and Ecology of Communal Resources."* Tucson .

Mathieu, P. Niasse M. et Vincke, P., 1986: "Aménagements Hydro-agricoles, concurrence pour l'espace et pratiques foncières locales dans la Vallée du Fleuve Sénégal, le cas de la zone du lac de Guiers" in: Crousse,B. Le Bris et Le Roy (eds): *Espaces disputés en Afrique Noire.* Paris.

Mathieu, P. 1996:"Pratiques informelles, gestion de la confusion et invention du foncier en Afrique." in Villers (ed) *Phénomènes informels et dynamiques culturelles en Afrique"* Editions l'Harmattan, Paris.

Mearns, Robin, 1995: Community, Collective Action and Common Grazing, the Case of Post- Socialist Mongolia: Paper presented at the Common property Conference: Reinventing the Commons, Bodø. 1995.

Miehe,S., 1990: "Inventaire et suivi de la végétation dans les parcelles pastorales à Widou Thengoly: Résultats des recherches effectués de 1988 à 1990 et évaluation globale provisoire de l'essai de pâturages controllé après une periode de 10 ans. Unpublished report, Projet GTZ Exploitation agro-sylvo-pastorale des sols dans le Nord du Sénégal. St. Louis.

Milleville, P., 1989: "Activités agro-pastorales et aléa climatique en region sahélienne" in Eldin, M. et P. Milleville: *Le risque en agriculture*. Paris, Editions ORSTOM.

Moore, Sally Falk, 1994:"The Ethnography of the Present and the Analysis of the Process, from: Brorofsky, Robert (ed): *Assessing Cultural Anthropology*. New York.

Moore Sally Falk, 1987a: Explaining the Present : Theoretical Dilemmas in Proccesual Ethnography" American Ethnological Society Distinguished Lecture, San Antonio, Texas,in *American Ethnologist 1987*.

Moore, Sally Falk, 1987b: "Law and Social Change: The Semi-Autonomous Social Field as an Appropriate Subject of Study" in Moore, S.F. *Law as Process; an Anthropological Approach*. Routledge and Kegan , London, and Boston.

Moore Sally Falk, 1986: *Social Facts and Fabrications, Customary Law on Kilimanjaro 1880-1980*. Cambridge University Press, pp.1-13.

Moorehead, R. and Lane, C., 1993: "Nouvelles orientations en matière de politique et de tenure foncière des ressources naturelles en terres de parcours" in: Rapport de l'Atelier Sous-Regional sur Le Foncier Pastoral et le Developpement au Sahel, Nouakchott 30 Oct.- 4 Nov. 1993. Annex I and II,IIED, London.

Moorehead, Richard, M., 1991:"Structural Chaos: Community and State Management of Common Property in Mali", Ph.D. thesis. International Development Studies, University of Sussex..

Moris, Jon 1988:" Failing to Cope with Drought: the Plight of Africa's ex-pastoralists". *Development Policy Review*, Vol. 6. SAGE, London.

Mortimore M.and William Adams 2001: "Farmer adaptation, change and 'crisis' in the Sahel", *Global Environmental Change* vol.11.

Mortimore, M., 1995: "Population growth, agricultural expansion and natural resource degradation, an oversimplified causality?", Paper presented at the 1995 Sahel workshop, Sønderborg, Denmark.

Morton, James 1994; "The Poverty of Nations; The Aid Dilemma at the Heart of Africa", British Academy Press, London, New York.

Müller, J.O.,1988: "The Land Laws and Community Reform as an Example of Institutional Change in Senegal; Legal Principles, Implementation and Preliminary Results from the Semi-Arid Land in the Ferlo" *Quarterly Journal of International Agriculture*, vol.27, no.1.

Müller, J.O., 1989: "Risiken der Sedentarisierung und Tranzhumanz-Verhalten "après-forage" von der Peul Nomaden im Koya (Nord-Senegal) Vortrag anlässlich des Symposiums "Tierhaltung im Sahel" Tropenzentrum Universität Göttingen 26-27 Oktober 1989.

Ndiaye, Ousmane, 1993: "Micro-level Small Ruminant Transaction Analysis and Livestock Policy in Senegal". Plan B paper for M.Sc. Michigan State University.

Ndione, Cheick Mbacke.1994. "Impact de la dévaluation sur les filières animales du Sénégal". ISRA. Saint Louis. (mimeo)

Nelson, Ridley: "Dryland Management- The Desertification Problem". *Environment Department Working Paper* 8. World Bank,Washington.

Niamir, Maryam 1990: "Herders Decision-making in Natural Resource Management in Arid and Semi-arid Africa" *Community Forestry Note* 4, FAO, Rome.

Niamir, M 1989:" Local Knowledge and Systems for Natural Resource Management in Arid and Semi-arid Africa. FAO, Rome.

Niane, I.C. 1990: "Note sur la situation des affectations foncières (1988-90) et les litiges foncières intra et intercommunautaires (Département de Matam, Podor et Bakel)" PNUD/Cellule Après-Barrage,Dakar.

Niane, I.C. 198?: "Du fonctionnement des conseils ruraux et des centres d'expansion rurales polyvalents de a Vallée du Fleuve Sénégal" Projet SEN/86.001.

Niang, Mamadou 1979: "Regimes des terres et strategies de developpement rural au Senegal (un exemple de la resistance du droit coutumier africain)" *African Perspectives* vol 1. No. 45-51.. Leiden.

Niemeijer, David, 1996: "The Dynamics of African Agricultural History: Is it Time for a New Development Paradigm?" *Development and Change* Vol 27.

North, D.C., 1990: *Institutions, Institutional Change and Economic Performance*, Cambridge, Cambridge University Press.

Oakerson, 1992: Analyzing the Commons: A Framework" in Bromely (ed.) *Making theCommons Work*. Institute for Comparative Studies, San Fransisco, CAlifornia,

Okoth-Ogendo, H.W.O., 1989:"Some Issues of Theory in the Study of Tenure Relations in African Agriculture" *Africa* vol 59, no.1. pp.6-18.

Olivier de Sardan, J.-P., 1991: *Anthropologie et Developpement*, Editions Khartala, Paris.

Oloko-Onyango, J. et al., 1993: "Pastoralism, Crisis and Transformation in Karamoja". *IIED Issues Paper No. 43*. London

Olson, Katarina, 1984: "Long Term Changes in the Woody Vegetation in N.Kordofan, The Sudan- Study with the Emphasis on Acacia Senegal". Lunds Universitets Naturgeografiska Institution in cooperation with the Institute of Environmental Studies, University of Khartoum.

Ortner, S. B.,1986: "Theory in Anthropology since the Sixties" *Comparative Studies in Society and History*, vol.28 no.2. London .

Ostrom and Keohane 1994: Introduction in Local Commons and Global Interdependence: Heterogeneity and Cooperation in two Domains. *Journal of Theoretical Politics*, vol 6. No. 4.

Ostrom, E., 1992: The Rudiments of a Theory of the Origins, Survival and Performance of Common Property Institutions" In Bromley (ed) 1972:

Making the Commons Work, Theory, Practice and Policy.

Ostrom. E., 1990: *Governing the Commons: The evolution of institutions for collective action.* Cambridge University Press, Cambridge.

Ostrom, Ellinor, 1988: Institutional Arrangements and the Dilemma of the Commons" in Ostrom,V. Feeny,D. and Pitch (eds) *Rethinking InstitutionalAnalysis and Development: Issues Alternatives and Choices.* San Fransisco.

Ostrom, Ellinor 1987: Institutional Arrangements for Resolving the Commons Dilemma, some Contending Approaches" in Mc Cay and Acheson (eds): *The Question of the Commons"* Tucson, Arizona.

Painter, T,M, 1994:"Situating User Based Governance: Peoples Livelihood Strategies and Natural Resource Management in West Africa. in Marcussen, H.S.: Improved Natural Resource Management. The Role of the State versus that of the Local Community. *Occasional Paper* no.12, IDS, Roskilde.

Panzacchi, Cornelia,1994: "The Livelihood of Traditional Griots in Modern Senegal", *Africa* 64 (2).

Pedersen, Jon, 1995: "Drought, Migration and Population Growth in the Sahel: The Case of the Malian Gourma: 1900-1991". *Population Studies,* vol 49.

Peet, R and M. Watts, 1996:"Liberation Ecologies, Development, Sustainability and Environment in an Age of Market Triumphalism" in Peet, R and Watts (eds.): *Liberation Ecologies; Environment, Development, Social Movements.* London.

Pellisier, Paul, 1966: *Les Paysans du Sénégal, les civilisations agrarires du Cayor a la Casamance*, Saint Yrieix, France.

Perrier, G. 1995: "New Directions in Range Management Planning in Africa", in Scoones: *Living With Uncertainty; New Diractions in Pastoral Development in Africa.* Intermediate Technology Publications, London

Peters, Pauline 1994: *Dividing the Commons; Politics, Policy and Culture in Botswana.* University Press of Virginia.

Peters, Pauline, 1992: "Manoeuvres and Debates in the Interpretation of Land Rights in Botswana" in *Africa*, vol 62, no.3.

Peters, Pauline, 1987: "Embedded Systems and Rooted Models; The Grazing Lands of Botswana and the Commons Debate" in Mc Cay and Acheson (eds) 1987: *The question of the Commons, the culture and Ecology of communal Resources*. Tucson.

Peters, Pauline, 1984: "Struggles over Water, Struggles over Meaning: Cattle, Water and the State in Botswana" *Africa* vol. 54, no.3..

Picardi, A.C and Siefert, W.W., 1976: "A Tragedy of the Commons in the Sahel". *Technical Review*, May 1976.

Pouillon, F., 1990: "Sur la "stagnation technique" chez les pasteurs nomades: Les Peul de Nord-Senegal entre l'economie politique et l'histoire contemporaine". *Cahiers des Sciences humaines* 26 (1-2).

Prévost Y., 1990: "Analyse spatiale de la pression animale comme facteur de desertification dans le Nord du Senegal". Publication CSE, Dakar

Profil de l'Environnement de la Vallée du fleuve Sénégal" 1990, "Euroconsult" and "Institut National de Recherche pour la Conservation de la Nature". Document préparé à la demande de la Direction Générale de la Coopération au Dévéloppement (DGIS). Ministère des Affaires Etrangères, Pays-Bas.

Republique du Sénégal, Ministère de l'Economie, des Finances et du Plan, Direction de la Prévision et de la Statistique, 1988: *Répertoire des Villages*. Saints Louis, Louga.

Reyna, S.P. and Downs R.E.,1988: "Introduction", in Downs and Reyna (eds.): *Land and Society in Contemporary Africa*, University Press of New England.

Ribot, Jesse 1995: "From Exclusion to Participation: Turning Senegals Forestry Policy Around?" *World Development,* Vol. 32, no.9.

Richter,M.,1991: "Les Peul dans la zone du projet" and other articles in Kasberger-Sanftl, G.,Richter, M. et Tluczykont, S. 1991: Le pâturage controlé: Un système d'exploitation sylvo-pastorale comme modèle pour la sauvegarde des ressources naturelles". Saint Louis, Senegal. Mission Forestière Allemande,GTZ.

Riesman, Paul, 1974: *Freedom in Fulani Social Life; an introspective Ethnography*. University of Chicago Press.

Riesman, Paul, 1990: "The formation of Personality in Fulani Ethnopsychology", in Jackson, Michael and Ivan Karp: *Personhood and Agency:The experiance of Self and Other in African Cultures*, Uppsala.

Roe, Emery 1993; "New Framworks for an Old Tragedy of the Commons and an Aging Common Property Resource Management" *Agriculture and Human Values*, Vol.11 no.1.

Roe, Emery M, 1991:"Development Narratives, or Making the best of Blueprint Development" *World Development* Vol. 19 no. 4. Great Britain.

Rondinelli, D. And Minis, H.P., 1990: Administrative Restructuring for Economic Adjustment; Decentralisation Policy in Senegal. International Journal of Administrative Sciences, SAGE, London. vol. 56.

Roseberry, W.,1989: *Anthropologies and Histories, Essays in Culture Histories and Political Economy*. Rutgers University Press, New Brunswick (Introduction p.1-14)

Runge, C.F., 1981 "Common Property Externalities: Isolation, the Assurance and Resource Deplation in a traditional Grazing context. *American Journal of Agricultural Economics* vol 63.

Runge, C.F., 1986: "Common Property and Collective Action in Economic Development" *World Development* vol 14, no. 25.

Salih, M.1990: "Pastoralism and the State in Africa" *Nomadic Peoples* 25-27 Uppsala.

Salzman, P.C., 1995: "Studying Nomads: an autobiographical reflection" *Nomadic Peoples* no.36/37.

Sandford, S., 1983: *Management of Pastoral Development in the Third World*, London.

Sandford, Steven, 1983: "Organisation and Management of Water Supplies in Tropical Africa" *ILCA Research Report No. 8*. International Institute for Livestock Centre for Africa, Addis Abeba, Ethiopia..

Sandford, Steven, 1982: "Pastoral Strategies and Desertification: Opportunism and Conservationism in Dry Lands" in Spooner and Mann (eds): *Desertification and Development; Dryland Ecology in Social Perspective*. London.

Santoir, C., 1994: "Décadence et résistance du pastoralisme. Les Peuls de la Vallée de fleuve Sénégal": *Cahiers d'Etudes africaines* 133-135; XXXIV-1-3.

Santoir, C. 1993: " D'une rive a l'autre; Les Peul mauritaniens refugiés au Sénégal (départements de Dagana et de Podor" *Cahiers des Sciences Humaines* 29 (1).

Santoir, C., 1990a: Le Conflit Mauritano-Sénégalais: la genèse; Le cas des Peul de la Haute Vallée du Sénégal" *Cahiers des Sciences Humaines* 26 (4).

Santoir, C., 1990b: " Les Peuls 'refusés'; Les Peul mauritaniens refugiés au Sénégal" *Cahiers des Sciences Humaines* 26 (4.

Santoir, C., 1983: *Raison Pastorale et Developpement. Les societes peuls face au amenagments*. Dakar, Travaux et Documents de l'ORSTOM no.166.

Santoir, C. 1982: "Contribution à l'etude de l'exploitation du cheptel. Region du Ferlo-Sénégal". Dakar, ORSTOM, multigr

Santoir, C. 1979: "Peuls et aménagements hydro-agricoles dans la Vallée du fleuve Sénégal". Dakar, ORSTOM, multigr.

Santoir, C., 1977: "L'Espace Pastoral dans la Region du Fleuve Senegal", ORSTOM, Dakar.

Sayer, A.1984: *Method in Social Science; A Realist Approach*, London and New York.

Schmitz, Jean, 1993: "Anthropologie des conflits fonciers et hydropolitiques du fleuve Sénégal (1975-91)" *Cahiers des Sciences Humaines* Vol. 29, no.

4,.

Schmitz, Jean, 1987:"Projet de la cuvette de Kaskas, fin de l'étude de la cuvette de Moutoul. SAED, ADRAO, Université de Wageningen et ORSTOM (Miméo).

Schmitz, Jean, 1986a:"Projet d'irrigation de Kaskas et situation des périmètres villageois de la zone".SAED, ADRAO, Université de Wageningen et ORSTOM.

Schmitz, Jean, 1986b:"Agriculture de décrue, unités territoriales et irrigation dans la Vallée du Sénégal" Communication présentée au seminaire " Aménagements Hydro-agricoles et systèmes de production, DSA-CIRAD Montpellier dec. 1986. *Les cahiers de recherche developpement* no. 12.

Schneider, Harold, K. 1959: "Pakot resistance to change" in Bascom and Herskovits: *Continuity and change in African Culture*. Chicago.

Scoones, Ian, 1995: "New directions in pastoral development in Africa" in Scoones (ed): *Living with Uncertainty: New directions for Pastoral development in Africa*, London.

Scoones, I., 1994: Living with Uncertainty: New directions for Pastoral development in Africa, Overview Paper from the workshop on New directions in African Range Management and Policy, Woburn, UK, June 1993.

Seck, S.M. 1991: "La Dynamique de l'irrigation dans la vallée du fleuve". In Crousse, B. Mathieu, P. And Seck, S.M. (ed): *La vallée du fleuve Sénégal*. Karthala, Paris.

Sepällä, Peka 1996: Negotiated development- A new paradigm for Social Dynamics in Rural Africa" *Nordic Journal of Development Studies* vol.5. no. 2. pp.84-98

Serres, H. 1977, Essai de bilan des politiques hydrauliques pastorales GERDAT-IEMVT, Paris.

Solway, Jaqueline S. 1994:"Drought as a 'Revelatory Crisis'; an Exploration of Shifting Entitlements and Hierachies in the Kalahari, Botswana." *Development and Change,* vol. 25.

Speirs, Mike and Ole Olsen, 1992:" Indigenous Integrated Farming Systems in the Sahel" *World Bank Technical Paper* no.179. Africa Technical Department Series.

Spittler, Gerd 1979: "Peasants and the State in Niger", *Peasant Studies* vol. 8 no.1.

Spittler, Gerd 1984: "Introduction; Peasants, the Administration and Rural Development," *Sociologia Ruralis No. 24*

Spooner, Brian 1993: "Ignoring Turbulence in Planning: Some Lessons, Experience and Principles of Chaos, Hazard and Conflict from the Horn of Africa".in Brimer et al: *Natural Resources and Social Conflicts: Proceedings from the 5th Sahel Workshop,* Sandbjerg.

Spooner, Brian, 1987: "Insiders and Outsiders in Baluchistan, Western and Indigenous Perspectives on Ecology and Development" in Little, Horowitz and Nyerges (eds): *Lands at Risk in the Third World,* Westview, Boulder.

Spooner, Brian, 1982: " Rethinking Desertification: the Social Dimension" in Spooner and Mann (eds) *Desertification and Development; Dryland Ecology in Social Perspective.* London.

Solway, Jacqueline, 1994: "Drought as a 'Revelatory Crisis': An Exploration of Shifting Entitlements and Hierarchies in The Kalahar, Botswana" *Development and Change* vol 25.

Stebbing, E.P., 1938: "The encroaching Sahara:The threat to the West African Colonies: A Paper Read at the Evening Meeting of the Society on 4 March 1935". *The Geographical Journal,* The Royal Geographic Society, 1938 vol. 85) London.

Stroosnijder, L., 1994: "Population density, Carrying Capacity and Agricultural Technology in the Sahel" in: *Proceedings from the 6th Sahel Workshop.* 6-8th January 1994. Aarhus, Denmark.

Sutter, J.W. 1987: "Cattle and Inequality: Herd Size Differentiation and Pastoral Production among the Fulani of Northeastern Senegal." *Africa,* 57 (2.

Swallow, B. 1989: "Strategies and Tenure in African Livestock Development", Draft, Land Tenure Center , University of Wisconsin, Madison, USA, Sept. 1989.

Swift. J.J., 1988:" *Major Issues in Pastoral Development with Special Emphasis on Selected African Countries*", Food and Agriculture Organization (FAO) Rome.

Swift. J.J., 1996: " Desertification; Narratives, Winners and Losers" in Leach and Mearns (eds): *The Lie of the Land; Challenging Received Wisdom on the Agrican Environment*.The International African Institute in association with James Currey, Oxford and Heinemann Portsmouth, N.H.

Thébaud, Brigitte, 1995: "Pastoralisme et degradation du milieu naturel au Sahel: Mythe ou réalité?, L'experience de pâturage controlé à Widou Thiengoli (Ferlo Senegalais) Document présenté dans le cadre du seminaire Sahel, Soenderborg janvier 1995.

Thebaud, Brigitte, 1994a: "Projet "Exploitation agro-sylvo-pastoral des sols dans le Nord du Senegal" (GTZ) : Bilan et identification d'un nouveau projet. Rapport de mission 28 mars au 5 mai 1994.

Thébaud, Brigitte, 1994b: "Projet Exploitation agro-sylvo-pastoral des sols dans le Nord du Sénégal" (GTZ) : Bilan et identification d'un nouveau projet. Rapport de mission 28 mars au 5 mai 1994.

Thebaud, Brigitte, 1993a: " Le foncier dans le Sahel Pastoral, situation et perspectives". Dec. 1993, article in press prepared for the Seminar of EHESS.

Thebaud, Brigitte, 1993b: "Causes et consequences de la désertification en Afrique: essai d'interprétation. Document preparé dans le cadre du Panel International d'Experts sur la Désertification. Genève nov.1993.

Thebaud, Brigitte and Camilla Toulmin, 1993: "Causes et consequences socio-économiques de la désertification en Afrique: la question pastorale". Document preparé dans le cadre du Panel International d'Experts sur la Désertification. Genève nov.1993.

Thebaud, B., 1990:"Politique d'hydraulique pastorale et gestion de l'espace au Sahel" in *Cahiers des Sciences Humaines* Vol .1 et 2, ORSTOM, Paris.

Thebaud, B., 1985: *Elevage et développement au Niger - quel avenir pour les éleveurs sahéliens,* BIT, Genève.

Thiam, Algor, 1995 :"Le rôle du système d'élevage extensif amélioré dans la production de viande au Sénégal: Contraintes et perspectives" Communication du Seminaire-Atelier sur la production de viande en Afrique Sub-Saharienne, 13-17 Mars 1995 à Saly Portudal, Sénégal, multigr.

Thomas, D.S.G. and Middleton, N.J. 1994: *Desertification: Exploding the Myth*, Chichester.

Thomson J.T.1989: "Options for Promoting User- Based Governance of Sahelian Renewable Resources (prepared for CILSS).

Thomson, J.T., 1991:" Sahel Decentralization Policy Report, Volume 1: Decentralization, Governance and Problem Solving in the Sahel". Agency for International Development.

Tiffen, Mary and Michael Mortimore, 1994: "Environment, Population Growth and Productivity in Kenya: a Case Study of Machakos District. *IIED Issues Paper* No. 47.London.

Tiffen, Mary, Michael Mortimore and Francis Gichuki, 1994: *More People, less Erosion; Environmental Recovery in Kenya.* Wiley Publishers, Chichester.

Tluczykont, Siegfried 1991:"Le modèle de pâturage contrôlé" in Kasberger-Sanftl, G. Richter, M. et Tluczykont, S. 1991: Le pâturage contrôlé: Un système d'exploitation sylvo-pastorale comme modèle pour la sauvegarde des ressources naturelles". Saint Louis, Senegal. Mission Forestière Allemande,GTZ.

Toulmin, C. 1993: "Combatting Desertification: Setting an Agenda for a Global Convention". Dryland Networks Progamme, *IIED Issues Paper* no. 42. International Institute for Environment and Development, London.

Toulmin, C., 1986: "Access to Food, Dry Season Strategies and Household Size amongst the Bambara of Central Mali" in *IDS Bulletin*, vol 17 no.3.

Toulmin, C., 1991: Natural Resource Management at the Local Level: Will this bring Food Security to the Sahel?" in *IDS Bulletin* 22-3.

Touré, O. 1991a: "Mission d'évaluation du Projet Sénégalo-Allemand d'exploitation agro-sylvo-pastorale des sols dans le nord du Sénégal-Rapport sociologique". Unpublished. Dakar.

Touré, Oussouby 1991b: "Développement pastoral et contraintes foncière dans la zone sahélienne du Sénégal." Publication du Centre de Suivi Ecologique, Unpublished. Dakar.

Touré, Oussouby 1990a: "Les sociétés peuls du Ferlo: continuité; changements, menaces." Publication du Centre de Suivi Ecologique, Unpublished. Dakar.

Touré, Oussouby, 1990b: "Where Herders don't herd anymore: Experience from the Ferlo, northern Senegal. Dryland Networks Progamme, *IIED Issues Paper* no. 22. International Institute for Environment and Development, London.

Touré, Oussouby, 1989: "Le zonage du Ferlo, Analyse des modes d'exploitation du milieu et de leur evolution." Publication du Centre de Suivi Ecologique, Unpublished. Dakar.

Touré, Oussouby and J. Arpaillange: *Peul du Ferlo*, L'Harmattan, Paris, Tourrand, J.F., 1993: "L'Elevage dans la révolution agricole au Waalo. Ruptures et continuité". Thèse d'Etat, Université de Paris-XII.

Tourrand, J.F. 1989: "Un pasteur devient agro-pasteur: Une étude de cas dans le Delta du fleuve Sénégal": Seminaire RESPAO. Accra, 1989,.

Tyc, Jean, 1994: Etude diagnostic sur l'exploitation et la commercialisation du bétail dans la zone des 'six forages', Rapport de mission, Projet d'exploitation agro-sylvo-pastorale des sols dans le nord du Sénégal (GTZ)..

UNCED 1992: *Convention on Desertification*. New York.

UNSO/PNUD 1994:"La gestion des Ressources Naturelles et les Politiques Pastorales Nationales" Compte Rendu de l'Atelier Sous-régional, Bamako Nov, 1993.

van Dijk, Hans, 1994: 'Livestock Transfers and Social Security in FulBe Society in the Hayre, Central Mali', *Focaal* no. 22/23.

Vedeld, Trond 1994: "The State and Rangeland Management: Creation and Erosion of Pastoral Institutions in Mali" London International Institute for Environment and Development. *IIED Issues Paper* no. 46.

Vedeld, T., 1992: "Local Institution Building and Resource Management in the West African Sahel" Draft, NORAGRIC, Norway.

Vengroff, R. and A. Johnston, 1985:" Senegals Rural Councils: Decentralization and the Implementation of Rural Development" Mimeo. Center for Applied International Development Studies (CAIDS) Texas Tech University, Report prepared for USAID.

Vengroff, R. and A. Johnston 1987:" Decentralization and the Implementation of Rural Development in Senegal: The Role of the Rural Councils" *Public Administration and Development* vol 7.

Wade, Robert, 1992: Common Poperty Resource Management in South Indian Villages" In: Bromley (ed) 1972: *Making the Commons Work, Theory, Practice and Policy.*

Warren, A and Agnew, C., 1987: *An Assessment of Desertification and Land Degradation in Arid and Semi-Arid Areas.* Dryland Paper no. 2. IIED. London,

Weicker, Martin, 1993: *Nomades et sedentaires au Sénégal*, ENDA-Editions, série Etudes et Recherches no. 139-140 Dakar, Sénégal.

Wilson, F., 1990: "The Study of Institutions and the Paradoxical Situation of doing Research" in *Occasional Paper* no.1. IDS, Roskilde.

Webb, James, L.A.,1995: *The Desert Frontier; Ecological and Economic Change along the Western Sahel 1600-1850.* University of Wisconsin Press.

Youmba, Malick Abdoul 1983: Rapport de stage: Hydraulique pastorale et villageoise" Ecole Inter-Etat des Sciences et Medicine Veterinaire, Dakar.

Anthropology and Development

edited by Thomas Bierschenk (Universität Mainz) and Jean-Pierre Olivier de Sardan (Ecoles de Hautes Etudes en Sciences Sociales, Marseille) for APAD (Euro-African Association for the Anthropology of Social Change and Development)

Pernille Sørensen
"Money is the True Friend"
Economic Practice, Morality and Trust among the Iganga Maize Traders in Uganda

The Ugandan economy was once solidly based on the export of cash crops such as coffee and cotton. The economic crisis and the civil war in the 1970s and 1980s however profoundly changed the agricultural economy, and marketing of traditional cash crops was replaced by marketing of commercialized food crops. "Money is the true friend" deals with the emergence of de-regulated food markets for maize in Eastern Uganda. The focus is not marketing as such, but rather a new social and economic field for local traders demarcated by the involvement in three maize markets: the relief market, the Kenyan market and the domestic market. The central problem illuminated in the book is the relationship between the liberalization of food marketing and the development of a new social and cultural practice – a morality – for trading which is both shaped by and shapes the marketing opportunities for the participating traders.
Bd. 4, 2000, 248 S., 20,90 €, br.,
ISBN 3-8258-4393-9

Halle Studies in the Anthropology of Eurasia

General Editors: Chris Hann, Richard Rottenburg, Burkhard Schnepel and Shingo Shimada

Chris Hann and the "Property Relations" Group
The Postsocialist Agrarian Question
Property Relations and the Rural Condition

"... anthropology needs a broader vision. It needs to shake off its strong association with the primitive and the exotic and become genuinely global in its comparisons. From this perspective, more sustained attention to Eurasia and a renewed focus on its underlying unity might launch the transformation of our parochial scholarly traditions into a mature cosmopolitan science." – Chris Hann, in his Preface to this series This is an age of neo-liberalism, in which the advantages and virtues of private property are often taken for granted. Postsocialist governments have privatized and broken up state farms and socialist cooperatives. However, economic outcomes and the social insecurity now experienced by many rural inhabitants highlight the need for a broader anthropological analysis of property relations, which goes beyond changes in legal form. A century after Kautsky addressed 'The Agrarian Question' in Germany, it is therefore necessary to address a postsocialist Agrarian Question throughout Central and Eastern Europe, the former Soviet Union and China. The studies collected here derive from the first cycle of projects at the Max Planck Institute for Social Anthropology. They are prefaced by a substantial Introduction by Chris Hann, a Founding Director of the Institute. Contributors: Susanne Brandtstädter, Andrew Cartwright, Barbara A. Cellarius, John Eidson, Patty A. Gray, Chris Hann, Patrick Heady, Deema Kaneff, Alexander D. King, Carolin Leutloff, Liesl L. Gambold Miller, Gordon Milligan, Mihály Sárkány, Florian Stammler, Wolde Gossa Tadesse, Davide Torsello, Aimar Ventsel, Lale Yalçın-Heckmann, John P. Ziker
Bd. 1, 2003, 488 S., 30,90 €, br.,
ISBN 3-8258-6532-0

L IT Verlag Münster – Berlin – Hamburg – London – Wien
Grevener Str./Fresnostr. 2 48159 Münster
Tel.: 0251 – 62 032 22 – Fax: 0251 – 23 19 72
e-Mail: vertrieb@lit-verlag.de – http://www.lit-verlag.de

Hannes Grandits; Patrick Heady (eds.)
Distinct Inheritances
Property, Family and Community in a Changing Europe
Questions about the respective roles of private and state property have been at the center of European political life for the whole of the past century. Much less publicity has been given to the ways in which rights to property are transmitted over time and how different inheritance traditions have affected European societies. The chapters in this book draw on historical and anthropological research to show how inheritance practices connect the intimate organization of domestic life with questions of economic development, political structure and religious belief. The book traces the story from the coming of Christianity, through the imposition and dissolution of different forms of feudalism, to the development of the modern economy. Several chapters deal with the impact of communism and its collapse - and demonstrate how ideas about the inheritance of property and status are continuing to shape, and be shaped by, economic and social changes in a continent that is moving beyond the ideological dichotomies of the Cold War. Contributors: Ulf Brunnbauer, Nevill Colclough, John Cole, John Eidson, Jack Goody, Hannes Grandits, Patrick Heady, Karl Kaser, Margareth Lanzinger, Robert Layton, Carolin Leutloff-Grandits, Hans Marks, Michael Mitterauer, Frances Pine, Andrejs Plakans, David Warren Sabean, Tatjana Thelen, Davide Torsello, Oane Visser, E.A. Wrigley
Bd. 2, 2004, 440 S., 29,90 €, br.,
ISBN 3-8258-6961-x; 39,90 €, gb.,
ISBN 3-8258-7334-x

Davide Torsello
Trust, Property and Social Change in a Southern Slovakian Village
Slovakia is a young and little studied country of the former socialist bloc. As in all postsocialist Eurasia, continuing transformations of everyday practices are still inadequately understood. This study combines anthropological and historical methods to search for alternative ways of "reading postsocialism" in the rural community. More specifically, it applies the notions of trust and property to map the outcomes of over a hundred years of turbulent social change, but not in the way that mainstream economists and political scientists have used these concepts. Trust and property acquire analytic significance only when contextualised into the practices and ideologies of the actors. This allows the observer to grasp the nuances of apparently ambivalent behaviour and "uttered mistrust" in other villagers and local institutions. Ambiguity veils subtle strategies for keeping up with the instability of the times and obtaining the best one can from the present. By providing a theoretically grounded ethnographic account of historical transformation the book makes an original anthropological contribution to the classic theme of social change in rural societies, while at the same time engaging constructively with other social science approaches to postsocialism.
Bd. 3, 2004, 264 S., 29,90 €, br.,
ISBN 3-8258-6962-8

Frances Pine; Deema Kaneff; Haldis Haukanes (eds.)
Memory, Politics and Religion
The Past Meets the Present in Europe
This collection of essays focuses on the haunting themes of religion, politics and remembering the past. Spanning Europe from Ukraine to Spain, the authors consider ways in which memory is used, at the local level, both to legitimate and to contest claims to power, status, and social and cultural capital. The result is a rich and innovative set of texts on memory and silence, on the place of the past in the present, and on the ideologies and practices which constitute memory at the local level.
Bd. 4, 2004, 320 S., 29,90 €, br.,
ISBN 3-8258-8051-6

Joachim Otto Habeck
What it Means to be a Herdsman
The Practice and Image of Reindeer Husbandry among the Komi of Northern Russia
Habeck takes the reader to the tundra in the Far North of the Russian Federation, descri-

bing and interpreting the practice of reindeer herding on the land. His vivid account of the everyday life of Komi reindeer herders and their family members as they interact with their bosses, the town, the market and oil companies, reveals both the reach of their agency and its limitations. Through a meticulous analysis of each of these domains, Habeck shows how public discourse about reindeer husbandry as a traditional life-style derives from outside the Komi reindeer-herding communities, yet it has powerful effects on the local actors' ability to frame their own existence. He argues that the concept of tradition, despite its many positive connotations, places Komi reindeer herders in a „golden cage" which leaves no space for acknowledging their drive to innovation and flexibility.
Bd. 5, 2005, 296 S., 29,90 €, br.,
ISBN 3-8258-8045-1

Modernity and Belonging
edited by Peter Geschiere and Birgit Meyer (University of Amsterdam)

Antoine Socpa
Démocratisation et Autochtonie au Cameroun
Trajectoires régionales différentes
Partout en Afrique, la démocratisation semble déchaîner une véritable obsession avec les identités locales, exprimée en termes d'autochtonie et d'exclusion des « allogènes ». Pourtant, l'articulation entre démocratisation et autochtonie suit des trajectoires différentes. Cet ouvrage compare les processus divergents de l'introduction du multipartisme dans deux régions du Cameroun: Yaoundé, marquée par des tensions entre « autochtones » Béti et « allogènes » Bamiléké; et le Logone-Chari où Kotoko et Arabes Choa se confrontent autour des mêmes idées qui ont pourtant une suite toute différente. Cette étude s'intéresse au rôle de ce qu'on pourrait appeler la politique de l'autochtonie.
Bd. 1, 2003, 352 S., 29,90 €, br.,
ISBN 3-8258-6997-0

Philip J. Havik
Silences and Soundbytes
The gendered dynamics of trade and brokerage in the pre-colonial Guinea Bissau region
Set in the pre-colonial Guinea Bissau region, Silences and Soundbytes deals with the largely ignored roles women – and men – played as traders and brokers in the Afro-Atlantic trade settlements emerged after first contact in the fifteenth century. Largely based upon unpublished archival material, the book traces the evolution of these riverine settlements and their populations until the military occupation by Portugal in the early twentieth century. It holds that the formation of settlement communities that operated the relay trade along the region's many rivers between the region's hinterland and the coast created opportunities for enterprising and well-connected women.
Bd. 2, 2004, 408 S., 29,90 €, br.,
ISBN 3-8258-7709-4

Marijke Steegstra
Resilient Rituals
Krobo initiation and the politics of culture in Ghana
How should modern Ghanaians relate to 'culture'? This is a hotly debated issue in Ghana, where the annual performance of the initiation rites for Krobo girls (dipo) is highly contested. Drawing on her extensive fieldwork and missionary and colonial archives, Steegstra shows how the contemporary performance of dipo relates to and is shaped by Krobo encounters with missionary Christianity, colonial intervention and modern nationalism. Krobo responses to global processes of change involved considerable resistance, and over time, ongoing local struggles but also a pursuit of cultural resilience.
Marijke Steegstra (Ph.D. University of Nijmegen, The Netherlands, 2004) currently holds a post-doctoral research position at the anthropology department of the University of Nijmegen.
Bd. 3, 2004, 368 S., 29,90 €, br.,
ISBN 3-8258-7786-8

LIT Verlag Münster – Berlin – Hamburg – London – Wien
Grevener Str./Fresnostr. 2 48159 Münster
Tel.: 0251 – 62 032 22 – Fax: 0251 – 23 19 72
e-Mail: vertrieb@lit-verlag.de – http://www.lit-verlag.de

History and Theory of Anthropology / Geschichte und Theorie der Ethnologie
edited by / hrsg. von Prof. Dr. Klaus-Peter Köpping (University of Heidelberg)

Klaus-Peter Köpping
Adolf Bastian and the Psychic Unity of Mankind
The Foundations of Anthropology in Nineteenth Century Germany
Adolf Bastian mapped a programme for anthropological research in the nineteenth century which is still accepted in the international scholarly community today, without the figure of its founder being known. This is the first time that seminal pieces of the work of this much-neglected scholar have been translated into English. Bastian had an impact, directly and indirectly, on geography, psychology, comparative religious studies, and ethnology in the twentieth century.
Bd. 1, 2005, 296 S., 20,90 €, br., ISBN 3-8258-3989-3

Christoph Wulf
Anthropology of Education
Educational anthropology constitutes a new and important field of education. It deals with central educational concepts from an anthropological perspective. As historical and cultural anthropology it takes into account the historicity and culturality of education. The book focuses on major issues of education: *The Problem of Human Perfectibility an the Difficulty of Human Change – Mimesis in Education, Culture and Anthropology – Global and Intercultural Education – Educational Anthropology: A New Perspective on Education.*
Bd. 2, 2002, 184 S., 24,90 €, br., ISBN 3-8258-5681-x

Eduard Matt
Ethnographische Beschreibungen
Die Kunst der Konstruktion der Wirklichkeit des Anderen
Ethnographische Beschreibungen dienen in der qualitativen Sozialforschung, in den Cultural Studies, in der Ethnologie und Anthropologie der Erforschung und Darstellung unvertrauter Lebenswelten. Das Verständnis des Anderen in seiner Normalität soll hierbei erfaßt und vermittelt werden. Nicht Ausgrenzung oder Nivellierung, sondern Anerkennung des Fremden ist das Ziel. Detailliert werden im vorliegenden Band die Bedingungen der Möglichkeiten des Zugangs angesichts der Pluralisierung der Lebenswelten diskutiert: Kultur als Text, die Bedeutung des Erzählens, das Fremdverstehen, der Zusammenhang von textlicher Repräsentation und Weltdeutung sowie das Verhältnis von Alltag und Wissenschaft.
Bd. 3, 2001, 224 S., 20,90 €, br., ISBN 3-8258-5672-0

Soziologie und Anthropologie
Kulturwissenschaftliche Perspektiven
hrsg. von Prof. Dr. Detlef Pollack,
Prof. Dr. Werner Schiffauer und
Prof. Dr. Anna Schwarz (Europa-Universität Viadrina, Frankfurt/Oder)

Rebecca Budde
Mexican and Central American L.A. Garment Workers
Globalized Industries and their Economic Constraints
Bd. 1, 2005, 160 S., 19,90 €, br., ISBN 3-8258-8397-3

LIT Verlag Münster – Berlin – Hamburg – London – Wien
Grevener Str./Fresnostr. 2 48159 Münster
Tel.: 0251 – 62 032 22 – Fax: 0251 – 23 19 72
e-Mail: vertrieb@lit-verlag.de – http://www.lit-verlag.de